Thinking a
Personal and Social Education
in the Primary School

Edited by
Peter Lang

BASIL BLACKWELL

© Peter Lang 1988

First published 1988

Published by
Basil Blackwell Limited
108 Cowley Road
Oxford OX4 1JF

British Library Cataloguing in Publication Data
Thinking about personal and social education
in the primary school.
1. Great Britain. Primary schools. Social
education
1. Lang, Peter
372'.01'150941
ISBN 0-631-15878-2
ISBN 0-631-15879-0 Pbk

Typeset in 11/12½pt Baskerville
by Joshua Associates Ltd, Oxford
Printed in Great Britain by T. J. Press Ltd, Padstow, Cornwall

Contents

iv

Preface

The idea for this book arose from a seminar held at Warwick University to consider current practice and future needs of personal and social education and pastoral provision in primary and middle schools.

The motivation behind its organisation was a belief that personal and social education is of fundamental importance in the early years of education and that, as a dimension of the formal and informal curriculum, it needs to be explicitly considered. The seminar was intended to provide an opportunity for primary teachers and headteachers, advisers and others involved in teacher education, to share and develop perceptions of the nature of social and personal education and to raise awareness of the ideas, work and research of others.

The 50 participants included a number of those most closely involved in these developments, particularly in the area of inservice training. Seven teacher training institutions were represented and advisers and teachers came from 15 LEAs. A number of the papers found in this book were originally presented at the seminar.

The development of the National Curriculum gives this book an added urgency as, in the attempt to map out an entitlement curriculum, many fear that the personal and social dimension of primary teachers' work with pupils will be marginalised.

The purpose of this book

Most primary teachers would agree that much of what they do in school concerns the personal, social and moral development of children. It is usually not difficult to persuade them that this is an important dimension of their work; it may be harder to convince them of the need to critically review what they do as a consequence of this. It may also be hard to persuade them that it is by no means certain whether the experiences children have in their schools necessarily foster their development in these areas in the ways that teachers, parents and other interested parties think is desirable.

One purpose of this book is to help nursery, infant, junior, first, middle and primary schools (which will normally be called primary schools for simplicity) recognise the need to examine, as part of a continuous curriculum review, the effect of the informal and formal curriculum on their pupils' personal and social growth. It is suggested that such an examination should lead to systematic responses in the school as a whole, as well as in direct teaching and learning experiences in the classroom.

The proposal that personal and social education should be an explicit dimension of the primary curriculum does not necessarily mean that it must receive a quantifiable time allocation, as may be designated for other parts of the formal curriculum, though in some instances there may be a case for this. Much of what is required can be realised through the day-to-day relationships and activities which take place as part of the school organisation. Personal and social objectives can also be achieved alongside objectives in other areas of the curriculum. What is clear, though, is that this vital area of the curriculum should not be left to chance. It must be carefully planned, implemented and evaluated. In effect then, as the title of this book implies, personal and social education in the primary school should be *thought about*.

In the first place, this book is intended to be a stimulus for thinking about personal and social education. As has already been indicated, we are dealing with an area that is recognised as important but also frequently taken for granted; this book challenges the 'taken for granted' dimension. Having encouraged the reader to think, the book seeks to help in this process. It provides help by indicating the ways such thinking can be developed, partly in the introduction and in particular papers where this is specifically dealt with, but also through the wide range of examples of differing dimensions and approaches presented in over 30 papers. These papers are provided as a source to be drawn on as appropriate; it is likely that the book will be best used as something to be returned to at regular intervals rather than read from start to finish.

The papers in this volume are of a number of different kinds, some descriptive and some reflective, some both. They are also pitched at different levels, ranging from the very practical to the fairly theoretical. The editor believes that this is entirely consistent with the book's aims; not only should personal and social education be thought about, but it should be thought about in different ways. Primary teachers engaging with PSE need straightforward sources for practical ideas, but they also need to be challenged to analyse and think. What unifies the papers included is not just that they are all about aspects of personal and social education, but that they all illustrate attempts to think about it.

Finally there is one thing that this book does *not* seek to do, it does not tell the reader *what* to think. What the reader thinks will, it is hoped, be based on an active dialogue between what the book has to offer and the particular circumstances and needs of the pupils, classroom and school in which they are involved.

Acknowledgements

To the ESRC which provided the financial support needed to run the seminar. To Warwick University for providing support in terms of resources.To NAPCE for the provision of resources and administrative backup. To Barbara Stagles whose ideas have been drawn on in the Preface and Introduction.

 Thomas

What did mummy do
to make you grow?

she
talked to me and she
wash me she exercised
me
and she gave me rest
2 a day and she gave
me fresh air and she
feed me
She loved me

Introduction
Peter Lang

The dilemma

There is clearly something of a 'Catch 22' situation as regards the current position of personal and social education in the primary school and the aims of this book. The role of personal and social education in the primary school is something that needs careful thought, analysis and planning – yet this is at least partly because PSE is likely to be one of the most 'taken for granted' aspects of what is believed to happen in the primary school. That is the catch, of course: precisely because of this 'taken for grantedness' it may be extremely difficult to get primary teachers to think about personal and social education at anything beyond a superficial level, or indeed to read books about it. This introductory chapter will explore the nature of this dilemma in more detail, attempt to draw out some of its implications, and briefly suggest the ways schools and teachers might proceed in dealing with these problems and questions about the nature of personal and social education.

The current problem

The writer who has made the greatest contribution to thinking about the nature and purpose of personal and social education and its significance as an aspect of education, is almost certainly Richard Pring (see, for example, Pring, 1984). This is not to say that other writers and texts relating to personal and social education have not been influential; for example the Schools Council Programme 3 *Personal and Social Education in Secondary Schools* has had a significant effect on the way practice has been promoted at LEA level and developed in schools (David, 1982). But there is a distinction between influences that affect people mainly in terms of encouraging them to undertake personal and social education (such as the Schools Council paper) and influences that encourage analysis and thought as the essential basis for such action. Richard Pring is one of the few writers whose work falls clearly into the second category.

As has already been made clear, this book's influence is intended to be of the second kind; the intention is that the 'why' shall always be linked to the 'how' of personal and social education. In the opening to his contribution in this book (page 39) Richard Pring provides his own clear formulation of this central dilemma in the development of effective personal and social education in the primary school. He both demonstrates the need for thought and provides a starting point from which such thought should develop.

It is seen as self-evident that Personal and Social Education (PSE) be at the centre of what we should be planning and should be doing in primary schools. And most teachers would claim that, in fact, they are indeed engaged in pursuing what is seen to be so obviously important.

But therein lies the problem, for what is seen to be self-evidently true, or what is seen to be obviously worth pursuing, rarely receives the critical examination and scrutiny that perhaps it requires. Rarely is that which is regarded as self-evident spelt out in detail. Certainly it is understood to be beyond the need for justification. And thus unfortunately anything might be acceptable under such bland and unhelpful titles as 'helping children to realise their potential' or 'facilitating growth' or 'encouraging personal autonomy'. When Personal Development (unlike mathematical or scientific development) is 'everywhere' in the school, then there is a need to be doubly cautious – first, because, whatever PSE is, it might just as easily be inhibited as promoted by the practices within the school; secondly, because something so all-pervasive may be denied the systematic thought it deserves.

Though it is seen as 'self-evident' among primary teachers that personal and social education should be at the centre of what is done in the primary school, this does not mean that PSE is regularly discussed in primary schools or much reflected in the documents produced relating to school policy. What it is more likely to mean, in most instances, is that when primary teachers are actually questioned about the importance of personal and social education, they will respond that it is central to all they do, both in their classrooms and in the school as a whole. They will probably add that in their view the personal and social education of their pupils is already well-catered for through their current practice. Thus even the 'taken for grantedness' of PSE is usually at an implicit rather than explicit level.

The context of confusion

Why then is it that personal and social education is acknowledged as important by primary teachers and schools but generally does not feature as a priority either for discussion or for action? The arguments presented in the first chapter of Alexander's book *Primary Teaching* appear to throw some light on this. Under the heading 'The Language of Child-Centredness' he states:

Nobody familiar with the culture of primary schools can doubt the pervasiveness of two elements. First there is the language of child-centredness, the verbal expression of an ideology which remains in the 1980s as powerful and some-times vehement as it was in the 1960s. This language has considerable potency for inducing a warm consensual solidarity. From the mouth of the non-teacher, viewed initially and inevitably with suspicion, the rhetorical question 'but we teach children, not subjects, don't we?' is a ticket to professional approval and acceptance; it disarms suspicion, sets heads nodding and confirms ally status. Second many primary schools, especially infant and first schools, have a physical appearance and interpersonal climate which seem to confirm the seriousness of the intentions . . .
. . . In developing a critique of some aspects of primary ideology, I wish in no way to deny the value of the kind of school climate with which, at best, it is associated. Rather my argument is that the primary school's strengths in respect of climate and interpersonal relations are sometimes offset by weaknesses in respect of curriculum and pedagogy − not always obvious to the uncritical outsider (or insider) since such

weaknesses may not significantly diminish the defining characteristics of 'busyness' and 'enjoyment'.

(Alexander, 1984)

There are three dimensions to the explanation that Alexander's
argument provides. First, if, as he suggests, child-centred ideology is
still a powerful force within primary schools it is hardly surprising
that the pupils' personal and social education is acknowledged as
important; to suggest otherwise would appear to contradict the
essential nature of child-centredness. However, in his conclusion to
the chapter Alexander comments on the language through which
primary ideology is expressed; he highlights its 'heavy use of
aphorism, false dichotomy, caricature, and other devices which serve
to diminish and debase basic educational concepts like 'curriculum', 'knowledge' and 'teaching' to the extent that a failure to
engage in serious discussion of them can be justified paradoxically,
as 'child-centred'. Clearly the same factors could well pre-empt
serious discussion of personal and social education.

Second, the climate of 'busyness' and 'enjoyment' described in
relation to child-centredness can also serve to convince the uncritical
outsider (or insider) that personal and social education is well
catered for. Third, though climate is important for PSE, so too are
curriculum and pedagogy; if there *are* weaknesses in these areas
these will undoubtedly affect PSE provision.

These problems are not confined to individual schools but can be
found on a much broader basis; the ambivalence, lack of clarity and
unwillingness to address the issue of PSE fully so far described can
be found reflected in the recent Parliamentary report *Achievement in
the primary school* (HMSO, 1986). The term personal and social
education does not occur in the main text (in spite of written
evidence given to the committee drawing attention to its importance)
but there are at least two statements which have clear implications
for PSE. In *Part One*, under the heading 'Education Achievement
and Values' comes the following statement:

2.2. But education is about a good deal more than this. As
the Secretary of the Catholic Education Council put it: 'surely
one of the purposes of education is to uplift'. The national
economy is important but ultimately a society stands or falls by
its social cohesion and by shared moral values. Education,

perhaps particularly primary education has a crucial role to play in promoting and safeguarding that cohesion and these values. Schools have the difficult task of being part of the community and at the same time standing for what is best in it as well as giving its children a glimpse of what is most valuable in our civilisation, aesthetically, morally and spiritually. Such aspirations are not beyond the primary school: many already possess this ethos, whether they fully realise it or not.

Three points about this passage are of considerable importance to the present discussion of personal and social education. First it must be a matter of some concern that only a year after the Swann Report (HMSO, 1985) a parliamentary report should contain a key statement which, if not directly contradicting Swann's recommendations, certainly ignores them. Compare the simplistic statements about the need for shared moral values and social cohesion (virtual invitations to well intentioned bad practice at school level based on an outmoded integrationist approach to ethnic minority pupils) with Swann's recommendation.

> If schools were seen by parents to be offering a more broadly based curriculum, which reflected the multi-racial, multi-lingual and multi-faith nature of Britain today we feel this would counter many of the anxieties which have been expressed.
>
> (Swann, 1985, p 509)

Though the Swann Report and multi-racial issues are mentioned briefly in later stages of *Achievement in the primary school* nothing is said that might counteract the impression given by the first statement.

Second, although much of what the statement says is over-simplified and thus open to misinterpretation, it does provide a rudimentary justification for the importance of PSE within the primary school. However, it reinforces the 'taken-for-granted' quality of the activity by suggesting that many schools may already possess an ethos which caters for these needs, though *they may not realise it* (my italics).

Later on the same page *Achievement in the primary school* appears to give further endorsement to the value of PSE in its tentative espousal of the definition of the aims of education found in the Warnock Report (HMSO, 1978):

> ... first to increase a child's knowledge of the world he lives in and his imaginative understanding, both of the possibilities of that world and of his own responsibilities in it; and secondly to give him as much independence and self-sufficiency as he is capable of, by teaching him those things he must know in order to find work and to manage and control his own life.

On the next page the report paraphrases the four aspects of achievement suggested in the Hargreaves Report (ILEA, 1984) suggesting that, though made in the context of secondary schools the Hargreaves' analysis of achievement is relevant to the primary stage as well. Here again there is implicit support for PSE; Aspect 3 of the analysis is expressed as being

> ... concerned with personal and social skills; the capacity to communicate with others in face-to-face relationships; the ability to co-operate with others in the interests of the group as well as of the individual; initiative, self-reliance and the ability to work alone without close supervision, and the skills of leadership.

Finally, in Part 6, under the heading 'The Curriculum, Methodology and the Timetable' comes the following brief reference to the hidden curriculum.

> 6.45. As will be apparent from our earlier comments on the curriculum, values and attitudes may be conveyed indirectly as well as directly by the form of organisation chosen, by where things are placed either in time or space, by tone of voice or gesture. We agree that this hidden curriculum is powerful and that it should as far as possible, not be a matter of accident.

Achievement in primary schools provides a graphic illustration of a number of the key points with which this paper is concerned. It shows that some consideration of areas that fall within the bounds of what would normally be described as personal and social education seems inescapable if the nature of achievement in the primary school is to be fully reviewed and understood. The statements quoted underline this point and suggest that the report's writers recognised it. However the statements quoted also illustrated the very general nature that often characterises such discussion; further, they often contain a degree of ambivalence and contradiction which raises doubts as to the nature and quality of practice likely to be developed from them. Having drawn attention to the significance of the personal, social and moral dimensions of the primary school's work and the effect of the hidden curriculum, *Achievement in primary schools* then fails to draw out the implications of this recognition, either in terms of effect or as recommendations. The report's limited and undeveloped treatment of those aspects of primary education which fall within the personal and social education umbrella demonstrates clearly the precise problems to which this book responds; personal and social education is acknowledged as important but not really thought about.

The approach characterised above can also be found reflected in the literature of primary education. For example, in a book on the primary curriculum (Boyd, 1984), clearly addressed to practitioners, the author draws attention to the research of Ashton *et al.* (1975). This research found that one of the three key emphases that primary teachers gave to their view of the aims of education was one concerned with 'children's personal development which included well-being and cheerfulness, a positive attitude towards school and the development of self-confidence and individuality' – indeed, much of what would normally be seen as PSE. Though Boyd includes these research findings, the implications remain undeveloped and there is no consideration of personal and social education included in the book.

Again, Alexander (ibid.) effectively summarises the central points of this discussion. In chapter three 'The Class Teacher and the Curriculum' he takes four recent studies of primary curriculum practice and draws out a number of general points from them. Under the heading 'The Formal Primary Curriculum: Scope, Priorities and Consistency' he includes the following observations in relation to personal, social and moral development.

The area is acknowledged as central but value-saturated. The solution to this dilemma is usually to dodge it: it is rare to find a school or LEA statement as full even as the APU's

24-page pamphlet (APU, 1981). Yet, of course, children develop personally, socially and morally whether or not schools conceive of such development in terms of specific timetabled curriculum activities: their learning in this area is promoted through their everyday interactions, the examples presented by teachers and fellow-pupils and by the 'hidden curriculum' of a school's norms and values relating to personal and inter-personal behaviour and relationships. The greater risk, it can be argued, is not of overt indoctrination but of a school being either so squeamish about the issue, or so ignorant of the actual mechanism of social and moral learning, that it fails to examine its actual impact on the child in this area, and the social/moral curriculum becomes 'hidden' rather than formalised, yet none the less influential. If the question 'How *ought* the child's personal/social and moral education to proceed?' seems too fraught, then the alternative 'What *is* the impact of this school's culture and practices on the child's personal, social and moral development?' is perhaps more acceptable and more essential.

Though Alexander's perspective here corresponds very closely with that of this paper there would be a difference of emphasis in relation to his last point. He appears to suggest that review of the impact of the school's culture and practices on the child is an adequate response in its own right; this paper would argue that such review can only be a starting point.

So far problems and questions in relation to the primary school curriculum, teachers' attitudes to this and the aims of education, and what these mean for the development of personal and social education have been raised. But the questions asked should not only be pitched at this level. The pedagogy used in the classroom also has major implications. For example, almost all practitioners or supporters of personal and social education would stress the contri-bution that is made to pupils' development through some form of cooperative or developmental groupwork. Questions about the successful practice of PSE in primary classrooms are raised by the comments of Bennett in a recent paper on changing research perspectives. Talking of the degree to which the prescriptions of the Plowden Report have been implemented he says,

> . . . the management of classroom groups is a good example
> of partial implementation. Teachers certainly organise their

class into groups, but these are no more than physical juxta-
positions of children engaged in individual work. Plowden on
the other hand envisaged that groups would be the focus of
teaching and would be involved in collaborative activities.

(Bennett, 1987)

Making sense of personal and social education

So far this paper has reviewed some of the key problems that confront
those concerned to develop effective personal and social education in
primary schools (and first and middle schools). The problems identified have been those that already exist within the system and those
that have arisen from the current ideas, understandings and ideologies that are to be found amongst primary teachers. The *thinking*
with which this book is concerned must involve a careful consideration of these background issues. Critically, thinking must focus on
the 'taken for grantedness' and the lack of 'critical examination' that
characterises the response to PSE of many primary schools and
teachers and much of the literature. Once this first stage of awareness
is reached and it is recognised that specific thought, planning and
action are needed to develop personal and social education, what
exactly does this mean and how should it be put into practice?

As has already been stressed, few people would argue against the
significance of personal and social education in primary schools. It is
also probable that at this general level they would not consider that
responding to this significance posed any particular problems. Yet,
as the discussion of Alexander's work above has already suggested,
the problems experienced are very real. 'The area is acknowledged
to be central yet value-saturated. The solution to this dilemma is
usually to dodge it' (ibid., p. 54).

Once people start exploring the area in greater depth they are
likely to find that it is more problematic than they imagined and that
there is considerably less agreement about what should take place.

The reasons for this lie partly in the fact that many people see
personal and social education as a way of producing individuals
suited to *their* view of 'a better society'. Since people vary as to what
constitutes a better society, the qualities they value are likely to vary
too. Most people do not articulate this in a very clear way, though
they will often select aspects of contemporary society that concern

them: 'rapid change and uncertainty', 'increases in moral and social problems', 'the decay of family life' and argue that children should develop qualities to respond to these.

For many people the desired qualities are not so overtly related to concepts of the good society but reflect their particular preference for certain types of persons (an aspect of PSE focused on by Pring in his paper on page 39 of this book). Such people justify personal and social education in terms of the benefits to individuals which come from acquiring these desired qualities. Many teachers believe that these personal qualities are not only important in their own right but also help children become better learners. They argue that it is part of their professional duty to be concerned about the impact of their attitudes and actions on their pupils' learning.

Other reasons given for the importance of personal and social education are concerned mainly with ease of management and teaching in the school. Teachers concerned about difficult or disruptive behaviour in class or school sometimes see personal and social education as a means of achieving more effective control. Such a purpose may well complement other objectives that teachers have for children's personal and social development, but it could also be a source of conflict with them.

The significance attached to PSE by some may simply reflect their commitment to one of the particular methodologies that tend to be associated with it, such as 'student centred learning', 'experiential learning', 'developmental groupwork'. These are often simplistically contrasted with didactic and cognitive models of teaching. (The writer recently encountered a manuscript on 'experiential learning' by a well-known trainer, where lack of rationale for this type of work was presented as a strength!)

Because there are so many different understandings of the purpose of personal and social education it is important for groups of teachers and other interested people to explore what they mean by it, what aims they have for children's personal and social development, and through what approaches these aims might be achieved. It is also important that the different groups of teachers, advisers, school governors, parents and maybe even pupils share the outcomes of these debates and are prepared to modify their own views as a result of coming to understand the perspectives of others.

What is personal and social education?

Where schools and individual teachers have started to develop conscious policies for PSE, lack of clarity about its nature and purpose has led a number of them to seek the security of a definitive definition of the area. However, it must be recognised that, at least to some extent, such a definitive definition is currently a chimera and to seek one may even be inappropriate. Even in traditional curriculum subjects this is difficult to achieve, and in an area where there is at present such a variety of analyses and approaches it is almost impossible.

Establishing a starting point

Considerably more important than seeking the reassurance of the 'gestalt' of an all-embracing and precise definition of PSE as a starting point for development, is to focus on the actual stages and process through which schools and individual teachers determine the appropriate personal and social education for their pupils. Though the starting point must be concerned with the establishment of needs, how this is done and what use is made of the outcomes must depend to a considerable extent on the nature, resources and situation of the particular school and classroom.

In relation to this, this paper will offer a set of very broad and general parameters within which people may establish their own aims for the children for whom they are responsible. It is suggested that discussions about what personal and social education is and ought to be are best held in a specific context and with specific children in mind; and that any discussion would need to take account of the fact that personal and social development is a lifelong process which happens to all people, regardless of their situation. We can, however, identify certain key aspects of the nature of personal and social education.

1 It has *longer term* as well as immediate implications. Thus it should involve some notion of a developmental (spiral) curriculum, and particularly careful consideration of the relationship between what happens in primary and secondary schools within the areas of personal and social education and pastoral provision, and the relationships between the two areas.

2 It involves taking account of *physical* and *psychological developmental processes* as well as *socialisation* within families, school, and other social institutions and social structures, including culture and class.

3 It has a *moral* component and is concerned with the development of values, attitudes and feelings as well as knowledge/ understanding and behaviour and skills.

4 It involves the growth of understanding and feelings about the self as an entity, as well as in relation to others and to the social groups of which one is a part.

5 It concerns the development of competence in communication, in one-to-one relationships and in groups.

6 It must be understood in the context of the relation of human beings to the natural world – especially, in the case of primary children, to animals and plants.

7 It has implications for, and should be involved in, many curriculum areas; other curriculum areas can also contribute to its development, particularly in terms of the pedagogical approach used.

8 It has implications for those who teach it – among other things they will need to seek to achieve a degree of self-awareness, and in some cases a certain amount of personal change may be required before a teacher can undertake effective work in this area. Primary schools may need to recognise that some members of staff are unsuited temperamentally to teaching PSE and must respond to the implications of this.

People may also find it valuable to draw on the work done by others as a source of information and clarification, but they should do this only in conjunction with thinking through the question for themselves. In this way they are likely to become clearer about their own conceptions of personal and social education and the reasons why they think it is important. They are also less likely to be disheartened or confused by the differing and in some cases conflicting conceptions and approaches they may encounter. Some LEAs have produced guidelines for PSE and in the writer's view these should be used in the same way as any other literature – to complement and possibly review the deliberations a school is already involved in.

The position of this book in relation to these recommendations is slightly different. It is specifically intended to promote thought and also to assist it; therefore it is intended that it might also be used as a starting point, a source of ideas as schools initiate their own responses, but equally as a resource against which schools' and teachers' own endeavours can be measured and reviewed.

Some questions and guidelines on the implementation of personal and social education

The successful implementation of any programme of personal and social education depends on systematic examination of what is already happening in the school, planning for what should happen and a careful system of monitoring and evaluation. This should be spearheaded by the head or, in a larger school, a co-ordinator who should ideally be a post-holder. All staff, however, must be involved and time allowed for planning – only in this way will they 'own' any developments. If this exercise is to be effective it should not be an 'afterthought' but a fundamental part of the school's policy and planning for each child's total curriculum experience.

1 Who should be involved in thinking and planning for PSE?

Teachers may not be the only people who should decide what kinds of personal and social education should take place in schools. Many claim that this is a matter in which parents and governors have a right to participate. It might also be thought that other members of the school staff and workers in agencies associated with the school should be involved. Some would wish to include representatives from the community and religious bodies. Perhaps even pupils should be consulted. Schools will need to consider carefully who should be involved.

2 What kinds of people do we want our children to be?

This paper has already laid out the parameters for a discussion of this kind and suggests that this is best done in a 'workshop' designed specifically for the purpose. As a starting point people might be asked to reflect on the kinds of persons they want the children to be.

14

Experience suggests that while there may be fundamental differences in the values underlying the aims which people express, at a practical level there are also many areas of agreement. Once these are identified it may be possible to establish principles for personal, social and moral education.

The following list of hoped-for outcomes from PSE was suggested by one of the groups of teachers, advisers, teacher trainers and researchers who attended the original Warwick seminar. It is provided as an example, not as a definitive list – though it might well make a useful basis for some preliminary discussion. The outcomes they identified were:

- mutual trust between child and child, child and teacher, teacher and teacher, teacher and parents;
- children regarding themselves and others as persons of value whatever their sex, colour, creed or appearance;
- children confident in relation to staff, parents, visitors, adults (welcome and unwelcome);
- children more interested in learning and better learners as a result of being regarded as persons rather than vessels for learning;
- children more able to cope with conflict, crises and transitions, success and failure, pain and joy etc;
- children having responsible attitudes to themselves and others and to their learning in and out of school;
- children understanding and relating to the groups of which they are part and becoming aware of the communities and societies of which these groups are part.

The process of identifying these outcomes is an essential part of any attempt to implement PSE. It is vital that all those involved take part in this exercise.

3 To what extent does the school make a positive or negative contribution to meeting these personal and social needs?

Teachers must ask how far the school ethos, the way in which it is organised, the approaches to teaching, the relationships with parents and the community and many other aspects of the *informal curriculum* help or hinder the school in achieving the desired goals for personal and social development. There are often many unexamined assumptions about the ways in which school experience is helpful to children and a closer examination may reveal the need for adjustment. This is particularly important where contradictions are revealed between what is taught in the formal curriculum and the attitudes, values and practices that are implicit in the day-to-day workings of the school. It is vital that these should complement one another.

One aspect of the informal curriculum is the pastoral provision offered by the school and the ways in which children are supported through major as well as minor crises. It is sometimes assumed that because of their small scale, primary schools automatically care for children's needs. Teachers need to ask if this is the case and whether staff have the counselling and groupwork skills, time and opportunity to relate to children individually about their concerns. Other professional agencies also have a role to play with children who are undergoing crises and it is important that teachers are aware of the welfare network that exists, know when to refer to appropriate agencies and are given the opportunity to meet with individual workers and attend case conferences.

Teachers must examine whether the *formal curriculum* is planned and offered in such a way as to help children gradually acquire knowledge and understanding, attitudes, values, beliefs and feelings, skills and behaviours which are in keeping with the agreed goals of the school's approach to PSE. This means looking very carefully not only at what is taught but at *how* it is taught. It is through the processes of teaching that children learn powerful lessons about their own value and the value of others. Some approaches to teaching are likely to give greater scope than others for children to take responsibility for their own learning and to engage in experience which will advance their personal and social development.

With regard to the introduction of topics and issues in the field of personal and social education, it is important for these to be revisited at different levels as the children progress through school. The notion of a developmental (spiral) curriculum is a helpful concept here. There will be times when themes which are central to personal and social education are addressed explicitly and for their own sake rather than as an adjunct to another part of the curriculum. On other occasions, however, planning for different parts of the school curriculum should include aims for personal and social education as well as for the topic in hand. The concept of twin objectives should be useful here.

4 *How can we know whether we are succeeding?*

The development of PSE involves monitoring and self-evaluation by staff and pupils alike; without this vital part of the process of curriculum review it is not possible to check whether originally agreed aims and approaches remain appropriate and effective. Monitoring and evaluation imply systematic reflection, actual observation, recording and analysis in which aims are related to practice and gains and losses assessed.

There are many real difficulties in setting attainment targets in PSE as in any other area of the curriculum and there are special problems in judging whether they have been achieved. But such problems should not prevent this being attempted, providing it is handled with sensitivity and caution. The danger of not doing so is that personal and social education will be regarded as an adjunct rather than a central part of the primary school curriculum.

Analysing personal and social education and the determination of needs

The point has already been made that the proper starting point for the development of personal and social education is to determine the needs that PSE should meet. It has also been pointed out that individual perceptions of the nature and purpose of personal and social education vary considerably – thus it will certainly be the case that individual perceptions of the needs PSE should meet will also vary. It follows from this, and the other arguments presented in this paper, that though the determination of needs and appropriate responses must be an essential part of the process through which effective personal and social education is developed, how individual schools undertake this and whom they involve in the process will depend on their individual situations and the skills, expertise and resources available. Clearly, some schools will be better placed than others in relation to the task of developing and implementing effective personal and social education. One purpose of this book is to provide a resource that can assist schools in overcoming this disparity, but schools may be further disadvantaged by the lack of generalised models relating to dimensions of PSE from which they can work. Ultimately it is to be hoped that as the literature of the theory and practice of personal and social education develops, so will the number and sophistication of the models available to assist schools. As a starting point the following tentative model for the formulation and analysis of needs is presented (Figure 1). This model is an illustration of the sort of analytic tools that could – and perhaps should – ultimately underpin the development of personal and social education.

Figure 1 *A model of the range of needs which underpin personal and social education*

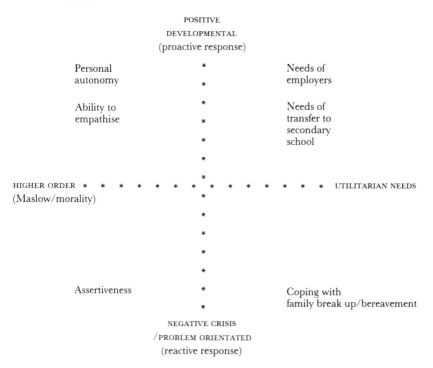

Needs can be located in relation to two continua; one ranges from the positive developmental needs of all pupils to the more negatively characterised crisis-orientated needs of individuals; the other continuum lies between needs which are basically utilitarian in character – relating to aspects of society, the economy, the school as an institution (these are likely to change over time) – to needs derived from conceptions of the individual as a person and what that implies. It is towards the latter that aspects of morality will be located (needs at this end of the continuum are less likely to change over time). Finally, in terms of response to different needs this model underlines the importance of a balance between a *reactive* and *proactive* approach to personal and social education and between response to problems and support for positive development. When schools approach their examination of the needs which should form the basis for their work in the field of PSE, the use of such a model may not only promote a greater depth of understanding and assist clarification, but may also encourage a more balanced and broader perspective on what constitutes the needs of their pupils. Indeed some schools might wish to add further dimensions to such a model. They might wish to include, for example, the range between quasi-psychological concerns such as drug misuse or child abuse, and encouragement with positive developmental tasks such as promotion of self-esteem; or they might add a continuum between focusing only on those dimensions of PSE which directly support effective study and cognitive development, through to focusing on areas of PSE exclusively concerning the 'affective' domain.

Conclusion

This paper has highlighted some of the problems that currently exist in relation to personal and social education in the primary school. It has sought to relate this to the need for a book such as *Thinking about . . . personal and social education in the primary school*. It has then indicated some of the areas that require thought, and provided some guidance as to how the development of PSE should be approached.

It is for the reader to determine how much of what has been said is relevant to their particular situation. More important than this, however, is that a careful reading of a range of the papers found on the following pages should provide a considerable stimulus for thought and a source of ideas. The papers that follow should provide both starting points and a means to review what is already being done, and in some cases to improve it.

References

Alexander, R, 1984 *Primary Teaching* Holt, Rinehart and Winston.

Ashton, P, Kneen, P, Davies, F, 1975 *The Aims of Primary Education: a study of Teacher's opinions* Macmillan Educational.

Assessment and Performance Unit, 1981 *Personal and Social Development* DES.

Bennett, N, 1987 'Changing Perspectives on Teaching-Learning Processes in the Post-Plowden Era' in *Oxford Review of Education*, 13(1).

Boyd, J, 1984 *Understanding the Primary Curriculum* Hutchinson.

David, K, 1982 *Personal and Social Education in Secondary Schools* Schools Council/Longman.

Education Science and Arts Committee, 1986 *Achievement in the Primary school* HMSO.

HMSO, 1985 *Education for all – the report of the committee of inquiry into the education of children from ethnic minority groups* (The Swann Report) HMSO.

HMSO, 1978 *Meeting special educational needs* HMSO.

ILEA, 1984 *Improving Secondary Schools* ILEA.

Pring, R, 1984 *Personal and Social Education in the curriculum* Hodder and Stoughton.

SECTION ONE
Background

Personal and social education cannot be developed in a vacuum, the fact that the work is being undertaken within a wider framework has to be recognised and taken account of.

Section One provides the context within which the discussion of personal and social education in the primary school should be set. The papers in this section provide a combination of background, overview and look to the future, while the place, nature and significance of personal and social education in the primary school is also considered. In the first paper Phillip Gammage provides a broad backdrop, a setting of the scene, or, as he describes it, a 'balance sheet'. He draws attention to some of the misinterpretations and misunderstandings to which views on primary education are subject, for example the popular and erroneous assumption that the typical primary school is excessively and obsessively child-centred. He also outlines many of the practical realities that underlie primary education today, the small size of the average primary school, the poor state of buildings and inadequate level of resourcing. His paper suggests that though much that is good can be said of primary practice today, there are also many critical observations that should be made, the large amount of time spent on a few traditional subject areas taught through a didactic, whole-class approach is one of significance to the theme of this book. Nevertheless Gammage is concerned to defend the spirit of 'Plowden', warning that some critics, in their enthusiasm to highlight the failures of the Plowden ethos, are in danger of 'throwing the baby out with the bath water'.

Patrick Whitaker produces an inspiring mixture of idealism and reality when he considers how the primary schools of tomorrow should respond to the problems and challenges of the world as it is likely to be then. He lays particular emphasis on the ability to cope with ambiguity and paradox. Finally Richard Pring provides a philosophical overview of the nature and place of personal and social education at the primary level. He considers the relationship between PSE and education generally and stresses the need for those involved in the area to reflect on the type of person that PSE should seek to produce.

Had this book been published at a later stage it might have been possible to include a paper in which the implications of the National Curriculum for personal and social education were considered and vice versa. The form this will ultimately take is still unclear. What does seem certain is that, whatever the outcome, there must be a place for some form of personal and social education within the National Curriculum's framework, both through the way that the prescribed areas are taught and also in that period of the week when the school is able to determine its own priorities. This book will provide much of the material needed to support arguments for such provision and also give some indication of the ways in which this might be done.

1 Primary education today: an overview

Philip G. Gammage

When we pick teams in the playground
Whatever the game might be,
There's always somebody left till last
And usually it's me.

I stand there looking hopeful
And tapping myself on the chest,
But the captains pick the others first,
Starting, of course, with the best.

Maybe if teams were sometimes picked
Starting with the worst,
Once in his life a boy like me
Could end up being first!

Allan Ahlberg

In education, the period 1967–1987 can be seen, in English (and perhaps in North American) terms as a period of 'growing disenchantment', as a period of 'increasing realism', as a period of high rhetoric and low reality. In primary education especially, there are milestones of note which most of us could recall. First, the *Plowden Report* (1967) which set out to legitimise good practice and which, as we know, in various ways got it right (the need for nursery education, the need for the children to be actively engaged, the need for greater parental involvement) and, in various ways appears to have got it wrong (the importance of group work, of child choice). Then, in the late 1960s and early 1970s, came the *Black Papers* which accused the primary schools of being too 'open' or too 'sloppy', and whose vitriol has cunningly and wickedly left strong residues in the public mind. The *William Tyndale Affair* (1974) became a 'cause célèbre' which focused much media attention on our sometimes inadequate processes of organisational and curricular control. The *Great Debate* commenced at Ruskin College in 1976, started by the then Prime

Minister, James Callaghan's too-ready association of social malaise with types of schooling. The publication of Neville Bennett's book *Teaching Styles and Pupil Progress* (1976) gave much publicity to the apparent failure of 'informal' teaching styles. The HMI *Primary Report* (1978) confirmed certain inadequacies, notably insufficient stretching of the more able. Publications following the *ORACLE Study* (Galton *et al.*, 1980) demonstrated that the much-vaunted ideal type of 'Plowdenesque' teaching was rare; moreover, that 'within teacher' changes in teaching style were perhaps more usual than was presumed. Barker-Lunn (1984), after a series of studies, showed that Plowden had, in effect, hardly happened in our 23 000 primary schools, that teaching was still like it had been *before* Plowden; and Mortimore *et al.* (1986) emphasised (as has Bennett in more recent publications – Bennett, 1987) that the focus on the task and upon its interrelated *processes* seems central to successful learning.

A corresponding 'litany' might be assembled from charting the different emphases on classroom processes research over the past 20 years or so, from the over-enthusiastic attempts to relate organisation to success, through the search for ideal teaching styles, and the glib connections between climate and pupil achievement, to the more sober assessments of the conditions of learning and the analysis of the task.

Others might wish to cite the economic, social, material and demographic changes which have affected our primary schools so profoundly. The drop in enrolments by over a million pupils during the 1970s, a 20% reduction, changed the structure of many classrooms, increased the amount of vertical grouping – and brought the average primary school size down to well below 170+ pupils. The variations in cost per pupil from LEA to LEA (ranging from £10.44 to £17.70 per capita in 1984) (Gammage, 1986) could well be taken to indicate increasing poverty in the system. The variations in teacher pupil-ratios which, as the recent *Select Committee Report* (1986) shows, run from 1:8 to 1:39 might also be mentioned. To those of us engaged in teacher education, the increasingly centralist tendencies of the DES, or the CATE criteria could loom large in our assessment of change. For their part, local politicians would be well aware of what the *Thomas Report* (ILEA, 1985) called 'increasing financing around the edges' of primary schooling.

But all this is a familiar enough story. Put together too starkly, it could remind one of the famous Hoffnung talk to the Oxford Union in 1956, in which he described the trials and tribulations of repairing a chimney – and which, as many know, ends up with the plea. 'Sir, I respectfully request sick leave!'

It is not my wish, in this brief overview and introduction to the business of caring *better* for children, merely to depress. There is still much to be proud of in English primary education, much that is vital and imaginative. But I wish to place this in a *real* social and historic context, and that context is one of a country still, in some respects, reflecting great inequalities of provision – and hence of opportunity; of a country of relatively small, accessible primary schools, but one in which 40% are based in old and deteriorating buildings. It is a country which, as the Select Committee (1986) reminds us, has a long history of funding secondary schools almost twice as well as its primary schools; a country which among its European partners allocates some of the smallest spaces to its primary children. It is, too, a country which long ago established provision for nursery education (in the 1918 *Fisher Act*), yet which, some 70 years later, has still to reaffirm (in that same all-party Parliamentary Committee) the importance of extending a system whereby currently only 30% or so of our three-year-olds have a pre-school opportunity for social and educational development.

Many teachers concerned with pastoral care come to that concern through a variety of routes, some may wish to add expertise to a strong inclination to act *in loco parentis*; some become inspired by actual experience of the change that can occur when a child's whole personality is engaged in the learning; others see teaching as a caring profession. All of us, however, have several things in common:

1 We assume that *content* and *transaction* are not easily separated in the business of teaching.
2 We recognise the contribution that *psychology* makes (however imperfectly) to educational theory and practice.
3 We are concerned that education should be about *human development*, not human failure.

This interest in children and their welfare is sometimes characterised as *professional* rather than *academic*. Indeed, the British Psychological Society had this to say, early in 1986:

The 'professional' or 'applied' contribution has tended to focus – though not exclusively – on the assessment, placement and assistance of individual children and young people who, for whatever reason, find difficulty in meeting the demands of a normal school. At the time of the Plowden Report a central notion had been the distribution of intellectual abilities between and within individuals. Gradually since then the emphasis of applied educational psychology has moved from a casework to a system level of application, the implication of which is to locate a child's problems more in his family and school environment rather than in features of the individual child.

(BPS, 1986, p 121)

This, like the changes in primary education over the last 20 years, is a change in emphasis with which we are all familiar. But be careful. Who was it who said that educational theories are like buses? If you wait long enough another one comes along! Theories, as many sociologists remind us, are often merely *what counts as valid knowledge at the time*. They are very much grounded in the contemporary perspective. Again, the briefest reflection on the developments and changes which have taken place in social psychology, that applied area *par excellence*, would confirm this. The social psychology of *The American Soldier* (Stouffer *et al*, 1949) was all about theories and research-work on relative deprivation, propaganda, resistance, that were concomitant with the war effort. More recent preoccupations with business success have spawned many of the current social-psychological analyses of management, communication structures, brand image, marketing, and so on. Some of these have been 'translated' (if that is the correct term) into direct educational contexts; this is not to decry them, but it is to emphasise the need for caution. Before we throw out the Plowden baby with the Sir Keith Joseph bathwater; before we wholeheartedly espouse the focus on learning task rather than teaching style; before we move totally from descriptions of normality/abnormality to context analysis, let us look again at the purposes, problems and conflicts inherent in primary schooling.

1 The children are young – for the most part pre-pubescent – and therefore strongly adult-oriented and in need of nurture.
2 Research studies show that primary education (including nursery education) has a powerful and pervasive effect on the later educational development of the child.

3 Childhood (though partly a 'social product') is undoubtedly a period when the individual may easily feel lost and confused.

4 It is easy to underestimate the roles which teachers play in helping children come to terms with *groups* of people – a vital journey in socialisation.

5 The integration of information in personally meaningful ways is central to each child's developing self-concept as well as to his/her development of a coherent world view of things.

6 Ideally, teaching should take differentiation and 'initial periods' of learning into account. Epstein, for instance, 'advocates that teaching should take into account the alternation in speed of growth: new ways of thinking should be introduced when the brain is showing rapid growth; during the intervening periods there should be consolidation of what has already been learnt' (Schmidt, 1984, p 18).

7 An increasing number of studies here, in Australia and in North America have demonstrated the effectiveness of involving parents and other adult workers and listeners in early years schooling.

8 Educational problems faced by a significant number of children 'are in part due to the organisation of the school as a whole, as well as to individual teachers within that school' (BPS, 1986, p 123).

And so, back to the beginning, to Plowden and to the apparent 'decline' in primary education. Did Plowden get it so wrong? Academic educationists may demonstrate the 'woolliness' in it all, the lack of detailed analysis of *how* it might all be done, but there was no lack of central concern for the child and his or her home, nor lack of concern that primary education should be exciting and challenging. Much educational writing of the earlier decades of this century was *inspirational*, concerned to present a vision. As Selleck says (quoting Boothroyd in the 1920s):

> In 1918 we Inspectors stood upon the mountain top, looking down into the Promised Land which we expected, shortly, to enter: our old men dreamed dreams and our young men saw visions . . .
>
> (Selleck, 1972, p 129)

Surely, it is in these lights, that one classifies primary education, and with it the ideology of what has been called 'of being on the child's side'.

Bond seems to me to have got the measure of it all when he says,

Only when the attitudes and relationships are right within the school and within the larger community will we achieve our educational goals. There has been no 'rise and fall' of the open school in its correct sense, nor has there been a 'back to the basics' effect in our schools. (How could there be when the vast majority of the schools have never left the basics?) Rather there has been, as happens always in change, a small movement forward followed by a consolidation period that only the foolish would call a regression.

(Bond, 1986, p 11)

Recently, I had the temerity to try to make a brief assay of the present state of English primary education. As part of that survey I composed a final balance sheet which I now up-date and present to the reader for consideration.

1 Our schools are relatively numerous yet small (some 23 000 – probably about 3000 too many in DES and recent political terms – but small schools can be 'clustered' or federated, and the political will to close schools probably does not exist).

2 The average primary school now has about 170 children and 5/6 staff.

3 There is a clear deterioration in buildings and resources that has been well documented in recent years. Yet there is an improved teacher:pupil ratio because of the effect of falling rolls. There is a growing need for a modest expansion in primary (especially infant) teacher-training output (*Select Committee Report*, 1986).

4 There are major differences between LEAs as regards general capitation and provision of resources. There are major differences between 'catchment' areas because of this and the increasing reliance on parental finance at the 'edges' of the system.

5 Because of recently falling rolls many primary schools (perhaps now the majority) employ mixed-age groupings and, less often, two part-time teachers to a class.

6 All primary schools devote considerable time to the basic subjects and much of this is taught in conventional class approaches. Surveys on the *extent* of commitment to the 'three Rs' vary, but some suggest that almost 70% of the week is devoted to them in some form or other.

7 There is an increasing central control of the curriculum content and a tendency for the DES (especially) to emphasise 'subject' expertise and curriculum leadership in primary schools, though there is no clear evidence of specialist teaching in the accepted secondary school sense.

8 All primary teachers entering the profession are now graduates. Primary teacher-training courses approved by CATE pay particular attention to there being a substantial element of specialist subject learning in the course. About half the new primary teachers entering the profession, however, are now destined to emerge from the degree-plus-one-year PGCE route, with all its concomitant and acknowledged weaknesses.

9 A marked increase in parental involvement has been assured during the last decade, through legislation, through requirements that schools better inform parents, through duties laid on LEAs and through the impact of research.

10 There never was a massive, uncontrolled, or highly child-centred approach to primary education. Any caricature of primary education as such does great injustice to the principles espoused in the original Plowden Report (1967) and flouts all known evidence. The reality has been repeatedly shown to be one of modestly child-centred and individual approaches mixed with a large core of class-teaching and recognizably planned and sequenced teacher direction.

(Gammage, 1986, p 82)

Yet it is important to remember the ideals of Plowden. At the heart of it all lies the child. It is all too easy to be lost in worries about leadership training, size of class, use of information technology and so on. Ben Morris probably got it about right when he said, in a talk in Australia in the 1960s,

The development of confidence in one's own genuine powers – however limited these may be – is the first essential of personal growth, and such confidence is rooted in an attitude to the world which finds it a good place and people in it worthy of trust and love. In the beginning, belief in ourselves depends on

someone else having believed in us, having cared for us having
loved us.

(Morris, 1972, p 261)

That still seems the worthy goal of it all and the essential underlying
leitmotiv for a good primary education.

References

Barker-Lunn, J, 1984 'Junior school teachers: their methods and practices'
in *Educational Research*, *26*(3), p 178–88.

Bennett, N, 1976 *Teaching Styles and Pupil Progress* London: Open Books.

Bennett, N, 1987 'Changing Perspectives on Teaching-Learning Processes
in the Post-Plowden Era' in *Oxford Review of Education*, *1*.

Bond, G, 1986 'Anglo-American Scene' in *Journal of National Association for
Primary Education*, *17*, p 8–11.

British Psychological Society, 1986 'Achievement in the primary school:
Evidence to the Education, Science and Arts Committee of the House of
Commons' in *Bulletin of the British Psychological Society*, *39*, p 121–5.

DES (1978) *Primary Education in England: A Survey by HM Inspectorate of
Schools* London: HMSO.

Galton, M, Simon, B and Croll, P, 1980 *Inside the Primary School* London:
Routledge and Kegan Paul.

Gammage, P, 1986 *Primary Education: structure and context* London: Harper
and Row.

Morris, B, 1972 *Objectives and Perspectives in Education* London: Routledge
and Kegan Paul.

Mortimer, P *et al.*, 1986 *The Junior School Project* ILEA Research and
Statistics Branch.

Select Committee on Education, Science and Arts 1986 *Achievement in
Primary Schools*, *1*, HMSO.

Schmidt, W H O, 1984 *Human Development: The Early Years* ECS, Alberta
Education.

Selleck, R J W, 1972 *English Primary Education and the Progressives, 1914–1939*
London: Routledge and Kegan Paul.

Stouffer, S A *et al*, 1949 *The American Soldier: Adjustment During Army Life*, *1*
& *2*, Princetown, NJ: Princetown University Press.

2 A speculative consideration of primary education and the future

Patrick Whitaker

Schools today are having to respond to a moving target of changing circumstances, values, ideas, structures and forces. A fundamental problem that teachers need to address as they prepare children for life in the future is that of uncertainty. It has become something of a cliché, these days, to say that the children now in our primary schools will be living out the whole of their adult lives in the 21st century. But behind this somewhat obvious statement lurk a range of implications, both for children themselves and for the schools in which they learn.

There is a growing literature on futures, some of it to do with the implications of living in a world where nuclear weapons continue to be stockpiled, where power and wealth are pursued by a few at the expense of the many and where the life-enhancing qualities of the planet's fabric continue to be ravaged at an alarming rate. Other writers about the future take a less pessimistic view and point to the need to raise our awareness of the importance of human relating and of being a person. Supporters of a more creative view of human groups suggest that it will be necessary to reinvent the tribe to help people to overcome the alienating effects of large institutions and structures. Much of the work on futures points towards a more holistic approach to knowledge and understanding. Scientific research is moving away from reductionist approaches to a more systemic and connective analysis. Such a stance can also be seen in work in philosophy, medicine, psychology, economics and education.

One of the inherent difficulties of educating, as we tend to approach it, is that of trying to offer a body of knowledge that will remain valid and valuable throughout a person's life. Fifty years ago Alfred North Whitehead observed that such an approach would only work if the time span of major cultural change was greater than the life span of individuals. But now:

We are living in the first period of human history for which this assumption is false . . . today this time span is considerably shorter than that of human life and accordingly our training must prepare us to face a novelty of conditions.

Within a life span there will be many phases of social change; if the five year olds now in our schools live out their 70 years or so they will experience a whole range of social, economic, political, scientific and technological changes. In such circumstances what is the value of an approach which is built on the basis of a body of knowledge? The preoccupation of the schooling system with facts, information and knowledge must be challenged. Learners need to develop a high respect for facts but only because they serve the purposes of solving human problems and dilemmas, not as ends in themselves.

Writing in *Future Shock* as long ago as 1971, Alvin Toffler drew attention to a seeming incapacity among people to cope with rapid change. Since then, change has continued inexorably. Within our specific concerns of pastoral care and education we are witnessing the growing phenomenon of child abuse with all its alarming implications. The role of the teacher is being modified to incorporate this social issue and teachers will need much in-service training if they are to be able to respond to it with sensitivity and imagination. But let me suggest one issue which has made an impact on all our lives, not since 1971, but 1981 – that of AIDS. How will the education system respond to this? In the six months between this talk and preparing it for publication a vast range of activities have been undertaken to raise public awareness. AIDS is likely to present the greatest social, medical and moral dilemma of the 20th century and its impact will be more far-reaching than leprosy was a thousand years ago. That is until the next issue comes along to take its place. For us as educators the challenges are enormous. They are more to do with helping the learners in our schools to develop strategies for dealing successfully with problems and dilemmas, however and wherever they occur, than with providing particular tactics for specific issues.

Toffler suggests three key considerations for schools of the future. The first of these is that the curriculum needs to focus on helping pupils to learn how to learn, so that in any novel situation they have easy access to the learning capacity that we are all born with. Far from concentrating simply on a body of knowledge, the learning process becomes more one of unlocking the learning potential of all the children we work with. Second, Toffler suggests that we should increase the work we as teachers do in helping children to relate one to another, to work in groups, and to work alone. As well as having an increased capacity to build effective relationships, the learner of tomorrow will need the capacity to cope with loneliness and the breakdown of relationships. In order to achieve this, schools need to help children to listen more effectively. Toffler's third suggestion is that learners in schools will need to be helped to deal with an increasing degree of choice – moral choices, social choices, economic choices, career choices, friendship choices and relationship choices. Our classrooms need to become places where decision-making skills can be learnt and practised; where pupils can learn to face the consequence of choices and to take responsibility for their actions.

This phenomenon of overchoice is already being experienced by headteachers in primary schools. Constant demands for responses to new policy initiatives, ever-increasing expectations of governors and parents, rapidly changing social phenomena and a crisis of confidence in the capacity of schools to deliver effective education, are creating conditions of overload in the management of schools and causing stress and breakdown in an increasing number of head-teachers. Heads working in these conditions at the edge of change will need more courage than ever before to say no to those things they must resist and to say yes to those things they know are essential to the healthy growth and development of their pupils.

I want to say something now about personal and social education and the pathological tendency. In *The Politics of Experience* R D Laing wrote:

> A child born today in the United Kingdom stands a ten times greater chance of being admitted to a mental hospital than to a university. This can be taken as an indication that we are driving our children mad more effectively than we are genuinely educating them. Perhaps it is our way of educating them that is driving them mad.

Learning which is conducted under the general heading personal and social education needs to avoid the idea that life is so awful that our children will need survival strategies to cope with an increasingly complex, confused and disoriented society. We must work hard to avoid the idea that personal and social education is a sort of emotional first aid. Good first aid kits are kept in a cupboard and used only occasionally, when they are necessary. I dread the possibility that personal and social education will come to be seen as one more example of 'remedial' work. Rather it needs to be seen as a process of rediscovering and reactivating those potentials and abilities which have become suppressed as a result of socialisation. Personal and social education in the future needs to be about setting up a framework for natural growth and learning which pays full attention to Maslow's idea of the actualising tendency – that natural capacity organisms have to develop to their full potential. Only when that natural capacity is interfered with and the growing conditions damaged does the tendency to full healthy growth become frustrated. The human organism enters a world of chaos and disorientation and unless personal and social education is placed right at the very centre of the learning process, schooling is likely further to damage its precious potential.

We also need to take account of research into the brain, which shows that the two hemispheres of the brain deal with quite different functions. The education system has tended to overdevelop the left side of the brain which deals with logical thinking, rational processes, convergent problem solving and mathematics, and to underdevelop the right hemisphere which deals with creativity, emotional and intuitive processes and the world of the imagination. This cognitive preoccupation was recognised by A S Neill, who asserted that most schools treated pupils as 'brains on sticks'. We need to look harder at the concept of the whole person as a complex system of interconnecting parts. The concept of holism requires us to set a pupil's learning within the context of daily life so that living and learning are inseparable threads in the unfolding of under- standing and awareness.

As we move into the future we must also try to overcome the need to re-educate adults in many of those qualities and learnings which naturally emerge quite early in life. The process of management training in education is an interesting example of this situation. I can speak of it with some authority because I have been involved in it as a trainer for many years now. When I go into nursery and infant classrooms and spend time with very young children engaged in their learning I see all the management skills in evidence around me.

The children can organise, they can motivate, they can plan, they can challenge, they can make decisions and work out the results of their endeavours. Yet when you become 40 or so you are sent on a management course to learn about these things. The fact is, of course, that these young children have not quite learnt that there is a special way of conducting learning and that is the way that the school decrees. Personal autonomy and individuality are not the qualities we prize most highly in our classrooms and the need for order and control loom higher in most schools' priorities than initiative and creativity.

I should like now to mention six points that come from a book which has made a strong impact on my thinking about the way that schools should be run. The book is *In Search of Excellence* by Peters and Waterman; it looks at the lessons to be learnt from America's best-run companies. The most successful companies seem to be the ones that have the most radical approaches to management and organisation, approaches which surely have implications for the way we run our schools. I will attempt to relate some of these points to schools and to personal and social education in particular.

First, good schools in the future will be those which have a capacity to respond creatively to ambiguity and paradox. Schools are full of inconsistencies and contradictions, and that is to be expected. People do not behave tidily, learners do not learn in uniform ways and teachers approach similar subject matter from many different standpoints. Many schools become preoccupied with removing inconsistencies and the pursuit of uniformity leads to frustration and despair. It is much better to accept paradox, to plan for the unexpected and to recognise the ambiguities inherent in human behaviour.

Second, Peters and Waterman talk about the need for 'ad hocracy'. This is often despised as a management approach, departing as it does from the ideal of carefully formulated plans and policies. Yet ad hocracy seems to be a feature which contributes to success. If one thing doesn't work, try another. It is the method children constantly adopt as they grapple with the problems of living. This is not to suggest that ad hocracy is an alternative to more systematic approaches but that in some cases it is the most appropriate, particularly when situations demand quick and flexible responses. In human situations like teaching and learning, rigidity of approach and uniformity of practice serve to release the innate capacities of pupils and teachers. We need to move away from institution-centred learning to a more person-centred approach which responds to human individuality and difference.

Third, there is the idea that the schools of tomorrow will be successful if they have a bias for action. In a fast changing world the capacity to get things done quickly is vital. Many schools seem to devote years to discussing curriculum change and very little time to the process of actually introducing new programmes and policies. We are living through a time when school accountability seems to be discharged through the weight of the documentation that can be produced about the curriculum, rather than through the quality of the learning experiences that pupils have access to. Sadly, many of the documents that are produced bear very little relationship to the work that actually goes on in classrooms. A bias for action would place far more emphasis on the implementation stage of any innovation or change; it is a sad fact that some schools seem to spend their time looking for something else new to do and very little time following up and supporting the new things they have just done. This is not to suggest, however, that the strategy attributed to an executive of the Cadbury organisation – READY ... FIRE ... AIM! – is the one to be adopted.

The fourth point is that good schools will be those which have a high tolerance of failure. Schools have long been far too concerned with mistake avoidance, with making sure that nobody gets anything wrong, with getting it right first time and in your best hand writing. Yet getting things wrong is a model for growth. Learning from your mistakes is often put forward as one of the most important ways of learning. But where are the schools which celebrate the fact that getting things wrong can be a source of growth? Creative risk taking is the very stuff of learning, as George Henson has stated:

> ... teachers and parents need to provide a safety net that encourages high-spirited mistakes that are not terminal. Some will learn one way and some another.

Fifth, Peters and Waterman suggest closeness to the customer as an essential ingredient for success. In schools this means that we have to get closer to the children we teach. 'Watch the child, the child will show you what to do' was Froebel's phrase. We need to extend that to listening as well, listening perhaps more than watching because it is in the words of the child that we gain insights into the inner world of being. As teachers we need to increase our capacity to sense what learning feels like from the learner's point of view. We certainly need to spend more time listening to our pupils than talking to them.

Sixth, we have the phrase 'simultaneous loose – tight properties'. What this means is that in good organisations there is a strong adherence to a central core of values but that individuals have freedom to work according to their skills and expertise, without undue supervision and excessive concern for uniformity of approach. What seems to happen in a lot of our schools is the exact opposite of this. There is a looseness of values and ideals at the heart of many schools but a rigidity of practice and procedure which inhibits the creativity of teachers. To change this to the pattern recommended by Peters and Waterman requires a process of very courageous management. This involves equalising educational enterprise. A clear framework of support and encouragement needs to be created so that the skills and creativity of children and teachers is released for the good of all. Creating an organisation in which everyone feels a sense of belonging, a feeling of achievement and of influencing the course of events depends upon the synthesising of a clearly understood and accepted central core of values.

All of these points are worthy of consideration. Few of them, however, will be much use in a school which has lost its capacity to dream. Daring to dream about good learning and good education is a vital activity for heads and teachers, just as daring to dream about the possibilities of their lives and futures is a vital activity for children. The bringing of dreams to reality is at the very heart of what we should be trying to do in our primary schools. In a world where the pursuit of the curriculum can so easily become very dire, it is essential to maintain a sense of vision. As teachers we need to 'let go' a bit more and help children to do the same. The relentless pursuit of barren, cognitive objectives will not produce healthy, intelligent and creative adults. We need to share with our pupils the joy and exuberance of learning when it is well done in a spirit of enquiry and curiosity.

3 Personal and social education in the primary school

Richard Pring

It is seen as self-evident that personal and social education (PSE) be at the centre of what we should be planning and should be doing in primary schools. Most teachers would claim that they are indeed engaged in pursuing what is seen to be so obviously important.

But therein lies the problem, for what is seen to be self-evidently true, or what is seen to be obviously worth pursuing, rarely receives the critical examination and scrutiny that perhaps it requires. Rarely is that which is regarded as self-evident, spelt out in detail. Certainly it is understood to be beyond the need for justification. Thus, unfortunately, anything might be acceptable under such bland and unhelpful titles as 'helping children to realise their potential' or 'facilitating growth' or 'encouraging personal autonomy'. When personal development (unlike mathematical or scientific development) is 'everywhere' in the school, then there is a need to be doubly cautious – first, because, whatever PSE is, it might just as easily be inhibited as promoted by the practices within the school; second, because something so all-pervasive may be denied the systematic thought and planning that it deserves.

What is the source of the problem I want to outline? On the one hand, the self-evident nature of the importance of PSE arises from the logical or conceptual connections between personal development and what it *means* to educate someone. The concern for personal development of young people is inseparable from the very educational enterprise that teachers are paid to carry out. On the other hand, the full implications of this conceptual truth are rarely made clear – understandably so, because deep down there is a suspicion of education, even among teachers, and thus of the personal development of young people, however much teachers might protest to the contrary. This apparent paradox I will try to outline in this chapter, together with the implications for curriculum planning.

Education and PSE

Let us start with a distinction between training and education. Parents or teachers train children to do particular things – to wash their hands before meals, to speak politely to one another, to articulate their thoughts and wishes, to read fluently, to count and to take away, and so on. These are specific skills, specific ways of behaving. What young people are trained to do (successfully, we hope) *may be* an important part of their education. But, on the other hand, it may not be. For instance, some might argue that early training in mathematics might be *mis*educative – if, for example, it gives the child such a poor impression of mathematics that he or she is put off the subject for life, or if the concepts acquired get in the way of subsequent learning. Similarly, successful behavioural training might be considered *mis*educative by some if it shapes a submissive attitude to authority or encourages too ready a conformity to dominant values. Training, then, is a very specific process whereby people (in this case young children) are enabled to do specific things. What is a successful outcome of a process of training may or may not be regarded as successful education. The latter depends on further considerations.

These further considerations lie in some account of what we consider to be valuable in life for these young people to learn. 'Education', unlike 'training', is a concept that implies that something worthwhile has been achieved. To educate young people is to introduce them to a worthwhile form of life – it is to say that these qualities, experiences, skills, and understandings are very important and that, having acquired or internalised them, children are able to live more effectively and fruitfully. You can claim to have trained someone (as a computer operator, as a bus driver, as a merchant banker) without raising the more fundamental questions of what is worthwhile. But you cannot claim to be *educating* someone without, implicitly at least, committing yourself to a moral stance as to what is of worth to him or her as a person.

We need to unpack the values that are implicit in our talk about educating people as opposed to merely training them, about introducing them to a worthwhile form of life as opposed to simply giving them specific skills or knowledge. The first point to note is that such an introduction to a form of life must affect them in a personal way –

it must transform their outlook significantly. For example, it is possible to be trained to use a computer so that this becomes a purely 'added-on skill', an acquisition of a way of working in specific circumstances which, in a real and important sense, leaves the child much as she was before, with her general outlook on life, and its possibilities, in no way affected. On the other hand, the child could be so trained that the very acquisition of that skill does transform her outlook – does raise questions about technology and its uses, about its potential for communication or for the storage and pursuit of knowledge, about the silly attribution of gender differences in technological ability – and thus becomes an *educative* experience. The child is affected significantly; in an important sense, she changes as a person; her understanding of subsequent experience is in small measure transformed; new possibilities and values are opened up.

Inevitably, however, there are major disagreements over what specific qualities or skills or understandings are to be considered worthwhile. Different people will have different perceptions of 'the worthwhile form of life' to which they think children should be introduced. And this is no more than a different way of saying that people differ over what they consider to be personal growth – the kind of person (displaying certain kinds of qualities, attitudes and abilities) that they would like the child to grow into. Parents certainly feel this, however liberal they deem themselves to be. The parents who want their children to be able to read and write, to enjoy certain kinds of books and films, to be able to argue effectively, to be tolerant and fair, to participate in decisions that affect their welfare, to be alive to political and to social issues – such parents have a clear view of the sort of person they want 'produced' and of the educative process intimately connected with it. Teachers, too, by reinforcing certain behaviours and curtailing others, by introducing certain forms of literature and discouraging others, by drawing attention to certain social and environmental issues and ignoring others, by organising physical and sporting activities in one particular way and not in others – such teachers do have implicitly a picture of what, for those children, are significant formative experiences and what, for them, is a worthwhile way of seeing and enjoying the world. There is a philosophy of education connected with a philosophy of personal development – often unexamined.

Such personal development cannot in practice be disconnected from social development, although it may be useful, for purposes of analysis, to keep them conceptually distinct. Let us take the important, though often ignored, capacity to engage in critical reflection upon generally accepted beliefs – a capacity that requires nurturing over a long period of time and that requires not only careful and well-planned teaching but also a favourable ethos within the school. Such a capacity, if acquired, will affect the way in which authority is to be exercised within the school; furthermore, it will bring with it certain expectations about how social institutions, which affect our lives and the distribution of opportunities, should be run. Thus, personal development, encapsulated in specific educational values, has wider social and political implications – and no doubt, for this reason, many (including teachers) feel that there can be too much education, too much personal development. After all, the educated person must be a challenge to the status quo. Therefore, instead of education, we so often see forms of socialisation that are *mis*educative and dominated by forms of social control within which the as yet unformed person is not permitted to grow. We must not complacently accept the apparent truism that all schools are concerned with PSE. Perhaps, on the contrary, many schools inhibit that very personal growth which they claim to promote, destroying maybe that sense of dignity and of personal worth, destroying too that independence of thought and of action, which must be at the centre of growth as a person – and thus at the centre of any activity that claims to be educative.

Clearly, PSE and education are logically connected. To educate someone is to transform in some small measure that person *as* a person in what is regarded as a valuable way. But therein lies the problem. PSE cannot be disconnected from the entire educational enterprise – from the values and from the social and political context within which the educational process takes place. Furthermore, those values and the desired context are inevitably controversial. Schools, in promoting PSE, cannot pretend that they are independent of wider political and social controversies about the shaping of society and of the individuals who will sustain, or subvert, the social institutions which constitute that society.

Educating persons

Too often teachers react to the consequences of the essentially controversial nature of PSE either by reducing it to trivia (demonstrated, in the secondary school, by the timetabled treatment, topic by topic, of job opportunities, income tax, interview technique, syphilis, nuclear power, etc) or by saying that it is what they are doing all the time in helping each individual to realise his or her potential. There is rarely any systematic reflection upon the values which should be promoted in the school or in each classroom, or detailed analysis of what is defensible as *personal* development. Education, or the process whereby individuals are helped to grow as persons, requires a clear idea of what counts as being a person. It is difficult to see how anyone can claim to be an educator (as opposed to a trainer) unless he or she has addressed him or herself to such an examination. In a recent book I tried to spell this out in some detail. Here I can only reiterate the points made, briefly and rather dogmatically.

First, one characteristic of being a person is the capacity to think, to reflect, to make sense of one's experience, to engage critically with the received values, beliefs, and assumptions that one is confronted with – the development, in other words, of the *powers* of the mind. The enhancement of that intellectual capacity is a personal right – a right that belongs to each individual *as a person* and as the recipient of a system that claims to be primarily concerned with *educating* the young. Of course, what is meant by 'developing the powers of the mind' does itself require explanation, and indeed the thinking school will never cease in its attempt to make sense in practice of this notion. But at least we can say that it will include the mastering or grasp of those ideas or concepts without which the child will not have an understanding of the physical and social world in which he is living and having to make choices about the future; it will include the cross-disciplinary skills of enquiry and of truth-seeking; it will extend and enhance the powers of imagination. There is something paradoxical about the too-frequent claim that a PSE course is successful where, in so much else, the person remains intellectually deadened by his school experience, uninspired, bored, put off the task of learning.

A second characteristic of being a person is the capacity to recognise others as persons – as centres of consciousness and reason like oneself. Hence, it is a peculiarity of being a person that one is able to relate to others in a person-like way, not using them as instruments for one's own ends, but as deserving of respect in their own right, worthy of being listened to, able to contribute a distinctive point of view. But this capacity to recognise others as persons does itself require nurturing – the gradual acquisition of that empathy, that sensitivity of feeling, that moral concern whereby the child gradually moves from the egocentric frame of reference, that Piaget describes so well, to a more impartial view of the world wherein one no longer remains the centre.

Third, it is characteristic of being a person that one acts intentionally, deliberately, and thus can be held responsible for what one does – not simply the unfortunate victim of forces beyond one's control. This must surely be the basis of moral attributes – of praise and blame, of being held responsible for one's actions and thus subject to reward and punishment, of those ascriptions of virtue such as loyalty, courage, or kindness. Yet, once again, such moral agency is not with us at birth. It requires the bit-by-bit acquisition of dispositions, understandings, and empathy with others. This gradual acquisition can be aided, or impeded, by the teachers' relations with, and instruction of, the children.

Finally, what is distinctive of personhood is the consciousness not only of others as persons but of oneself – a sense of one's own unity as a person, one's own value and dignity, one's own capacity to think through a problem, to persevere when things get tough, to establish a platform of values and beliefs whereby one can exercise some control over one's own destiny. This growth of what is often referred to as 'ego strength' is probably central to all else – the readiness to develop the powers of the mind (which so often requires perseverance and courage), the capacity to engage in meaningful relations with others fearless of rebuff or of failure, the readiness to accept responsibility for one's actions and for one's future.

Here, then, pronounced dogmatically maybe, are the characteristics of personal growth which are the central concern of education – the creation of individuals who are empowered to think and to reflect, who can engage with others in a meaningful and sensitive way, who can take on responsibility for their own actions and destiny, and who have a sufficiently strong sense of their own worth and dignity that they are not deflected from the task.

Curriculum planning

The points I have made can be questioned – questioned as a valid account of what it means to be and to grow as a person, questioned too in terms of how such abstract notions might be unpacked into specific classes, or teaching strategies, or institutional arrangements. But curriculum planning, concerned as it ultimately is with the development of persons, ought to begin (and to continue) with such questioning. For if what I say is in any way near correct, then it follows that PSE is not the kind of thing that can be hived off to one small part of the timetable. Far from it – the whole curriculum experience either enhances or diminishes the very qualities and skills which are essential to growth as a person. For example, the constant experience of failure, subject by subject, will only dent that slowly evolving sense of personhood which is common to all young people. Too often school has offered no more than the confirmation of failure, of unimportance, of worthlessness. Lack of attainment or of achievement, if constantly experienced, can only destroy inner confidence and sense of dignity.

Therefore, question number one in curriculum planning must be: what do we *mean* by personal and social development? But the second question should be: in what way does the experience of the pupils as a whole assist, or resist, such development? What is the impact of the curriculum upon the gradual acquisition of those qualities and understanding which seem essential to being fully a person?

The pursuit of this question will, if rightly conducted, require some examination of *what* activities enable *which* children to have a sense of achievement. It will seek to find out in what ways children are encouraged (slowly, stage by stage) to accept greater responsibility for their actions and for those decisions which affect them. It will look closely at how authority is exercised and relationships established between teachers and children. It will require an account of *how* children learn rather than of *what* they learn – cooperatively or competitively, from curiosity or for the sake of extrinsic reward, requiring initiative or dependent on authority.

Furthermore, one would (in examining the impact of the curriculum as a whole upon the child) be able to suggest detailed solutions to those problematic situations that arise. Thus, there are ways in which cooperative modes of learning can be positively aimed at; there are skills and habits of independent learning which can be introduced even among five and six year olds; discussion as a mode of exploring issues can be taught; the capacity to listen and to communicate can be developed. And, indeed, unless the foundation of these qualities and skills is laid during the primary years, it will be difficult for them to be achieved at the secondary phase.

PSE, therefore, should not be confused with a subject, a slot on the timetable, a particular curriculum innovation. Rather is it about the development of the person – an aim which is as broad as the educational enterprise itself. PSE requires a particular vision of personal growth, rooted in a concept of person that needs to be examined and justified. It requires a close examination of the experience which children receive in all areas of school life and of the ways in which teaching, curriculum content, and relationships shape that experience. Such an examination must have one eye to the child's future – the way in which present experience contributes to (or detracts from) that gradual acquisition of independence of thought and responsibility in action which the mature personality possesses.

In this book, there are many specific suggestions for assisting with personal and social development. But in concentrating on particular curriculum content and activity one must not lose sight of the wider philosophical perspectives. Otherwise one will be left with the outward signs of personal development, the fringe achievements, the appearances, but there will be no substance.

SECTION TWO
Pupils and teachers

What pupils and teachers do and think, whether or not they consider what they are involved in to be personal and social education, has important implications for how it is understood and how effective it is.

The general focus of the papers in this section is on personal and social education as it relates to pupil and teacher action, understandings and experience. As in several of the sections of this book, this central theme is, in fact, very loosely interpreted; some papers could as easily have been included in other sections. Patrick Whitaker focuses on the style that the teacher should adopt in the classroom, effectively incorporating aspects of personal and social education and pastoral care into the way that all teaching is approached. However, his concept of the 'person-centred teacher' is by no means the loose and amorphous notion that its title might suggest, and indeed evidence is included which links this style of teaching to enhanced pupil achievement.

In Tony Charlton's paper the concern is with one aspect of the teacher's approach to teaching, though in fact the group counselling approach which he describes is a notion that overlaps with some aspects of Whitaker's person-centred teaching, and will also, it is suggested, result in enhanced pupil performance.

Peter Lang sounds a word of caution by drawing attention to the results of some of his research, which showed that as yet the attitudes of teachers and their awareness in relation to PSE will need to change, before some of the objectives for effective work in this area suggested in this book can become a reality in many schools.

The other papers focus specifically on pupils and their perceptions: David Ingram and Noreen Wetton and Alysoun Moon demonstrate ways of working with pupils; Jim Campbell and Peter Lang, on the other hand, are concerned with the implications of how pupils perceive things and how this might be investigated.

4 The person-centred teacher
Patrick Whitaker

The 20th century has witnessed a developing debate about just what it is that pupils should learn in school and the struggle to achieve the right prescription has become something of a preoccupation in the management of the education service. Of the vast financial resources that have been allocated to curriculum development, most have been concentrated on the content and objectives of what pupils should learn and very little on the actual learning process. Radical critics of the education system such as Illich (1973), Reimer (1971) and Goodman (1971), achieved some attention during the early 1970s, but more often because of the power of their rhetoric than their capacities to suggest practical solutions to the problems they identified.

The late 1970s and early 1980s saw an increasing interest in the notion of person-centred learning. Carl Rogers' seminal book *Freedom to Learn* (1964) has been a key influence on a number of teachers. More recently, writers such as Theodore Roszak (1981), Marylin Ferguson (1982) and Fritjof Capra (1983), have articulated the need to change the emphasis of our education from one of teaching to one of learning. They stress the need to see learning as a natural part of healthy living and growing, and argue that in our formal institutions we need to create conditions in which pupils can find space, time and encouragement to learn during the most formative stage of their personal journey through life.

Pastoral care

At the same time as these developments has come the rise of pastoral care as a key function in the organisation and management of schools, particularly in the secondary sector. There can be few comprehensive schools which do not have a pastoral system, with a discrete management structure of roles and responsibilities. This development is symptomatic of a schooling system in a bad state of repair. As Schumacher observed in *Small is Beautiful*

If western civilization is in a state of permanent crisis it is not far fetched to suggest that there is something wrong with its education.

(Schumacher, 1974)

It would be foolish to believe that simply through pastoral care we have the capacity to make the schooling system the enriching and deeply satisfying experience it should be for both pupils and teachers. This is not to denigrate pastoral care, or those who work in it. In fact so successful have those teachers been who work within this system that a major crisis caused by pupil disaffection has so far been avoided. The point is, that while pastoral care continues to alleviate the problems caused by the learning process as it is presently conducted by the majority of teachers, then it can be little more than remedial work.

As pastoral care has grown there has been a tendency to separate it from the formal learning process of the school. Although many teachers find themselves fulfilling both curriculum and pastoral responsibilities there is a danger that pastoral care will come to be seen as an alternative to the curriculum. Already it is possible for teachers to pursue a career which is almost exclusively pastoral. Some schools have separate management teams attending to their own distinct set of interests and concerns. Increasingly, complaints are made that pastoral care is diverting resources from the curriculum and creaming off the best teachers. Those of us who work predominantly in pastoral care must do what we can to avoid this tendency to separate the learning and living aspects of pupil development.

A new paradigm

The healthy future of formal education within a schooling system lies in its capacity to integrate rather than to separate. Those who work in pastoral care are perhaps especially equipped to be aware of this necessary holism and in a better position to work towards its realisation. The libertarian Brazilian educator Paulo Freire (1972) has stressed that learning must be tied to the 'life force' of the learner. This places a pupil's personal growth as the central core element of the curriculum. If pupils are to become more involved in the process of learning they need to be helped out of 'the culture of silence' – that oppressive condition in which people are not aware of the social forces working them. This requires, Freire argues, a process of conscientisation. By learning to perceive the social and political contradictions in their lives people grow in awareness of their social reality and become more capable of transforming it. Pastoral care is very much about this transformational process, about helping pupils to rise out of their cultures of silence. Often it is the school itself which is creating oppressive conditions through a punitive ethos and instruction-centred curriculum. Cultures of silence are rife in management teams, staffrooms and classrooms as well as in the outside lives of pupils.

One way to achieve a more holistic approach to schooling lies in a more creative integration of the curriculum with the notion of pastoral care. This implies much more than the generation of a pastoral curriculum which runs alongside the more prestigious cognitive curriculum. It involves a complete re-examination of the principles and assumptions upon which approaches to teaching and learning are built. In an attempt to help us see the schooling process from the pupils' point of view Carl Rogers (1969) has suggested that teaching in schools is built on a number of basic assumptions, summarised as follows:

1 Pupils cannot be trusted to learn.
2 An ability to pass examinations is the best criterion for judging potential.
3 What a teacher teaches is what a pupil learns.
4 Learning is the steady accumulation of facts and information.
5 An academic procedure is more important than the idea it is intended to investigate.
6 Pupils are best regarded as manipulative objects, not as persons.

A number of significant changes will need to be made if the transformational process in education is to be successful. First, there needs to be a major shift from passive to active learning. Passive learning places great emphasis on conforming, memorising, meeting requirements and 'getting on'. Active learning places emphasis on the releasing of natural energy for learning through creating, problem solving, planning and evaluation. Most passive learning in school is lifeless, sterile and quickly forgotten, whereas active learning creates space for that most precious commodity – insatiable curiosity.

A second important departure from tradition needs to be an acceptance that by the time pupils enter the schooling system they are already skilled learners. As John Holt (1971) observes:

> Almost every child, on the first day he sets foot in a school building, is smarter, more curious, less afraid of what he doesn't know, better at finding and figuring things out, more confident, resourceful, persistent and independent, than he will ever again be in his schooling or, unless he is very unusual and lucky, for the rest of his life.

In our work with pupils we need to take full account of this capacity for free or natural learning. We learn to speak and walk by this method – two tasks arguably more complicated than anything the schooling system might require of us later, and which are accomplished without deliberate and organised teaching. Seymour Papert (1980) has suggested that natural learning has many of the features that schools should envy.

1 It is effective – all children get there.
2 It is inexpensive – it requires neither teacher nor curriculum development.
3 It is humane – children do it in the same carefree spirit without external rewards or punishment.

Like Holt, Papert suggests that it is the schools themselves which create difficulties for learners:

> Children begin their lives as eager and competent learners. They have to learn to have trouble with learning.

The key to achieving success in transforming attitudes and assumptions lies in accepting an enhanced view of human potential. Maslow (1968) and Rogers (1961) have both argued that individuals have within themselves vast resources for healthy and successful living. These resources become suppressed and minimalised during the process of socialisation but can be reactivated if a supportive psychological climate is provided. Such an actualising tendency is a characteristic of human beings but is also present in all living organisms. Unfortunately, schools have tended not to create the right psychological climate in which to promote and celebrate this directional process and many, perhaps the majority of, pupils leave formal education thwarted and unfulfilled. Theodore Roszak (1981) has summarised it well:

> This is what all of us bring into life and school: a wholly unexplored, radically unpredictable identity. To educate is to unfold this identity – to unfold it with the utmost delicacy, recognizing that it is the most precious resource of our species, the true wealth of the human nation.

The person-centred approach

With the increasing momentum created by the spread of personal education and the pastoral curriculum comes a steady permeation of active and person-centred education into the schooling process. If the transformative process is really to take hold there needs to be an accompanying acceptance that person-centredness is the concern of all teachers. Above all it is necessary to work to avoid a developing belief that active and experiential learning methods only have a place in the 'soft' areas of the curriculum. Those teachers working in the cognitive domain need to be helped to realise that person-centred approaches are very 'user friendly' and can bring positive benefits in the form of increased academic performance. Carl Rogers (1969) has drawn attention to a growing body of research evidence which supports a person-centred approach to education. In particular he describes a study undertaken in the United States and several other countries, which set out to determine which particular teacher behaviours were correlated with different kinds of learning outcomes. The research involved the study of 3700 hours of taped classroom activity from 550 primary and secondary schools. Three particular teacher behaviours turned out to be especially significant:

1 The teacher's ability to understand the meaning that classroom experience is having for each pupil.
2 The respect and positive regard the teacher has for each pupil as a separate person.

3 The ability of the teacher to engage in a genuine person-to-person relationship with each pupil.

It was found that pupils in classes with teachers who demonstrated these qualities to a high degree made significantly greater gains in learning. They

- became more adept at using higher cognitive processes such as problem solving;
- had a higher self-concept;
- exercised greater learning initiatives in the classroom;
- exhibited fewer discipline problems;
- had a lower absence rate.

What is particularly interesting and important is the conclusion that with specific training teachers can begin to change their attitudes and develop the sort of facilitative styles described above. The other main characteristics of such teachers were that they

- had a more positive self-concept than lower level teachers;
- were more open and self-disclosing to pupils;
- responded more often and more positively to pupils' feelings;
- gave more praise and encouragement;
- were more responsive to pupils' own ideas;
- engaged in formal didactic teaching less often.

The way forward

The idea of pastoral care and personal and social education needs to be extended to include the concept of person-centred learning. All teachers need to recognise and accept a full share of pastoral responsibility in their classroom work with pupils. The growing schism between pastoral care and the cognitive curriculum in secondary schools will be difficult to break down. The primary sector provides an altogether more conducive climate for exploration. But it is important not to be complacent. Recent evidence (Barker Lunn, 1984; DES, 1984) suggests that far from being havens of progressive and person-centred activity, primary classrooms are managed in much the same formal way that characterised teaching in the immediate post-war period.

The way forward is to bring together into a much closer relationship, concepts of pastoral care, personal and social education and classroom teaching. Pastoral care needs to be implicit rather than explicit, both in the rational expression of educational aims and in the practical processes of classroom management and teaching methods. The pastoral care community needs to concern itself with programmes and policies to develop the idea of person-centredness as the central concern of each and every teacher.

References

Barker Lunn, J, 1984 'Junior School Teachers: their methods and practices' in *Educational Research*, 26(3).
Capra, F, 1983 *The Turning Point* Fontana.
DES, 1984 *Education Observed – a review of published reports by HMIs* HMSO.
Ferguson, M, 1981 *The Aquarian Conspiracy* Granada.
Freire, P, 1972 *Pedagogy of the Oppressed* Penguin.
Goodman, P, 1971 *Compulsory Miseducation* Penguin.
Holt, J, 1971 *The Underachieving School* Penguin.
Illich, I, 1973 *Deschooling Society* Penguin.
Maslow, A, 1968 *Towards a Psychology of Being* Van Nostrand.
Papert, S, 1980 *Mindstorms – Children, Computers and Powerful Ideas* Harvester Press.
Reimer, E, 1971 *School is Dead* Penguin.
Rogers, C, 1961 *On Becoming a Person* Constable.
Rogers, C, 1969 *Freedom to Learn* Charles Merril.
Roszak, T, 1981 *Person/Plant* Paladin.
Schumacher, F, 1974 *Small is Beautiful* Abacus.

5 Images of the working world in an infant classroom
Jim Campbell

Background

St Faith's Church of England Infants School is a voluntary aided school, with some 140 children, five teachers and the headteacher. The catchment area is suburban, socially mixed, with parents mainly in skilled manual and professional occupations. The school is a semi-open plan design, which enables teachers to work collaboratively, where they consider it appropriate. In 1982, the school was encouraged to develop an industry-linked project by the local authority's Schools/Industry Liaison Officer; the idea was particularly attractive to the head, and to one of the classteachers of the top infants (6+ to 7+) class. The quality of the initial project was such that it was reported in a Schools Council publication (Jamieson, 1984).

Each year since then, there has been a project linked to a local firm, intended to enable the pupils to learn about industry. Parents were fully consulted, and several participated in project activities. A characteristic of the projects of the last two years has been that the pupils formed themselves into a mini-company, took shares in it by investing money, and designed, made and marketed a product in collaboration with the linked firm.

We make mugs – a simple project

In 1984/5, the project was developed with a pottery firm. It was called 'We Make Mugs' and two classes of top infants participated, during most of the spring and summer terms. There was a visit to a pottery museum to see how pottery was made at the turn of the century, followed up in school by making pottery in a range of ways. After consolidating the historical background pupils visited the modern factory, where they talked to employees, and followed the production of a mug from the clay preparation through to the packaging and display of the finished item. The visit stimulated the children to write and record their impressions of the trip and when the firm's personnel director and his assistant visited the school, they expressed surprise at the interest of the children and the range and quality of the work they had produced. The teachers developed the pupils' project into considerations of the site of the pottery firm, the location of raw materials and the transportation routes involved – including not only the present roads, but also the local canal system. The project spilled over into all areas of the curriculum, with work on volume in mathematics, written language and talk, and art/craft/design, involving a range of work in clay, models of contemporary and historical factories, and designs for different clay products. Science was included in the project as children experimented with clay, learned about materials required to make slip at the factory, and saw the results of firing poorly-made models. They also found out about electric circuits and switches to give some simple understanding of control of machines.

To help the children understand the running of a factory, they played a simulation exercise, in which they produced paper flowers, folded and coloured. The 'managing director' of two companies was a manager from the linked factory, the 'banker' was a teacher, but the roles of production line workers, supervisors, quality controllers, sales managers and purchasing managers and customers were taken by children. The impact of the simulations upon children's grasp of the financial base of industries was considered significant by the teachers.

They increased their knowledge about raising capital, buying and selling. Pay and bonus payments were discussed and they saw the importance of a good quality product.

A distinctive dimension to the project was the mini-company set up in order to sell mugs bearing designs made by the children. The teacher described the setting up of the company as follows:

After talking to the children about the roles of management and workers, they voted for the most important positions of Managing Director, Sales Manager, Accountant etc. They were very astute in their choice and turned out to have elected the children which we ourselves would most probably have chosen.

The children then set about the task of borrowing money (£100 from the school fund at 10% interest), opened an account at a local bank, ordered mugs with the children's designs on them from the linked firm, and advertised them throughout the local area. They sold the mugs in the school hall, at the junior and secondary schools, outside local shops and supermarkets, in churches, at the local polytechnic, and in the open-air market. When the company was wound up in June its accounts showed a profit of £379.78. At the outset each child had bought a 10p share in the mini-company, and they voted to pay themselves a dividend of 10p – 100% return on their investment. This project received the Education for Capability award from the Royal Society of Arts in 1985, and the citation notes the ability of the pupils to talk impressively and with confidence about the different roles and processes in industry and commerce.

Thus the project represented many aspects of good primary practice: integration of children's interests across the curriculum; learning through first-hand experience; collaborative group work; simulation and role play; parental involvement; great variety of contexts for children's talk; incorporation of relevant knowledge and skills. Similar educational qualities seem to be reflected in other projects based on Education/Industry links in primary schools, for example those reported by Waite (1984) and Ross (1984, 1985), and according to the brief analysis by Jamieson (1985).

Social and personal development

I visited the school in 1986, as part of a larger study of children's understanding of the adult world. The project in 1986 was linked with a different factory, and the children had designed, commissioned, and marketed small sweet dishes (some 11 cm in diameter) selling for £2.50. Like other visitors I was impressed by the enthusiasm and self-confidence of the pupils, and the educational quality of their work. (I must also have been impressed by their sales patter, since I came away with three dishes, rather than the one I had intended to buy!) I spent two days in the classrooms with the pupils, talked to the teachers and the head, conducted a group discussion with some of the pupils, and had informal, individual conversations (lasting about 25 minutes each) with three pupils. My main purpose was to capture something of the ways in which these very young pupils had construed their experience. My interpretations are presented very tentatively, not as criticisms of the participants, but as questions about the personal and social values embodied in the images of the world of work transmitted to the children in such projects. They are presented under three headings below.

Two clusters of values – leadership and loyalty?

The children seem to have picked up the idea of two alternative value orientations operating in industry. On the one hand there are a set of values associated with risk taking, decision making, initiative, responsibility, excitement and the exercise of power – 'leadership' for shorthand. The contrasting set of values is associated with obedience, lack of interest, and passive productivity – 'loyalty'. The former cluster of values is seen by the pupils to be characteristic of the managerial jobs, and to be attractive; the latter cluster is seen as connected to production-line operations and does not have great salience for the pupils. Thus Paul, who has played the part of banker to the simulation company:

> The first time, I was the banker, I enjoyed that job. As soon as we started, I had to lend the company 50 counters. Then every day, Mrs. Stone said I had to go and collect tax, five counters, from the company. I enjoyed that very well . . . Really I should have nicked some money out of the back ones and gone round and got some more Smarties (laughs) . . . Then the second one (i.e. the second simulation exercise) I was the cutter and drawer – you had to draw circles out of paper and then cut them out to make the bottom parts of the plates – we kept running out of paper because we were working so fast, and we were getting behind with the colouring because we were going so fast – I liked it less. It wasn't really exciting just cutting out, but it was good as the banker you could go round giving out money.
> *Is it like that in a real factory?*
> The banker does interesting things, he goes and collects money and goes out to other banks. It's the best way.
> *And the production line, the cutting and drawing?*

60

Well, that wouldn't suit me really.
Because?
I'd rather be banker, you get more money.

Or Jean, who described how she saw the different jobs involved in running a firm:

> The most important is probably the advertising manager or the sales manager. The advertising manager would have to advertise so she could get the company going . . . and the sales manager has to go out, like he often rushes out in a car or it might be a big lorry, and takes the dishes to the shops so that the shops can sell them.

This view is held by Jean, even though in the actual factory visit she said that the job she had liked the most had been a skilled production line job – setting the cameos onto plates. Paul, on the other hand, held a more ambitious view, describing his preferred career as a steady progression up through the ranks to managing director, because it would be more interesting, better paid and harder to do than other jobs, adding that he like hard jobs more than easy ones.

It will be an irony if a project enabling children to understand the world of work also helps to reproduce in them the polarised values characteristic of relationships between workers and management in much of British industry.

The enterprise culture – on the make in the infant school?

A second set of values was a scaled down version of what in the adult world has become known as the enterprise culture, that is the commitment to competitive marketing and profit-making in the market place economy. One aspect of the project that most clearly engaged the children's energies and involvement was the advertising and marketing of their company's product. Thus Jean:

> We all put money – it was 20p – to buy a share in the company, and we all have to work together hard and at the end, when we've sold all the dishes, we'll get our money back and if we've

done well, if we've sold a lot, we'll probably get another 20p as well.
What about – what will happen if a child hasn't bought a share, didn't buy a share at the beginning?
They won't get anything at the end.
Will they have worked hard like everyone else?
Well I don't know if anyone didn't buy a share, but if they didn't get a share they'll not get any money at the end.

Another aspect of the enterprise culture was built into the project through the competition for the best designs, but a particularly interesting aspect arose in the activities of two boys 'sacked' from the production line making plates in the simulation exercise, for messing about and not participating properly. According to Jean they set up an unofficial economy in 'misshapes' – plates that didn't come up to the standard required.

Shane and Craig went round buying the plates that weren't very good for seven counters instead of ten, and then they tried to sell them. But they got told off and had to stop it.

It might not be too fanciful to see this project on contemporary industry reproducing in pupils the values of the free market economy represented in the Britain of the 1980s. If so, in what ways are such values contributing to pupils' sense of their own worth and that of others?

The inevitability of hierarchy

When the pupils were asked about the organisation of industry, they referred more often to the simulation exercises than to the visits to the real factory, probably because the former were designed to provide experiential learning of company role structures. A dominant managerial perspective emerged in their descriptions – very much a traditional, hierarchical, 'top-down' model, with control and sanctions residing in the superior positions. Thus Mary:

The managing director, Jenny is ours, and she has to make sure that people aren't doing things wrong.

What would doing things wrong mean – what would be doing things wrong?
Well, they might be messing about, or maybe, probably they would not be doing their job properly.

And Paul:

> Say you have the managing director here, and the production line worker here, and say the worker was just walking about, the managing director would say 'hey you!' and the worker would go back to work.

Self-interest, however, would dictate that the manager behaves humanely, according to Jean:

> Jenny shouldn't be too bossy – if the other managers weren't doing their job properly she might give the sack, but she'd probably give them a second chance – say if the advertising manager had done an untidy poster, she'd not be too strict or bossing people about, because if she did there'd be no-one left to work for her.

We can see this top-down model operating most clearly when the pupils were asked to attribute blame for a hypothetical failure of the company to sell its products. Apart from the incidental reference by Jean above, all blame was attributed to production line workers, who were variously seen as 'messing about', 'not able to do the job properly', 'not checking the quality of the product'. In Paul's view, even listening to pop music while working was a cause of inefficiency on the factory floor which he would put a stop to if he became managing director.

Thus pupils were not getting an idealised sense of industry as friction-free; in both the simulation and the visits there was acknowledgement of the potential for conflict in work situations. But at a time when sunrise industries are developing more open structures, and when the value of partnership and interdependence between managers and workers is being recognised, pupils may be picking up an anachronistic model of the social relationships of the workplace.

Conclusion

This study was a small-scale and exploratory one. There is no suggestion that what has been observed at St Faith's is generalisable, if only because experimental approaches to the establishment of industry/education links in primary schools are at an early stage, and restricted to a relatively small number of interested teachers and local authorities.

From the point of view of pupils' personal and social development, however, the study raises an interesting issue. It concerns the possibility that the 'personal' and the 'social' may sometimes be contradictory, or at least not all the same thing, and that we ought to be rather more careful about the way in which the 'personal' and the 'social' are linked almost automatically. Some pupils in this project were indeed having their personal qualities realised and developed; they were being encouraged to show initiative, were being offered considerable opportunities for decision making and for taking responsibility for the consequences of their decisions – for exercising leadership. In addition the project helped the pupils develop a greater sense of confidence in their relationships with adults, in their ability to work cooperatively, to articulate their intentions and purposes for their own learning, and so on. All of these things seem to me inevitably bound up in the concept of personal development.

Against this, however, it is difficult to believe that the children I talked to had developed socially. They seemed to have had reinforced some of the more questionable values of individualism; the notion that what applies to others does not necessarily apply to me, that people not fitting in with my purposes should be punished, that getting on at the expense of others in a fundamentally competitive context is a matter in which to take automatic pride. Furthermore the acquiescent and deferential attitudes to perceived authority, together with the anticipated delight in its prospective exercise, would be difficult to designate as 'social development'.

In fact perspectives from studies of personal and social development may not help us understand what might have been happening at St Faith's. For that understanding we need to go to those studies of the relationship between schools and society called correspondence theory (eg Sharp and Green, 1976) or cultural reproduction (Bernstein, 1973; Bourdieu and Passeron, 1977) which suggest that

64

primary schools, however innovative, act as largely passive agencies for the reproduction of the social relations of the workplace and the economy at large. On this analysis, we can interpret the children's responses to the project by saying that the values of the Thatcher period are being reproduced in the children in the school. This might be attractive to neo-Marxists, if only because it is so simple a correspondence. For me it is plausible but too facile, and we urgently need further studies of children's interpretations of the world of work as it is transmitted to them through the primary school curriculum.

References

Bernstein, B, 1973 *Class, Codes and Control, 3*, Routledge and Kegan Paul.

Bordieu, P and Passeron, J C, 1977 *Reproduction in Education and Culture* London: Sage.

Jamieson, I (ed) 1984 *We Make Kettles: studying industry in the primary school* Longman.

Jamieson, I (ed) 1985 *Industry in Education* Longman.

Ross, A, 1984 'Planning a primary/industry project' in *Social Science Teacher, 13*(3).

Ross, A, 1985 'The workplace in the classroom' in *Education 3–13, 13*(2).

Sharp, R and Green, A, 1975 *Education and Social Control* Routledge and Kegan Paul.

Waite, P, 1984 'Industry and the Primary Classroom' in *Education 3–13, 12*(1).

6 Using counselling skills to enhance children's personal, social and academic functioning

Tony Charlton

Despite the extent of primary schools' concern for, and involvement with, the pastoral needs of young children, counselling has rarely been a prominent feature of their work. There seem to be two key reasons for this neglect.

First, counselling has often been construed, quite erroneously, as a practice undertaken exclusively by trained specialists, away from the classroom, with children experiencing severe emotional problems. This misunderstanding has been due, in part, to fairly widespread confusion concerning the meaning of the term 'counselling'. All too frequently there has been a failure to differentiate between those complex skills and strategies used at a level where counselling refers to a specialism beyond the scope of most, if not all, teachers, and those used at a lower (but no less important) level which can be put to good effect in classrooms. Occasions when children are being bullied by (or are bullying) peers, are upset by family bereavement, worried about aspects of their academic work, anxious about pending transfer to secondary school or concerned about the onset of puberty, represent but a few of the host of personal, social or academic problems and concerns which may well be alleviated by the efficient use of individual or group counselling skills by teachers in their classrooms.

Second, even when teachers have accepted that counselling is a perfectly legitimate, indeed invaluable, practice for them to adopt, their initiatives in this area have often been hampered by the failure of their initial training to equip them with a knowledge and understanding of the skills required. Unfortunately, this omission is indicative of the low priority which colleges of higher education and university departments of education often afford to areas concerned with children's emotional development, and the associated strategies/skills which teachers can use to help monitor and optimise such growth (David and Charlton, 1987).

Whilst the nature of pupils' problems and concerns may, at times, demand referral for outside agencies' support, there will be many occasions on which teachers can meet pupils' needs in their day-to-day work in classrooms, given the appropriate skills.

Charlton and Hoye (1987) have argued that counselling skills practised in classrooms can be usefully perceived in three differing – though not necessarily exclusive – contexts.

1 They may be used in a *reactive* sense, where a response is made to pupils' problems which teachers themselves have become aware of, or which have been brought to their attention by the pupil(s) concerned, or others. These problems, although they will be dealt with by the teachers, may at times be sufficiently complex, serious or sensitive to warrrant a brief, or even extended, counselling session conducted in privacy.

2 They may be so *well integrated* within the day-to-day teaching activities that no true separation is discernible between teaching and counselling. While imparting knowledge and information, teachers remain vigilant, and more-or-less immediately responsive, to potential or prevailing problems within their class. Usually these types of problems will be relatively minor, perhaps transitory, and refer to pupils' difficulties with material which is being taught, or facets of general classroom behaviour.

3 They may be employed in both a planned *proactive* and *reactive* sense. Teachers may use counselling techniques, in preference to more formal didactic methods, to promote some aspect of their children's personal and social well-being. On such occasions all pupils can be involved, either in groups or as an entire class. It may involve, for example, 'teaching' an explicit element of the personal and social curriculum. The proactive element refers to teachers' initial input and the reactive one to teachers' responses to, or consequent interaction with, pupils' analyses of (or other responses to) the teachers' input.

In recent years the third of the above-mentioned counselling descriptions has been used with good effect to enhance children's self-concepts and general coping strategies. Of particular interest are the occasions when these enhancements have been shown to produce associated gains in children's academic performance levels (eg Lawrence, 1971; 1972). The simplicity of the counselling skills used in such studies and, in one (Lawrence, 1972), the ease with which lay professionals acquired them, suggest that if elementary skills of this type do not already exist within teachers' skills repertoire, they can be easily incorporated.

Lawrence's earlier works (1971; 1972) did much to pioneer this awareness. Noting that unhealthy affective states – or feelings – (such as low self-concepts) frequently characterised children encountering difficulties in learning to read, he reasoned that these negative aspects of their personal functioning impeded satisfactory responses to reading skills instruction. To test this hypothesis he examined the differential effects of three treatments upon young children's reading performance (ie 'remedial reading'; 'counselling'; 'remedial reading and counselling'). Whilst 'remedial reading' focused upon improving the mechanical skills necessary for efficient reading, the counselling intent was to enhance children's self-esteem. Surprisingly – though consistent with Lawrence's reasoning – it proved to be the 'counselling' treatment which produced the greatest reading gains over a period of several months. As already mentioned, the counselling skills employed were uncomplicated. Teachers (and lay professionals in the later study) were required to establish empathic relations with their children which were characterised by a listening facility communicating warmth, interest, encouragement, unconditional acceptance and understanding; skills fundamental to many counselling strategies.

Aspects of Lawrence's research have been questioned (see Coles, 1976) but his reasoning has remained attractive, and provided inspiration for subsequent, and more refined, investigations which have often been supportive to his findings (eg Cant and Spackman, 1985; Murfitt and Thomas, 1985; Lawrence, 1985).

The investigations referred to in the previous paragraph looked at the relationship between children's academic and personal functioning within the context of self-concept theory. Other, similar, research has involved the *locus of control*. This is an important construct within Rotter's (1966) social learning theory. It refers to the beliefs people hold about the influence their personal behaviour has upon what happens to them. In the academic setting, for example, pupils who believe that success in reading, high test marks or teacher praise are attainable as a consequence of their own behaviour (eg by being industrious and persistent, particularly in the face of failure) are referred to as internals. Internals believe that the locus (source) of control over what happens to them, is located within (or internal to) themselves. Conversely, other pupils believe that no matter how much time and energy they expend, they can never achieve such 'success' – such individuals are identified as externals. Externals believe that the source (locus) of control over what happens to them, is outside, or external to, them. Their experiences are felt to be determined by such factors as luck, chance or fate – influences which they are powerless to control. It is understandable, therefore, if these feelings of helplessness discourage individuals from making meaningful efforts to exercise some control over the events which happen to them. Within the classroom setting, such feelings are likely to discourage children from practising the types of achievement-striving behaviours (eg effort and persistence) which are known to help guarantee academic success.

Like internal beliefs, external ones are learned; they are learned from past experiences. It is unfortunate for the external that s/he has learned what can often be a handicapping belief in the classroom, and elsewhere. Charlton (1985) contended that external beliefs frequently present as an unhelpful state which:

> ... seems to inhibit achievement-striving behaviour and encourage feelings of incompetence, both of which may precipitate or compound learning and behaviour problems. Consequently, a contention that externality in the school setting will be associated with poor achievement-striving behaviour, low academic achievement and a range of maladaptive behaviours seems logical.
>
> (Charlton, 1985, p 28)

This contention has been supported by research findings where students' external beliefs have often been found to be associated with a range of behaviours and feelings commonly regarded as unhealthy or undesirable, including delinquency, emotional disturbance, conduct disorders, poor interpersonal relations, high anxiety and low self-concepts (see Gilmore, 1983). Similarly, in the educational setting, externals have tended to evidence fewer achievement-strivings and receive lower academic achievement test scores as well as inferior report grades than their more internally oriented counterparts (see Findley and Cooper, 1983).

In conclusion, there is much research evidence to suggest that young children, as well as older students, who hold internal locus of control beliefs tend to be more industrious, more adjusted and higher academic achievers than their peers who hold external beliefs. These findings suggest, first, that internal beliefs present as a more competent, positive and educationally attractive orientation and, second, that externality appears as a hindrance to children's healthy personal, social and academic development.

In view of the above findings there appear to be reasonable grounds for suggesting that schools should encourage the development of internal locus of control beliefs in their pupils. Enhancing pupils' feelings of mastery over what happens to them (ie internality) should help motivate them in their academic work. Along these lines Phares (1976) reasoned that 'to enhance individual's capacity to cope with the world successfully one must influence the generalised expectancy for control' (ie promote internality). Similarly, Lefcourt (1966) noted that external beliefs 'seem common to many people who do not function in a competent way'.

The two separate studies examined below were pilot studies reporting on the effectiveness of:

- group counselling and operant conditioning programmes in enhancing junior school pupils' internal beliefs;
- the above group counselling programme in improving junior school children's reading performance.

Study 1

In this enquiry (Charlton, 1986) the subjects were fourth year junior school boys (N=92) and girls (N-81) in seven mainstream schools.

In two classes the children (N-55) were given a group counselling programme by their teachers. Prior to the commencement of the programme the teachers received in-service training to familiarise them with the aim and content of the counselling. At the beginning of an 11-week intervention period (11 sessions – one each week) the teachers spent one session discussing problems which they themselves had encountered when they were at school. Where applicable they emphasised how their own behaviour had created, or contributed to, the problems (ie behaviour-outcome contingencies). During the second session, pupils were invited to talk to the class about problems they had experienced. After each contribution, and only if the pupil concerned gave approval, the peer group questioned him/her in order to work out how the pupil's own behaviour may have contributed to that problem.

The remaining sessions (N=9) were based on a series of recorded audio scripts which portrayed youngsters in failure situations (ie experiencing problems in the home, play and school settings). After listening to each play, pupils were encouraged to identify, and then role-play, the youngsters' behaviours which directly caused, or otherwise contributed to, the problems encountered. After this has been completed, the class then suggested alternative behaviours which could have been used to avoid, resolve, or minimise the problems.

Towards the end of the 11-week counselling period pupils formed small groups and scripted two brief plays (each lasting a minute), both of which were to be based in the same setting. The first demonstrated how desirable/appropriate behaviours led to success outcomes (ie problem-free), and the second included undesirable/inappropriate behaviours which resulted in failure outcomes (ie problems). During the scripting and rehearsing of the plays the teachers monitored the groups' work and, where necessary, offered advice concerning the inclusion of, and clear emphases upon, the required behaviour-outcome contingencies. After each play was presented, the 'audience' were expected to account to the 'actors' for the emergence of problem, or problem-free, situations.

The teachers administering operant conditioning to pupils (N=51) in two other classes provided token (ie housepoints) and social (eg praise, attention, smiles) reinforcers for desirable behaviour. They were familiarised with these techniques during a number of in-service training sessions held before the programme commenced. Behaviours to be reinforced included on-task (ie effort and persistence) and prosocial behaviours as well as academic achievements. When reinforcers were administered teachers were encouraged to make clear to each pupil the behaviours which elicited reinforcements. For example a neat piece of written work could be praised by saying 'That is a neat piece of work; you must have taken a great deal of care when you were writing it'.

Pupils (N=67) in three other classes received no intervention programme, and served as a control group.

Pupils' locus of control beliefs were measured before and after the intervention period using the abbreviated Nowicki-Strickland locus of control scale (Figure 6.1).

Figure 6.1 *Mean locus of control scores for groups on pre- and post-intervention occasions*

Group	N	Preintervention		Postintervention	
		M	SD	M	SD
Control	67	8.5	2.5	8.3*	2.7
Counselling	55	7.7	2.8	4.9	2.4
Operant conditioning	51	8.2	2.8	6.8	2.4

* The lower the mean the greater the internality

Statistical analyses (analysis of variance/Tukey test) revealed that while counselling and operant conditioning programmes both effected significant improvements in children's levels of internality, the counselling produced the greater effects.

These findings suggested that teachers can modify their pupils' locus of control beliefs in the direction of internality by using basic counselling skills as well as techniques drawn from behaviour modification. The purpose of the next study, therefore, was to observe whether enhancing internal beliefs, as expected, led to improved academic (ie reading) performances.

Study 2

In the second enquiry (Charlton and Terrell, 1987) the hypothesis tested was that the group counselling intervention outlined in Study 1 would lead not only to the enhancement of pupils' internal beliefs, but also to improved reading performance through increasing achievement-striving.

The subjects in the pilot study were drawn from second year junior school classes (N=2) in two inner-city primary schools serving similar catchment areas (ie in terms of parents' socioeconomic status). One class (N=35) served as a control group, whilst the treatment class pupils (N=33) received 11, 40-minute group counselling sessions spread over a period of nine weeks.

The *Neale Analysis of Reading* (word accuracy test) was administered to all pupils in the week prior to the commencement of the counselling programme, and in the fourth week after the conclusion of the programme (a pre/post test period of approximately 13 weeks). Additionally, a Deeside Picture test given to all pupils before the commencement of the programme showed the mean intelligence scores of the two groups to be similar. Figure 6.2 includes the mean reading scores, on both testing occasions, of the two groups.

Figure 6.2 *Mean reading ages (years/months) and gains (in months) of groups on pre- and post-intervention occasions*

Group	N	Preintervention		Postintervention		Gains
		M	SD	M	SD	
Counselling	29	8.6	21.2	9.2	21.0	8.0
Control	32	8.2	17.3	8.6	18.0	4.0

Statistical analyses (one-tailed t tests) indicated no significant differences between the pre-intervention reading scores of the two groups. However, significant differences were found between the groups' post-intervention reading ages, and mean gains in pre/post intervention reading ages. On both of these occasions the counselled group evidenced significantly higher reader ages/gains than the control group.

Despite the limitations of the research design (ie small sample size, no controls for possible teacher/school/Hawthorne effects) the study's findings provide an indication that group counselling designed to promote internal beliefs simultaneously produces gains in children's reading performances.

Implications

The findings from both these studies add to an already extensive body of research which has deepened our understanding of children's personal and social (mal)functioning and how it is influenced by, and affects – healthily or otherwise – their academic performance in school.

It seems reasonable to suggest that the lack of success some children experience in school and elsewhere is, at times, associated with their unhealthy affective states, including feelings of helplessness to bring about any improvements in their lives (in school or at home). Within Rotter's social learning theory the locus of control construct offers teachers a theoretical framework within which to shape teaching strategies to help optimise pupils' all-round development. Some of the more salient techniques/skills employed in the two studies to enhance pupils' locus of control beliefs seem to have important contributions to make to the formulation of these strategies. They include the need for:

- *positive reinforcements* (praise, attention, smiles) to be regularly, yet judiciously, distributed among all children for desired behaviour (eg effort persistence, achievement, prosocial behaviour). Wherever practicable teachers should make clear to pupils the actual behaviours which are being rewarded. ('Good' may not always be adequate: it may be more helpful to say 'Your work is tidy. You must have taken a great deal of care with it'.) The award of reinforcements in this manner helps demonstrate to pupils the efficacy of their efforts and achievements in obtaining favourable outcomes.
- *listening facilities* to be made available to pupils. A distinction is made here between 'hearing' and 'listening'. Hearing suggests only a sensory input. Listening means much more; in addition to the sensory input it has an outgoing communication element which conveys a genuine concern for, as well as an understanding of (or a wish to understand) what a child is saying.

By listening (and observing) teachers become aware of children's feelings including their perception of behaviour-outcome causal contingencies. This awareness is derived more from an understanding of, than a knowledge about, children.

- *pupils to practise analysing problem situations* Like adults, children learn, and derive benefit, from analysing the problems others – or they themselves – have encountered, or are encountering. Through this practice they become more aware of their own behaviour-outcome experiences and, hopefully, more reflective and sensitive in their selection of appropriate behaviours in situations they encounter. By providing them, for example, with stories, audioscripts and videos depicting failure climates, they. can be encouraged (with the teacher's help) to analyse and discuss behaviour-outcome links. The subsequent stage is for the pupils to suggest and practise alternative behaviours likely to facilitate success climates.

- *pupils to acquire and practise social skills* In schools rather less time is given to the learning and rehearsing of personal and social, than is given to academic, skills. A failure to develop and become proficient in using such skills may precipitate failure and help inculcate the feelings of helplessness associated with external beliefs. Conversely, the more skills pupils acquire and become proficient in using, the more likely they are to develop feelings of competency and mastery in terms of their ability to exercise reasonable control (ie through problem solving/coping/avoidance) over events which befall them. Role-playing is an invaluable vehicle to use in these situations. It provides the extra dimension of 'doing' rather than merely discussing, and it is an activity which young children are instinctively attracted to.

  Analysing situations (as in point 3), acquiring new skills and learning to deliberate upon, and be selective in, their use will hopefully help enhance children's life-coping proficiencies.

- *feedback* Without frequent and explicit information concerning the consequences of their behaviour children may remain ignorant of the precise nature of their strengths and weaknesses. Whilst most children are intuitively 'tuned' to accept praise they are often less able, or inclined, to accept and benefit from references to their weaknesses. Healthy development is incomplete unless pupils learn to accept responsibility (and positively respond to that acceptance) for their *failures* as well as their *successes* (ie internality for failure and success outcomes).

With some justification the appropriation of the term 'counselling' to refer to the strategies used in the two studies can be challenged. Admittedly, the activities undertaken, or directed by the teachers, differ, at times, from traditional counselling practices where two individuals meet; one with a problem and the other seeking to help resolve it. Arguably, however, while the setting is different from the traditional one, the skills are very similar. Both studies· involved the teacher employing listening/analysing/ guidance/and rehearsal techniques; all of which, in combination, were ultimately intended to help optimise the healthy all-round functioning of the pupils. In the best classrooms teaching and counselling skills activities may be so inextricably intertwined that no true separation is practicable. The counselling referred to in this paper may illustrate that inseparability.

References

Cant, R and Spackman, P, 1985 'Self-esteem, counselling and educational achievement' in *Educational Research*, *27*(1), p 68–70.

Charlton, T and David, K (in preparation), *Personal and Social Education: School Teachers' Perceptions*

Charlton, T, 1985 'Locus of control as a therapeutic strategy for helping children with behaviour and learning problems' in *Maladjustment and Therapeutic Education*, *3*(1), p 26–32.

Charlton, T, 1986 'Differential effects of counselling and operant conditioning interventions upon children's locus of control beliefs' in *Psychological Reports*, *59*, p 137–8.

Charlton, T and Terrell, C (1987), 'Enhancing internal locus of control beliefs through group counselling: effects upon children's reading performance' in *Psychological Reports*, *60*, 928–931.

Coles, C, 1985 'Counselling and reading retardation' in *Therapeutic Education*, *5*(1), p 10–18.

David, K and Charlton, T (1987), *The Caring Role of the Primary School* Macmillan.

Findley, M J and Cooper, H M, 1983 'Locus of control and academic achievement; a literature review' in *Journal of Personality and Social Psychology*, *44*(2), p 419–27.

Gilmour, T M, 1978 'Locus of control as a mediator of adaptive behaviour in children and adolescents' in *Canadian Psychological Review*, *18*(1), p 1–26.

Lawrence, D, 1971 'The effects of counselling on retarded readers', in *Educational Research*, *13*(2), p 119–24.

Lawrence, D, 1972 'Counselling of retarded readers by non-professionals' in *Educational Research*, *15*(1), p 48–54.

Lawrence, D, 1985 'Improving self-esteem and reading' in *Educational Research*, *27*(3), p 184–9.

Lefcourt, H M, 1976 *Locus of Control: Current Trends in Theory and Research* Erlbaum.

Murfitt, J and Thomas, J, The effects of peer counselling on the self-concept and reading attainment of secondary aged slow learning pupils' in *Remedial Education*, *18*(2), p 73–4.

Phares, E J, 1976 *Locus of Control in Personality* General Learning Press.

7 Pupil experiences
David Ingram

All learning is based on experience which leads to a restructuring of skills, knowledge and attitudes. The focus here is on social experience and social and moral learning. Since 1973 I have been engaged in the development of curriculum materials based on a systematic study of children's experiences. Currently I am working with a group of Leicestershire primary teachers, all of whom are heads or deputies. We are developing a social and moral education programme for primary schools. Pupils in the schools involved in the project were asked to write about their social experiences in response to the questions:

> *Write about a time when it was difficult to make up your mind about what you should do.*
> *What did you do?*
> *What happened?*

The following responses give some of the flavour of the concerns of the pupils in these schools:

> Last Friday my rabbit called Prince had to go to the Vets. But on Fridays I go dancing. I did not know whether or not to go with my dad to the Vets or go dancing. In the end I went with my dad because Prince is my rabbit.
>
> Claire (aged 7)

> Once when I was coming home from school I was thinking about either going to the temple or going to the Brownie disco. It was on a Friday and we went to the temple on a Friday too. I wanted to go to the temple because it was a special occasion and my aunty had made me a new suit and I wanted to wear

78

that. It was peach and white. Well I wanted to go to the Brownie Disco because I hadn't been to one for quite a long while. Well I made my mind up. I said to myself that I better go to the temple because my religion is more important than a disco.

Aprita (aged 10)

About a month ago my cousin Debbie had a baby and it wasn't very well. It had to have two operations and was just getting better when it had a chest infection and nearly died but now it's much better and can come home soon. One day I got home and my mum asked me if I wanted to go and see the baby, Andrew. I said yes but the next day my friend rang me up and asked me if I wanted to sleep at her house. I said yes but as soon as I'd put the phone down I realised that I was going to see Andrew. All that night I was awake thinking about it. I had an idea. I would go to see the baby in the morning and go round to my friends at night.

Joanne (aged 10)

One day I was really bored. So I went to the window and watched my sister riding her bicycle when all of a sudden a car was reversing out of a drive. My sister put her brakes on too hard and went over the handlebars. I saw what happened and dashed up the stairs to tell Mum what had happened. My dad and mum ran down the stairs and brought her inside. She had a cut right down the back of her ear and she had cut her chin. Carolyn had to be taken to hospital. Next day was Friday and I always go swimming. And it is a lot of fun. But also on that day I was going to visit Carolyn. I was thinking hard on this. But eventually I went swimming and I thought I would visit Carolyn tomorrow.

Christian (aged 10)

These stories were collected by the children's class teachers during normal lesson time. The children were asked to think carefully and choose an incident which mattered to them and which could have happened recently or some time ago.

This work follows the pattern of 'Critical Incident Survey'

research developed by Peter McPhail in association with Michael Argyle, first reported in *Moral Education in the Secondary School* (McPhail *et al*, 1972). In 1973 I joined Peter McPhail's team on the Schools' Council's *Moral Education Project* (*8–13*) which produced a series of curriculum materials under the series title 'Startline' together with a research report, *The Moral Situation of Children* (Ungoed-Thomas, 1978).

The 'Startline' project enquiry into the social experiences of children involved 3475 children aged from 8 to 13, in schools throughout England and Wales. Teachers, under the direction of project staff, asked children three open-ended questions, which they answered in confidence.

1 *Write and draw about a time when somebody made you feel pleased or happy.*
  Describe what you did as a result.
2 *Write and draw about a time when somebody made you feel frightened, angry or unhappy.*
  Describe what you did as a result.
3 *Write and draw about a time when you were with somebody else (or other people) and you were not sure what to do.*
  What did you do?

The Schools' Council Project's study identified nine categories of themes.

Personal and home life
Siblings: trouble
Siblings: cooperation and
  concern
Grown-ups and home
Stairs
Food
Pets and animals
Moving home
Separation and reuniting

Other children
Peer groups and pressures
Boy/girl relationships
Friendship

Activities and pastimes
TV
Informal play and hobbies
Organised activities and sports
School work and activities
Shops and shopping
Vehicles

Special occasions and occurrences
Presents: giving and receiving
Christmas and birthdays
Social occasions
Public celebrations
Outings and visits
Staying away from home

80

Special occasions and occurrences
Births and christenings
Engagements and marriages
Public appearances

Behaviour difficulties
Misbehaviour
Provocation
Drink, drugs and smoking
Law breaking and delinquent
  behaviour
Adult/child disagreement

Critical situations
Getting lost
Strangers
Fear and the dark
Fire hazard
Hostile supernatural
  occurrences

Accident and injury
Illness and operations
Death or disappearance

Problems
What do I do?
What do I choose?
How do I occupy myself?
How do I do it?
Losing, finding and forgetting

Expectations
Expected happenings
Unexpected happenings
Striving
Praise
Temptation
Unfairness
Taking responsibility
Concern for others

Within the 'Startline' package the series of six pupil books *Choosing* made direct use of children's writing, as in this story from Book 3:

Standing up for my friend

In our class there was a girl called Wendy who was very argumentative. She always wanted her own way and if she didn't get what she wanted she used to be angry with us. Most girls of our class were frightened of her so they tried to be friendly even when she behaved badly. One day, about two years ago, this girl Wendy fell out with my best friend Sharon and, of course, everybody rushed to get on her side.
Sharon was left alone in the corner while the others were yelling horrible, untrue things at her. I had tried to keep out of the argument but when I saw Sharon alone in the corner I decided that even if everyone else did fall out with me I would go to her. When they were all shouting at Sharon I turned round with an angry face and said to all the girls 'You're all a cart load of babies all ganging together. You ought to be ashamed of yourselves'. To my surprise all my other friends came over to us and said, 'We're sorry we fell out with you'.

Wendy stormed off. I said, 'Now how about a game?' So we all got together and started to play.

The suggested questions which accompanied the story were:

1 *What sort of help can you expect from a good friend?*
2 *Act out a play based on this situation or one like it which you have experienced.*
3 *Why do you think the girls shouted 'horrible untrue things'?*
4 *It only took one girl to make the others change their minds, but do you think it was easy? What would you have done if you had been the friend?*

Throughout the *Choosing* series a general approach was suggested which consisted of the following activities and questions which could be put by the teacher.

1 *Have you ever been in this sort of situation? If so, decribe from your own point of view what happened.*
2 *Imagine you are one of the people in the situation which is described and say how you feel and what you would do.*
3 *Act out in your group what you think would happen next.*
4 *Discuss with the others what you think it would be best to do.*
5 *Act out what you decide is best and consider its effect on everyone involved.*

These materials were intended to provide a vehicle for deepening children's understanding of their social experiences, helping them to explore the situations which confront them in their lives and to acquire the skills, both cognitive and social, to be able to make decisions and to act upon them.

In the case of the 'Startline' project, it was reported that for some teachers the pattern of children's concerns seemed small scale and their achievements trivial – washing their own hair for the first time; taking a ride on a bus to town with a friend; cooking a meal, and so on. But these seemingly minor achievements are important in the development of the self-confidence which is necessary for action and the everyday decisions children take in the course of their play activities, such as what to do, where to go and with whom to play. These are not necessarily moral questions in themselves, but in order to resolve them children need to consider their relationship with others. This understanding of personal relationships and treatment of others is of central moral importance.

The data provided by such a critical incident survey can be

directly employed in the development of curriculum materials. The production of 'Startline'-based material in Japan and Hong Kong was preceded by such a research survey. In my own work, the 'Road Safety Attitudes and Education Project' at Cambridge University stemmed directly from 'Startline'. The Road Safety project led to two pupil books, *Going Places* and *Getting There* (Ingram V and Ingram D, 1983). The questions asked were:

1 *Write about a time when you were in or near traffic and you were frightened, angry or unhappy.*
2 *Write about a time when you were in or near traffic and you did not know the best thing to do.*

The pupil responses showed that, for the most part, children of school age appear to know the safety rules in the *Green Cross Code* and are well-intentioned towards them. The root of their difficulties seemed to lie in the gap between knowing the rules and attempting to apply them in diverse and unexpected situations, 'I looked for traffic lights and there were none. I didn't know what to do.' (Ingram D and Ingram V, 1981) As in the 'Startline' project the children's own writing was included in the curriculum material. The following story is taking from *Going Places*:

A few years ago when I had a dog called Spike a car nearly hit him.
My Dad had a shed over the road where he kept pipes, washers, nuts, screws and everything because my Dad was a plumber. We went to get some pipes and we crossed over and went into the shed. Spike followed us. We got the pipes and crossed back over. Spike followed us. As we walked across the road a car came round the corner. The driver slammed on the brakes and just missed Spike. I was frightened because Spike could have been killed. I was angry at the same time because Spike should have stopped on the pavement.

Direct use of children's writing need not necessarily follow. The 'Dudley Project' (Brownjohn P and Ingram D, 1987) conducted a survey of school leavers to identify missing elements of social education which it was thought would have eased the passage from school to 'employment'. In this project the teaching material uses fictionalised case studies supplemented by factual information.

The Leicestershire Primary Writing Group is incorporating the pupils' concerns and experiences into a series of stories. Furthermore the presentation is drawing on the North American experience of working through moral dilemma discussion, an approach developed by Lawrence Kohlberg and his colleagues at Harvard. This requires that the incident is portrayed in such a way that there is a tension between different moral concerns and commitments.

An example of such a story in which a number of moral concerns are in conflict is given below.

Holly's dilemma

Holly is an eight-year-old girl who likes to climb trees. She is the best tree climber in the neighbourhood. One day while climbing down from a tall tree she falls off the bottom branch but does not hurt herself. Her father sees her fall. He is upset and asks her to promise not to climb trees any more. Holly promises.

Later that day Holly and her friends meet Shaun. Shaun's kitten is caught up a tree and can't get down. Something has to be done right away or the kitten may fall. Holly is the only one who climbs trees well enough to reach the kitten and get it down, but she remembers her promise to her father.

Should Holly help Shaun and the kitten by climbing the tree to get the kitten down?

Why or why not?

(Gomberg S H *et al*, 1980)

Obedience, loyalty to one's friends, and concern for the welfare of animals are all involved and a central task for the teacher is to challenge the thinking of the children by asking questions related to principles other than that which they have used to justify their proposed solution.

The experience of teachers working with the 'Startline' materials was that if pupils could identify with the situations presented to them, they provided good starting points for classroom discussion and role-play. However many reported incidents took place in the home or its immediate environment. The key people in these events were most often parents, siblings, and close relations as well as friends. In *Choosing*, Book 4, this story was included:

Helping each other out

One day my friend Sally asked me if I would like to go
swimming with her. I said I would like to but would have to ask
my dad. When I got home my dinner was nearly ready and
when I asked my dad if I could go swimming he seemed to be
in a strange mood. He said, 'I couldn't care less what you do.'
When I was putting my things together he made comments
about my bikini and said that I was too fat to wear such a little
swimming costume. That upset me and I didn't really want to
go to the pool but when I got to my friend's house she cheered
me up. She said, 'Don't upset yourself.' We chatted all the way
to the pool and I began to feel much better. We had a
marvellous time at the pool.

Clearly there is every chance that children will talk about their
relations with their parents, especially in view of the suggested
question *Have you ever been in this sort of situation?* referred to earlier.

Teachers need to be sensitive in their handling of such issues,
respectful of the privacy of pupils' lives and protective, so that
children are not embarrassed or hurt by self-disclosure. In this
particular case emphasis could be placed on the helpfulness of the
friend rather than on the unkindness of the father.

The Leicestershire group of primary teachers has come to the conclusion that, although much moral learning takes places implicitly
through the life of the school as a community, time needs to be set
aside for social and moral education. It might be that some of the
work done in the time could relate to events within the life of the
school, the immediate and shared social experience of the pupils. In
moral education classes within the Belgian school system, time is set
aside for the discussion of issues and experiences chosen and
introduced by the pupils. The Belgian experience suggests that
teachers need to create a framework of classroom methods and
interpersonal relationships which will facilitate such work.

Teachers who worked with 'Startline' reported that after a while
they became familiar with the responsive way of working with their
classes required by the programme. Their classes became used to
small group discussion, had acquired listening skills and had
become used to examining choices in terms of likely consequences.
Then those approaches could be used to handle issues from their

daily lives and the work moves on beyond the materials. This is confirmed by the current work of a Hampshire teacher, Ruth Conway, at Tiptoe Primary School, whose pupils identify and bring to the class dilemmas which they can work on together.

The aim, however, is not to use structured material only as a means of acquiring procedures which can then be employed more flexibly. The Leicestershire group sees a place for continued work with ordered material which can be proactive rather than reactive, and prepares pupils for events and relationships which the surveys indicate are common. The programme should not only relate to the pattern of children's experience but also to stages of development revealed by research. Finally the material should be ordered so that a coherent conceptual structure can be developed, along with decision-making skills and the social competences through which they can be enacted. This calls for an ambitious programme of development.

The Leicestershire group have produced a range of classroom materials using photographs, drama and discussion which are currently being used experimentally. The following two examples are taken from their pack.

Going to the match

Your friend invites you to go with him to an important football match. The match is in a big city about two hours' drive away. You go in your friend's dad's car. Your friend's uncle goes as well. About half-way there you stop at a pub. Your friend's dad and uncle are generous. They buy you a glass of coke and some crisps. They give you some money to play on the Space Invader machine. The men have a pint of beer each and then another pint. You know about the dangers of drinking and driving. But the men have been very nice and it seems ungrateful to say anything to them. You decide to ignore it. But then they decide to have another drink. They are both red in the face now and laughing a lot.

Hammy is missing

(*This simple story is accompanied by a set of large pictures.*)
Simon is looking after Hammy this week.

86

He is allowed to stay in at play time to change the water and give Hammy some food.
Paul comes in and asks Simon if he can hold Hammy. Simon wants Paul to like him and lets him pick up Hammy.
Paul drops Hammy who runs away and hides.
Miss Jones asks Simon to tell her why Hammy's cage is empty.

References

Brownjohn, P and Ingram, D, 1987 *Social Education in a Community Context* RMEP.

Gomberg, S H *et al*, 1980 *Leading dilemma discussions; a workshop* Carnegie-Mellon University.

Ingram, D and Ingram, V, 1981 'The road safety attitudes and education project' in *Safety Education* (151).

Ingram, D and Ingram, V, 1983 *Getting There* RoSPA.

Ingram, V and Ingram, D, 1983 *Going Places* RoSPA.

McPhail, P, Middleton, D and Ingram, D, 1978 *Startline: Moral Education in the Middle Years* Longman.

McPhail, P, Ungoed-Thomas, J R and Chapman, H, 1972 *Moral Education in the Secondary School* Longman.

Ungoed-Thomas, J R, 1978 *The Moral Situation of Children* Macmillan.

8 Primary and middle school teachers' attitudes to pastoral provision and personal and social education

Peter Lang

The motivation for the investigations briefly reported in this paper lay in a belief in the importance of personal and social education and pastoral provision in primary and middle schools, and a resulting concern that there was a need for some data on teachers' attitudes to and beliefs about these areas; the relevant types of practice in which they engaged; and, crucially, the relationship between their ideas and this practice.

Implications of personal and social education and pastoral provision

In the investigation no attempt was made to provide a definition of personal and social education or pastoral provision, the aim being to see how these were understood by the teachers involved. However, for the purposes of considering practice some conditions considered necessary for effective practice were tentatively drawn up. It was felt that schools and teachers must demonstrate:

- some systematic consideration of school ethos and hidden curriculum;
- some attention to the nature of and skills required (counselling?) for effective interpersonal work with individual pupils;
- some practice of planned group work, involving at least some emphasis on the experiential dimension of this activity;
- some attention to an effective structure of referral;
- some indication of a willingness to reflect critically on one's own practice;

- some concern to take account of factors beyond the immediate school environment, both in terms of future education and society and cultures generally.

Even at the point of embarking on the research it was recognised that these conditions might not be immediately acceptable to all those involved in personal and social education in primary and middle schools. In the light of the range of approaches covered in the papers in this book it might be necessary to add further conditions.

Preliminary observations and discussion

The first stage of the investigation involved informal discussions and unstructured interviews with some 40 heads and teachers from primary and middle schools in four Midland, two Home County and one Northern LEA. Extensive but generally unstructured observation was also undertaken in about ten primary schools and one middle school. The majority of those involved in these discussions thought that personal and social education and pastoral provision were important at the level at which they taught; typically, however, they felt that, though important, this provision was not something that required particular thought or planning – due to the special nature of Primary and Middle Schools, and particularly the way they contrasted with secondary schools. Key elements of the argument tended to be that personal and social education was 'taught not caught' or that it happened through a process of osmosis. Such arguments were generally associated with statements about the warm, caring ethos of the school. Also often mentioned was the special class-teacher relationship and the use of group work. Though not always referred to directly, it was clear that this belief, that matters were already in hand and required no thought or review, was closely associated with ideas relating to the child-centred nature of their school, classroom and practice. It seemed apropriate to describe these beliefs as a 'conventional wisdom' similar to that found by Best, Jarvis and Ribbins (1980) in relation to pastoral care in the secondary school.

My own observations, however, tended to suggest that this generally held view did not always match with the reality of practice. In some classrooms there seemed to be little evidence of anything taking place that contributed very positively to the personal and social development of pupils. In the case of certain teachers the approach used, though almost certainly unintentionally so, seemed calculated to inhibit this aspect of pupils' development.

Ideas from the literature and research

Before continuing with a more systematic investigation some brief consideration was given to the literature and reports of research. In general, findings supported the general hypothesis 'that what primary teachers said and believed about their practice diverged considerably from what they actually did '. There seemed every reason to suppose that this would be as true of personal and social education as it appeared to be for other areas.

Robin Alexander is one of several writers to draw attention to the existence of a primary ideology of child-centredness.

There is the language of child-centredness, the verbal expression of an ideology which remains in the 1980s as powerful and sometimes as vehement as it was in the 1960s. This language has considerable potency for inducing a warm, consensual solidarity.

(Alexander, 1984)

He goes on to criticise this ideology and particularly the language through which it is expressed. One particular feature that he criticises is what he has called the 'cocooning effect'.

The child-centred cocoon enfolds the teacher as well as the child . . . Teachers may want the warmth and security of a child-centred cocoon for their pupils, but if their activities are to have any relevance to the world beyond school in which the child is growing up they must recognise that their own place is outside the cocoon facing and engaging with social realities, working out the best form of curricular response to them.

Drawing on recent research, several writers have stressed the divergence between the prevalent ideologies current among primary teachers and their actual practice. Anne Yeomans, in a paper focused on collaborative group work in both Britain and the USA

(Yeomans, 1983) provides a clear example of this, which it may be useful to quote at some length.

She opens her paper by attributing to the Plowden Report of 1967 the idea that group work was widely practised in the English primary classroom; she suggests that this gave rise to a model (ideology?) that was not only extremely influential in this country but also abroad, a model she describes in the following terms:

> This model represented the typical classroom as a hive of activity where pupils, when not working individually, were engaged in cooperative group work where knowledge and learning were generated by the pupils through free flowing discussion.

Yeomans goes on to summarise the findings of the ORACLE study (Galton *et al*, 1980):

> Individualised learning, ie pupils working individually on a task, was the most common form of classroom practice. Whole class teaching was far less frequently used, and group work was an even rarer occurrence, although pupils often sat together as a group at a table whilst working on their individual tasks. This latter arrangement is grouping but it is often referred to by teachers as group work.

She emphasises the point that in fact these two terms refer to very different processes.

> . . . grouping is a method of classroom organisation and group work is a way of learning. In the classroom studied, most pupils spent most of their time sitting at a table with other pupils working on individual tasks and a large proportion of their work was devoted to basics.

In the classrooms studied, very little discussion took place. Sustained conversation between pupils, or between the teacher and the pupils were extremely rare, and cooperation between the pupils was usually confined to the sharing of materials.

Joan Barker Lunn, commenting on the evidence from a NFER research project conducted in 1980 (Barker Lunn, 1984) adds to this less than encouraging picture:

What is clear from the 1980 survey, however, is that the most recently available evidence shows that the vast majority of junior school teachers are firmly in control of their classrooms. They determine what activities their pupils will undertake; they prefer a didactic approach rather than a reliance on discovery methods; they are making increasing use of class teaching and there is no need to exhort them to go back to basics.

This evidence from the work of others provided general support for the conclusions I had drawn from my preliminary work. Teacher beliefs and ideology (conventional wisdom) were not only likely to be at variance with their practice but would also function to make them feel that a review of this practice was unnecessary; thus the potential for effective personal and social development was limited. In relation to this last point, of particular significance was the general finding that little actual group work was used. One encouraging point in connection with this, made by Yeomans in relation to the ORACLE findings, was that though most teachers did not use group work many would have liked the opportunity to acquire the skills to do so. In her paper Yeomans also refers to a considerable body of research, both in this country and the USA, which has provided evidence for the effectiveness of collaborative group work as an approach to personal and social education. On the basis of my preliminary findings and this review of relevant research and literature a further small scale piece of questionnaire research was conducted. The focus of this enquiry was both on pastoral provision and on personal and social education.

Second stage of research

A questionnaire was completed by 53 teachers from primary and middle schools in both the North and South of England; about 50% of those responding were in fact heads. Observation was undertaken in ten primary schools and one middle school in the Midland area, this averaged out at about two hours per school.

The picture presented by the responses to the questionnaire was a fairly complex one. The majority of teachers expressed considerable concern over both pastoral provision and personal and social education, and some indicated awareness of the problems already described in this paper. There was a clear desire on the part of some teachers to have the opportunity to acquire the appropriate skills and a number did not feel well supported in this area. But there was also considerable evidence of the widespread existence of the 'conventional wisdom' already discussed – heads in particular often seemed to feel that this was an area already satisfactorily catered for. One significant aspect of the conventional wisdom expressed in a number of the questionnaires was the power attributed to the often very simplistic notion of the 'caring school' ethos – some heads in particular seemed confident that this ethos would satisfactorily meet all pastoral and personal and social needs.

In an earlier piece of research (Lang, 1982) I had already developed the notion of 'Pastoral incantation':

> Pastoral incantation is where the constant, or at least frequent repetition of warm, reassuring phrases provides a sense of security, and at least at a subconscious level insulates people form actual practice and the need for action.
>
> (Lang, 1982, p 229)

The frequency with which the statement 'This is a very caring school' or its equivalent has been made to me and the occasions where practice did not seem to support this belief fully leads me to suggest that this may need to be interpreted as a parallel case of incantation.

Questionnaire findings and examples of responses

There were very varied views on class-teacher relationships. Most thought it was better than in secondary schools, but not all felt that pupils would necessarily go to the class teacher with a problem.

> *Children don't normally go to class teacher, she/he needs to go to them.* (Female head)
> *Teacher isn't always the best person.* (Class teacher)
> *Not all teachers are approachable and even those who are may not relate to any one child.* (Class teacher)

The majority felt the problems they confronted had got worse. One head wrote – *Number on role 354, one-parent familes 71%. 22% pay for their meals – no, you've not read it wrong – 71%.*

All expressed a need for counselling skills.

Most did not see group work as a problem because they felt it already took place, though one head commented

Group work could do this in primary schools but in my experience rarely does, because it is not planned for this and opportunities are neglected because of lack of insight on the part of teacher.

Replies to the question which asked how teachers helped pupils with problems suggested a much greater reliance on cure than prevention and on what might be described as acts of faith rather than planned strategies.

Acts of faith rather than planning also appeared to be the rule when it came to ways of helping pupils get on with one another. Again the general rule appeared to be that it was the head rather than the class teacher who was involved in a case conference.

The observation tended to support the ORACLE findings, and certainly revealed classrooms where the atmosphere was decidedly frosty and in two cases quite punitive.

Overall both the questionnaire and the observation raised questions about the existence in many schools of some or all of the necessary conditions for personal and social education, as outlined at the start of this paper.

Systematic consideration of school ethos and hidden curriculum did not often happen – indeed a number of examples were found, particularly in relation to gender and health, where even the most superficial reflection would have called current practice into question. Both personal teacher skill (counselling) and group work were seen as important and many felt that they would have liked greater expertise in these areas. However in terms of actual practice the amount that took place was strictly limited, especially in the case of group work.

The study did not suggest that either pastoral or personal and social education were areas that primary teachers thought about in depth, particularly in terms of reflecting on their own practice. There were few examples of connections being made to broader society, or of any developed system of referral.

Conclusion

Though the findings of my research could not fairly be described as encouraging, they do, I feel, demonstrate that the potential for development exists. They must also be seen within the broader context of the positive approaches and critical thought illustrated by the papers in this book and of the increasing evidence from different parts of the country that teachers, heads (and perhaps, to a lesser extent, advisers) are becoming more aware of the issues that effective personal and social education and pastoral provision raises. However it is equally important that those seeking to promote personal and social education and pastoral provision should recognise the possibility of the existence of the type of perspective and attitudes discussed in this paper.

References

Alexander, R, 1984 *Primary Teaching* Holt Education.
Barker Lunn, J, 1984 'Junior school teachers: their methods and practice' in *Educational Research*, 26(3), November.
Best, R, Jarvis, C and Ribbins, P (eds) 1980 *Perspectives on Pastoral Care* Heinemann.
Galton, M, Simon, B and Croll, P, 1980 *Inside the primary school* Routledge and Kegan Paul.
Lang, P, 1982 'Pastoral Care: concern or contradiction?' Unpublished MA dissertation, University of Warwick.
Lang, P and Marland, M (eds) 1985 *New Directions in Pastoral Care* Basil Blackwell.
Yeomans, A, 1983 'Collaborative group work in primary and secondary school: Britain and the USA' in *Durham and Newcastle research review*, 10(51), Autumn.

9 Starting where children are: health education in the primary school

Noreen Wetton and Alysoun Moon

Health, said Katherine Mansfield, is 'the power to live a full, adult, living, breathing life in close contact with what I love – I want to be all that I am capable of becoming'.

The World Health Organisation established health for all by the year 2000 as an ideal to be strived for by every group and every nationality in every country. Preventive health is a key component of that ideal, with health education at its core. To be most effective, education for health has to start with the youngest children and schools are becoming increasingly aware of the need for health education programmes.

It is not easy to plan or provide a planning framework for health education in the primary school, for children who, between the ages of four and eleven move so far – from leaving babyhood behind to the threshold of adolescence. Nor is health education seen as one of the 'basic' subjects requiring detailed comprehensive planning. Compare the number of reading or mathematics schemes with schemes for health education. Records of a child's attainment and progress may include nothing about health education.

Today's growing concern for health and health-related issues is having its impact on schools, often putting pressure on them to tackle specific and immediate problems. Yet, for health education to be effective, valued and valuable, it must be planned and practised as a broad-based programme which starts with the youngest children in school, takes account of what they bring to their own learning and builds up – and on – their experiences, their explanations, their personal language.

Programmes and packs of materials designed to tackle specific problems or isolated topics will have little lasting impact without this broad base. Programmes and materials devised for older children and simplified or watered down to provide introductory steps for younger children fail to take account of where these children are and each one's unique contribution. There is no health-related topic, no issue, no activity, no new learning which does not have its roots in some health-related activity of the youngest children. Successful programmes are constructed by building an upward spiral of learning and learning activities.

Surveys by HMI have shown that, while there was ample evidence of primary schools incorporating health education into the curriculum at classroom level, there was little evidence of overall and coordinated planning. Pockets of good practice were seen to exist, but the national picture was one of a piecemeal or fragmented approach where teachers were pursuing their own work without the benefit of a coordinated plan or coordinating person. The surveys emphasised the need for a coherent, broad-based, flexible programme.

For many children, particularly in their early years at school, health education may be something which the teacher introduces incidentally, sparked off by some local or national event, incident, or accident. It could arise after a visit (perhaps to the local fire station or to a farm) or as the follow-up to someone invited in to share their experience with the class. It may be the offer of help from a health professional, or the opportunity to try out new materials, which structures the health education session. In the hands of a sensitive teacher, such spontaneous learning can be relevant and rewarding. If, however, this is the total of health education, then much may be missed, while other areas are repeated and overemphasised. Children may find it difficult to make lasting links between this learning and their own health-related attitudes and behaviours.

For other children, health education may happen as part of topic or project work. It may provide the major theme of a topic such as 'People who care for me', 'What is a friend', 'Moving and growing', or it may be one of many strands in a topic with a wider theme, for example, 'Victorians', 'Transport', 'Our town'. In these forms health education is part of an investigation. It is offered as one way of looking at an area of interest and is not isolated as a subject. But there may be a danger that the health-related content is chosen to fit the topic and important areas missed or glossed over.

A series of television programmes may provide the starting point and structure round which a health education programme is planned. Some teachers may start with packs of materials, perhaps devised as the result of research projects. From such starting points, relevant programmes can grow and expand. Other teachers will be using schemes or programmes which they themselves have devised, working closely with colleagues, other schools, families, health and community workers and other professional advisers.

As a result of this multiplicity of approaches, the place of health education in the day-to-day organisation will vary. It may occupy a regular slot once or twice a week, 'timetabled' to fit in with topic work or the availability of a television programme. It may be seen to belong in a specific subject area such as science or environmental studies, and only be found in that area of activities. It may be seen as a multi-faceted subject and planned across the curriculum, allowing the nature of each health topic or issue to suggest where it might best be developed – one health theme in language, literature, play, creative activities – another in science, physical education, music. Some schools will be going through the process of debating and developing or reviewing their health education programmes, consulting with what they see as the most closely concerned groups and individuals.

What kind of health education is wanted by these concerned groups? If we had asked that question some few years back, we might have had very different answers from those of today. Today's responses will be coloured by more than changes in consultation. People's attitudes to and knowledge of the many hazards to children's health, safety and well-being are changing. Many who would have wanted a health education programme which preserved childhood innocence and trust will now be reconsidering that view, or being forced to rethink it. Many will be wondering how soon and in what detail sensitive issues can be tackled without arousing fear and mistrust or encouraging too early experimentation and risk taking.

Some will ask for health education programmes which protect children from both present and future hazards, while still preserving something of childhood innocence. Others will want to focus on ways in which children themselves might be enabled to become strong and independent in health decisions, valuing themselves, others, the environment and life itself.

How can teachers provide a programme which goes some way towards satisfying some of these requirements? What can they offer as a personal and social health education in which they work as partners with families and the community? What kind of help is

98

needed? Is it possible to provide a non-prescriptive framework for planning and for day-to-day practice which provides this support and takes account of the widely differing experiences of the children? These experiences will have contributed, and be contributing, to the children's personal education in health. Their perception of what it is to be healthy, what well-being is or could be will influence everything they are asked to learn at school. We ask – and will ask again – 'Are schools consulting the real consumers of their health education programmes – the children – who will bring to their learning their own programme, their own contribution to their education in health?'

A successful programme would take account of this and have built into it ways of tapping, charting and using these perceptions. Perhaps the key to a health education programme that really works is to start, not from what other people think should be in the curriculum, but from the way children perceive, explain, describe and illustrate their experience of being healthy and happy, and to value each child's individual contribution.

No single prescriptive programme, no one package of materials can do this. When teachers and health professionals are asked about the kind of planning framework which would be most helpful, they say: 'Something *we* can use to get the best for and from the children, the best out of ourselves and out of the resources and materials. And whatever you provide,

- make it *flexible* We want it to work with the classes we've got now and the ones we'll get next.
- make it *simple* We want to take a holistic view of health education, to look at the whole person; to explore the way bodies work and change and grow, mental health and how people relate to each other; to think about caring for others and for the environment, about work and play, about medical and other resources – and so much more. But we need help in putting all that into a manageable programme.
- make it *relevant* – to the children we're teaching now, to their families – to us.
- make it *practical* Don't be prescriptive, but do suggest different strategies for understanding what children already know, for extending their experience and skills, for helping them to shift the focus of some of that knowledge.
- make it *work* Provide some strategies which enable children to

make sense of all the messages which bombard them, so that they internalise experience and understanding and put this into practice.

- make it *reach out* Help us to draw in and draw on the knowledge and expertise of the children's families. At the same time point out some ways in which our schools can go beyond supporting to promoting health.'

How do we start to develop a framework to meet such different needs and criteria? How do we provide a balance of support and flexibility, ensure relevance for all the children, control the mass of health-related topics and yet leave room for the unexpected? Perhaps it might help if we look at the tasks in health education which confront primary teachers, those non-specialists expected to be specialists in everything. They are constantly being fed health-related messages from outside the classroom, messages which not only shift and double shift, but also conflict. With these messages come pressures; these may come from conflicting sources or conflict with the teachers' own values and attitudes. But this is only part of the picture. Another set of messages has to be heard, the messages which the children have to give us, if we will give them the opportunity to tell us, to communicate and explain them. In the clamour of messages from outside the classroom, from government, local authorities, research, parents, governors and the media, the children's messages may be ignored. Part of the task for the teacher is to explore and chart these messages, their sources, how and when they change, what it is that signals the change and how to balance all this against the other messages and pressures.

To fail to do this may be to court disaster. Effective personal education in health requires that we get to know the world of health as the children perceive and explain it, the idiosyncratic logic which underpins those explanations, the language they use, the pictures they draw, the conventions and stereotypes they use. Only then can we make individual and relevant use of planning guides, materials, and resources, make choices about starting points and classroom strategies and know where to pitch conceptual and linguistic levels. Only then can we make the right match between where children are and what we or the activities demand of them.

Once we have discovered what the children bring to the task, the task for the teacher becomes clearer and simpler. It means achieving some balance among the messages about what it is to be healthy, what a healthy lifestyle is, what well being means and demands.

It is difficult to find baseline data which illuminates trends in children's changing perceptions or which gives even an outline picture of the link they make between their own activities and safe, healthy, happy outcomes. What kind of a view do children have? Is it a narrow or holistic one – and how are we to find out?

Research techniques for use with groups of young children are difficult to find, especially those suited to the field of health education. Question and answer techniques which may yield encouraging results with older children do not prove productive with younger ones. Techniques which ask a child to rank given responses or to hold a range of answers while searching for the most appropriate one, are conceptually too complex. Techniques which require children to respond to printed language pose other problems. Many children of this age are struggling with the skills of reading and of becoming a reader and these may demand all their mental and physical energy, leaving little or none for the subject matter itself.

There are always problems in providing children with a range of answers to choose from, in selecting criteria which suit the majority of children. Findings suggest that it is more profitable to encourage children to use their own language, their own ways of communicating, asking them to clarify where necessary, rather than to comprehend and reply using other people's verbal products.

Recent research with 9500 children aged 4–8 in 11 local education authorities in England, Wales and Northern Ireland[1] made use of a new technique based on the day-to-day classroom activities of drawing and writing in response to an open-ended invitation.

The research took place in the normal classroom situation. Without any previous discussion or prompting, children were invited to draw all the things they did to make and keep themselves healthy and to label these activities. The activity of labelling varied. Some children happily wrote for themselves, using their own invented spellings. Others used the teacher as a scribe, whispering the dictated label or statement. The research sought to tap some-

[1] *A Picture of Health – What Do You Do That Makes You Healthy and Keeps You Healthy?*, Report of an Investigation into the Perceptions of 9583 Children aged 4–8 Years, Wetton, N; Moon, A; Williams, T. Health Education Authority, University of Southampton. To be published.

eat lots of regtibals

Dont Glue snif

medson keeps me healthy

EXISIS keeps me healthy.

milk yogurt medicine apple banana

I am frowing some bolls and I am healthy

xasideis

E Xi SiS

e czers iz

Exus is e ing

ecs is e ing

X asis

Exesseses

breving

lifr
waiting

boing Summer
Solts Keeps me
healthy

Furt is
healthy

vedgtoballs

opreshun

Nee ups

body bilding

thing of the children's changing perceptions of the link they made between their own activities and their view of being and staying healthy. What was revealed was much more than this. Although only the written statements were coded and analysed, the illustrations showed the children as acute observers of the world of health, with an ability to capture and communicate much of what they perceived.

Far from being empty vessels waiting to receive a measure of health education, what the children brought was a wealth of information, often filtered through their own, unique explanations. They made sense, too, of what they had only partly grasped, manipulating it to fit with more established, but sometimes inappropriate, knowledge, using their own child logic. Teachers and children alike were reluctant to part with the response sheets, which still continue to provide the research team and many others with new insights, surprise, pleasure and delight. Every child in every class was able to take part, despite language and/or learning difficulties.

Many children for whom language was a real problem were able to make their unique contributions. Much was revealed of children's skill at illustrating, their ability to convey what they wanted to say and their struggle to master the complexities of written language.

Fifteen main categories of response emerged, but within these, a large number of sub-categories were identified, analysed and recorded. The overall picture was one of children who, from the age of four, were increasingly able to make a link between what they did (or thought they could be doing) and becoming and staying healthy. 60% of all the four year olds responded with at least one example of their health-related activity; by the age of eight, 98% were responding with a wide-ranging number of examples. As children moved from four through to eight years of age, so their perceptions of the significance of day-to-day health practices and routines – washing, resting, sleeping, cleaning teeth – changed. Four year olds, whose view of being healthy was of being happily cared for, tended to see such routine practices as unnecessary adult impositions, rather than health-related. Seven and eight year olds showed a much clearer understanding of the link between these activities and being healthy.

The analysis of the changing perceptions of these children has provided a springboard for discussion, further classroom based research and the development of a curriculum framework for primary school health education. The technique itself, inviting children to participate through drawing and writing, has provided teachers with a simple, adaptable tool for discovering something of where children are in their thinking and how they are able to record and communicate this. It has also provided teachers with a new starting point, where they begin by looking at what the children bring to their own education in health, the source of what they bring, the perceptions, the misconceptions and the logic which underpins these. Teachers are realising the importance of exploring all this with the children before moving on to new learning. Parents and others who make up the community of the school are being invited to share in this valuing of the children's contribution.

So much has been revealed, in the analysis of this research, not only about the children's changing perceptions, but about the way they order, organise and communicate their thinking, and their delight in capturing this on paper and sharing it with others. The Draw and Write technique has now been extended for use with children from four to eleven years in further health-related research.

Five key areas – relationships, keeping safe, healthy eating, the world of drugs and exercise and rest – have been explored to discover something of the ways in which children have internalised their own experiences and made their own sense of the information and messages which bombard them.

In all of these researches, a constantly recurring theme put forward by the children at every age has been the importance of relationships. It is clear that they understand the complexities of relationships and their own part in establishing or changing them.

No-one who has explored this view of the world of health would wish to start anywhere other than where the children are. No-one, having seen them at work or play, could undervalue the understanding and experience they bring, the acuity of their observations of the world, their lack of inhibition in expressing what they feel and see, and competence in their own education for health.

10 Do children know what they need? Talking to children about personal and social education

Peter Lang

At one level it is clear that children will know what they need, equally, at another, it is likely that they won't. There is nothing particularly surprising about this – it is often true of adults as well! None of us, enmeshed in the 'here and now' as we are, is always able to perceive what is in our best long term interest. The point of posing the question in the title, is to highlight the importance of an area that, this paper will suggest, teachers rarely bother to consider or raise questions about. In the writer's view it is precisely these sorts of questions that they should ask. If and when teachers do ask questions like this, they will find that the answers can only be found through talking to their pupils, in talking moreover in ways that they have never done before. This would be particularly the case in relation to personal and social education.

The aim of this paper is to emphasise two things:

- the value of the contribution that pupils themselves can make to the development and effectiveness of personal and social education at every level of schooling;
- the barriers that currently exist to their contribution being fully exploited at the primary level.

Work with primary pupils

At the primary level there are few examples in the literature in which the seeking of pupil views has been a significant element. The work that does exist demonstrates the illuminative value of such an approach. Take, for example, two studies concerned specifically with issues of gender; the studies and their conclusions were substantially based on data collected from discussions with small groups of primary girls which sought to elicit their understandings and perspectives. Both raised some important points and came to a number of significant conclusions.

> Children are not thought able to understand the complexities of the social world which we inhabit. However, in this chapter I suggest that children, in this case ten year old girls, often have an intuitive grasp of the social processes which mould their lives. In particular I argue that the girls I interviewed understand the nature of sexism but have not accepted its inevitability.
>
> (Holly, 1985, p 51)

Holly's discussion demonstrates both the level of sophistication these girls have in their understanding of sexism as it operates in their school, and also some key aspects of that sexism. In this her work highlights two key points regarding pupil perspectives. Pupils, even those still at the infant stage, are capable of quite sophisticated understandings and it is important for teachers to endeavour to engage with these. Where pupil perspectives are sought and examined they will often provide the basis for some aspects of a valuable critique of the school's current organisation and practice.

> The girls I talked to have not passively accepted themselves as victims of a system which defines them as less naughty than boys, less deserving of the same amount of space and incapable of kicking footballs. They see the injustice of all this and they struggle against it. However because being a girl means getting softer treatment they know that they have some advantages.
>
> (Ibid, p 61)

The second study raises issues about the methodological approach that underlies the neglect of pupil perspectives.

> Whilst schools are in many ways idiosyncratic they are nevertheless depressingly uniform in others. One aspect of their commonality, so researchers claim, is their gender stereotyping and differentiation in favour of males. Most such research has been undertaken from the perspective of pre-ordinate method-

ological or theoretical positions adopted by the researcher rather than from the perspective of the subjects (objects?) of their research ... Much of the research undertaken in the *Sex Stereotyping and the Early Years of Schooling* project attempted to tap into this latter perspective by attending to the perceptions of pupils as well as those of the researchers, who in this case were teachers.

(May, 1984, p 51)

Though only part of May's work is concerned directly with pupil perspectives it includes some revealing analysis supported by illustrative direct quotation.

Where the girls express interest in machinery and the development of technology, this interest is confined either to those industrial machines with which women were traditionally involved – as in weaving – or to contemporary machines which they might expect to use in a factory or the home – such as sewing machines and washing machines. Boys rarely mention these kind of machines as of interest to them, but when they do so, they have the following to say:

Interviewer: Why is the topic called 'Men and Machines'?
Boys: 'Because men invented the machines ... and women got all the enjoyment out of it.'
Interviewer: 'You think so, do you?'
Boys: 'Yeah'.
Interviewer: 'But women work with a lot of machines, don't they? In factories as well as at home?'
Boys: 'They don't have to graft. They've got electric irons and everything.'
Interviewer: 'And don't you think that's hard work?'
Boys: 'No'

(Ibid, p 69)

Both the papers quoted above use the data collected to develop fairly radical critiques of primary school organisation and curriculum from the perspective of sexism. But they also demonstrate the potential that the collection and analysis of pupil views has for raising questions about areas such as a school's organisation and curriculum, and which should contribute to the first stage of developing personal and social education within a school.

Concern over the effects on pupils of their move from primary to secondary school has been shown by teachers at both levels for a number of years. In this connection a study based on conversations with pupils before and after transfer produced significant insights about pupil concerns. It also showed that:

> ... while teachers on either side of the primary-secondary divide try to neutralise the vocabulary of streaming, the views of the children in my study would seem to indicate a much sharper break between primary and secondary school than the 'official' version and this despite the efforts of teachers to the contrary. One of the most significant factors contributing to this break is possibly that arrangement in secondary schools which labels children by stream or band and about which so much pupil talk and concern is directed.
>
> (Thorp, 1983, p 50)

Earlier in his paper Thorp, talking of transfer, focuses on one of the key problems about the assumptions that are made about pupil needs (that they are unproblematic, that teachers have a clear idea of what they are, and can therefore respond to them on the pupil's behalf), he also states the case for taking pupil views into account.

> Many teachers, like myself, have contributed to discussion about children's transfer to secondary school, considering continuity in the curriculum, personal liaison between primary and secondary teachers, record-keeping, testing and the use of test results. But all too often our discussion is blinkered by these basic assumptions. Our objective is usually to make transfer easier, less stressful and therefore more efficient. But from whose point of view? The children's experience of transfer is definitely neglected. As teachers, we make assumptions about their needs. We consider what we think best and our programmes of induction reflect our concerns. How much more meaningful would our professional discussion be if we considered the experience of our 'clients' – those children who have to live their daily lives under the constraints we impose.
>
> (Ibid, p 46)

Through the analysis of pupil perspectives Thorp also raises questions about some of the 'commonsense' assumptions made about the effects of transfer on pupils – assumptions which would certainly influence the nature of the personal and social education provided at both primary and secondary levels. He comments:

> A large part of teachers' conventional wisdom of transfer sees it as a traumatic experience for children. It is commonly thought to cause anxiety, stress, tension, even to be 'disorganis- ing' in some way . . . However in the overall context of the conversations I had with the children these fears represent only a very small proportion of their 'talk'. Most children were looking forward to transfer. The move was eagerly anticipated even though their talk revealed confusion about the kind of school they were entering and why they were going to that particular school.
>
> (Ibid, p 47)

Thorp's findings were recently supported by an MEd research project undertaken by Woods (1986) who also found little evidence of excessive anxiety or trauma amongst the pupils investigated in his study, either before or after transfer.

Apart from these and other isolated examples it is true that the views of primary pupils are still generally ignored at the level of research, broad policy, curriculum development and work in individual schools. The area of pastoral care and personal and social education, where these perspectives might be thought to be of particular significance is, in fact, no different in this respect to any other educational concern.

A structural explanation of neglect

The reason for this general neglect must be sought in terms of the distribution of power and status within the education system, together with teachers' professional identity and concerns. Nearly ten years ago Meighan (1977) observed that schools were reluctant to grant their pupils 'client' status; rather, they treated pupils as the recipients of the schools' 'benefits'. Meighan (1978) is particularly concerned with the status accorded pupils' own version of their experience. He points out that

> existing definitions of the situation appear to take teaching as more important than learning, the teachers' activity as more central than their pupils ... *despite the official rhetoric of educational writing and debate that makes claims for the pupil's welfare as the central focus*.
>
> (Meighan, 1978, p 136)

More recently Cohen and Manion (1981) drawing on the work of Calvert (1975) have made much the same points.

But what of the pupils? How do they see their school environment? What sense do they make of it all – the system's efforts to educate them, the teachers at the centre of the task, even work itself? In setting out to look for answers to these questions we are immediately confronted with a dearth of empirical studies in this area, the few that are available to us making up a mere handful of pieces in the total jigsaw. That there should be such relative neglect of the pupils' viewpoint is due, it has been suggested, to the low status of the pupil role.

Like the position of the child, and the position of the patient, (the pupil's role) lacks status; it commands little respect. Behaviour appropriate to a disvalued position tends to be defined for the occupants of that position by those who occupy related positions of greater status: the role of the child is defined by the adult, the role of the patient by the doctor or nurse, and the role of the pupil by the teacher.

> (Calvert, 1975)

Though the material quoted above was all written over six years ago it seems that the situation is still much as these commentators and my own work has suggested. It is most unlikely that many primary schools have undertaken systematic but unreported investigations into their pupils' perspectives into anything, let alone personal and social education. Thus, to return to the question asked in this paper's title, it is not so much 'Do children know what they need?' but rather 'If they do, is it likely that anyone will ask them?'

and 'If they *are* asked, will their answers be given the status they deserve?'

Problems particular to primary schools

As has already been suggested, there are particular characteristics of primary schools and teachers that may create further barriers to the serious consideration of the contribution that can be made by including pupil perspectives in the development of personal and social education. There are two key factors that need to be examined and understood in relation to this:

1 The prevalence of 'taken-for-granted' assumptions about the primary teacher's classroom practice.
2 Primary teachers' perceptions about the way children learn and the effects of home environments.

Many teachers would claim that they consider pupil views important and that, due to the special nature of their primary classroom situation and the relationships they are able to develop within it, they not only know and understand the views and understandings of their pupils, but are able to take account of these views. However, as many of the chapters in this book illustrate, there is often a significant gap between primary teachers' beliefs (taken-for-grantedness) and their practice.

In September 1987 a group of postgraduate students undertaking their initial school observation conducted a small-scale investigation in some 17 primary classrooms, over a period of two days. Their study provided some significant, if basic, data on the nature of teacher-pupil interaction in these particular classrooms. Although the primary teachers involved had regular individual interaction with all the pupils in their classes, in terms of time spent during the two days some pupils were involved with the teacher for up to ten times as much as others. Also, most interactions observed involved only very short periods of time. Though a very limited sample, it is likely that what was observed in these classrooms was fairly typical of a situation to be found more generally. It may be that primary teachers need to reassess the implications of their normal teaching styles and interaction with pupils. Some schools and classrooms do not really allow the time and space needed for the development of the kind of interaction and relationships through which pupil perspectives and views may begin to be understood.

Recently, a number of secondary schools have recognised the kind of problems outlined above, and have started to take organisational and structural initiatives to overcome them, for example by withdrawing pupils from class regularly to spend uninterrupted time on an individual basis with their tutors. These initiatives are not only directed to ensuring that pupils' perspectives are appreciated and understood, but also to providing a safety net in terms of such problems as child abuse.

The development of various forms of pupil profile in secondary schools and the need for teachers to negotiate with pupils in the development of these, has led a significant number of teachers to reconsider the appropriateness of the skills which they currently possess. In connection with this, recent research has suggested that there is increasing interest among secondary teachers in the acquisition of basic counselling skills (Hooper and Lang, 1988). It would be ironic if primary schools' inability to analyse fully the realities of their classroom situations and the level of specialised human relationship skills needed by teachers resulted in them understanding their pupils less well and responding to their needs less effectively than secondary schools.

The number of children of primary age responding to voluntary counselling initiatives (for example, phone-in services for those suffering from abuse of one kind or another) must raise questions about the level of care, availability of support and quality of relationships within at least some of the primary classes to which the children belong.

The second barrier special to the primary situation – primary teachers' perceptions of the way their pupils learn and the effect that their home environment has on this – could be described as the teachers' ideology of child development and cultural disadvantage.

Many primary schools see themselves as providing the only real basis for the proper development of their pupils; the notion that they are effectively compensating for the children's background is implicit in many aspects of the way these schools approach their work. Alongside these views is often a strong, if unrecognised view that pupils' development progresses through clearly defined stages.

The powerful, if somewhat ill-defined, concept of 'readiness' is an obvious manifestation of this view, though few would still maintain that the Piagetian stages of development are fixed stages which relate to particular ages. Research conducted by Margaret Donaldson in the late 1960s (published as *Children's Minds* in 1975) demonstrated the weakness of Piagetian research and showed how the rationale powers of young children had been underestimated. Nevertheless, the stages view has remained influential, in views about moral development as well as intellectual and cognitive development. So, for example, the Schools' Council Working Paper – *Primary practice* (1983) describes the three stages from intuitive to abstract thinking and states that '. . . children go through these stages in the same order', although it is also noted that 'they do not go through them at the same rate'.

Tizard and Hughes, in *Young Children Learning* (1984), show that the idea of a strict progression through the stages is not tenable. They show that pre-school children are capable of exploring abstract topics, that they can see cause and effect, work out what other people can see; and calculate or infer what another person might know – or what they might need to know in order to carry out a particular action. The context of this research was young children in the home context, and its findings turn upside down the commonly held belief that professionals know better than parents how to educate children. The children's talk with teachers in fact lacked the richness, the depth and the variety of the children's talk at home, it also lacked the sense of intellectual struggle and mutual attempt to communicate. At home, the children talked freely about a whole range of different ideas which they explored persistently and logically, puzzling over how to grasp and understand events around them and showing that they were capable of complex and sophisticated understandings.

Research shows that what pupils think, feel and understand is likely to be at a level and of a quality that can make significant contributions to the development and practice of personal and social education in a number of ways and at a number of levels. It also raises questions about the level at which personal and social education is pitched; where a 'stages' view of development is too influential, the type of PSE developed and the experiences in which the pupils are involved may not extend them fully. Where schools have balanced the implications of the stages of pupil development with high expectations of their potential at all ages, they have been able to develop skills and qualities in pupils at very early stages of their education. Finally, the research quoted suggests that many schools may need to think through their attitude to parents' involvement in and contribution to their personal and social education programme.

Why seek pupil views?

What then are the different contributions that pupils' views can make, and how can they be involved?

Before answering these questions it is appropriate to reflect briefly on the justifications for seeking pupil views and also the ways through which they might be obtained.

Of all areas of the curriculum the nature of personal and social education most clearly demands a direct involvement of pupils; the spirit of PSE is such that the pupil's 'client' status must be accepted. If a crucial dimension of the area is the insistence that all members of the group/institution should be valued, then there is an inescapable obligation to consult all these members. Where this is not done the school's work in personal and social education is likely to be unnecessarily impoverished.

Where schools are committed to developing personal and social education, seeking pupil perspectives provides a fuller understanding of what is being done and may also give a clearer view of what *should* be done. The initiatives a school is undertaking in PSE should be reviewed and evaluated at least partly on the basis of how the pupils feel about and understand them.

Where pupils' views are regularly sought, albeit in different ways, this is likely to enhance their own personal development. They may gain in confidence and feelings of self worth. When they later become involved in the negotiation necessary for the production of a cumulative 'record of achievement' this early experience may make them feel that they have more of value to contribute, and help them engage in the process more fully.

Ways of seeking pupil views

There are a number of ways in which pupils' views may be sought but they all share certain characteristics. They will be the result of a conscious, thought-through and systematic approach which is specifically intended to overcome the assumption, found in many schools and classrooms, that these things are already clearly understood. Pupil views may be sought by the class teachers themselves, by headteachers, or through schools working in cooperation with each other; in some cases it may be appropriate to use an outside consultant. The methods used can involve informal discussions and interviews, as well as structured ones. In some cases the use of questionnaires may be appropriate. Other ways may be more appropriate for seeking pupil views in particular instances and in relation to particular topics (see, for example, Wetton and Moon's chapter on pupil writing and drawing). The seeking of pupil views may be undertaken as a one-off initiative or at irregular intervals but ideally it should be an integral component of a school's personal and social education programmme.

The contribution of pupil perspectives

Important insights can often be gained by investigating pupil views and understandings in relation to the school's organisation, ethos, formal and informal curriculum. In some cases, however, the insights may be of an even more significant nature. Campbell's paper in this section provides a good illustration of this. The top infants that Campbell talked to had carried out a project to help them learn about industry – and certainly they learned an awful lot about the way industry is organised, possibly more than the teachers who were teaching them knew. Through their simulations these children developed ideas about hierarchical relationships in industry which clearly replicated industrial relations in Britain, between management and workers. Pupil workers also found ways of using the system to create their own black market. The value of Campbell's investigation is threefold: at a general level it demonstrates how pupil views can enhance our understanding of an activity in terms of its contribution to pupil's personal and social development. The study also illustrates how what pupils are really learning may be very different from the school's taken-for-granted assumptions about this; finally it shows once again how pupils, in this case fairly young ones, are capable of quite sophisticated understandings of their social world.

It is vital that schools take into account pupil views and perspectives in identifying the particular needs that PSE provision should be responding to. For example, it is clear that 'had they been asked', the black primary age children of the mothers whose views appear in Cas Walker's paper (Section Five) could have contributed significantly to such discussions in their respective primary schools. Further, pupil views and feelings should form part of the material for personal and social education (David Ingram's paper in this section provides a clear illustration of this). The review and evaluation which, it has been argued, must be an integral part of the development of personal and social education will have little validity if it does not include some attempt to consider pupil perspectives and understandings.

Finally, as has been said, where pupils regularly experience the type of involvement which not only entails their view being sought but also visibly taken into consideration, this will make a significant contribution to their personal and social education.

Conclusion

This paper has raised a number of issues regarding the contributions that pupils could and should make to the process of PSE, which is after all intended for their benefit. To do this I have spent considerable space on examining the range of factors that appear to have contributed to the current neglect of pupils' views. An awareness of these implicit barriers should encourage teachers and schools to recognise that to fully utilise the potential contribution of pupils, they will need to plan and think things through in ways that have so far not been undertaken. 'Taken for granted' assumptions must be questioned from a positive viewpoint and strategies evolved to overcome them, particularly in terms of the interactive and investigative strategies developed both in and out of the classroom. Pupils have got things to say about what they need; we must talk to them (and listen to them) about personal and social education.

References

Calvert, B, 1975 *The Role of the Pupil* Routledge and Kegan Paul.

Cohen, L, and Manion, L, 1981 *Perspectives on classrooms and schools* Holt, Rinehart and Winston.

Donaldson, M, 1975 *Children's Minds* Fontana.

Holly, L, 1985 'Mary, Jane and Virginia Woolf: ten-year-old girls talking' in Weiner, G (ed) *Just a bunch of girls: feminist approaches to schooling* Open University Press.

Hooper, R, and Lang, P, 1988 'Counselling Revisited' in *Pastoral Care in Education*, 6(2).

Kitteringham, J, 1987 'Pupils' perceptions of the role of the form tutor' in *Pastoral Care in Education*, 5(3).

Lang, P, 1983, 'How pupils see it: looking at how pupils perceive Pastoral Care' in *Pastoral Care in Education*, 1(3).

Lang, P, 1985a 'Taking the consumer into account' in Lang, P and Marland, M (eds) *New Directions in Pastoral Care* Blackwell.

Lang, P, 1985b 'Schooling and Welfare: taking account of the views and feelings of pupils' in Ribbins, P (ed) *Schooling and Welfare* Falmer Press.

May, N, 1984 'Bees make Bees – not honey' in Shostak, F and Logan, T (eds) *Pupil Experience* Croom Helm.

Meighan, R, 1977 'The pupil as client: the learning experience of schooling' in *Educational Review*, 29(2).

Meighan, R, 1979 'A pupil's view of teaching performance' in *Educational Review*, 30(2).

Schools' Council, 1983 *Primary Practice* Methuen.

Tattersfield, R, 1987 'Sixth form students' perceptions of pastoral grouping' in *Pastoral Care in Education*, 5(3).

Thorp, J, 1983 'Evaluating practice: Pupils' views of transfer from primary to secondary school' in *Pastoral Care in Education*, 1(1).

Tizard, B and Hughes, M, 1984 *Young children learning and thinking at home and school* Fontana.

Woods, G, 1986 *A Comparative study of primary secondary transfer* Unpublished MEd dissertation, University of Warwick.

SECTION THREE
Schools and teachers taking initiatives

No matter how much personal and social education is analysed and discussed, however rigorous the analysis of primary schools' current practice, this in itself will make a limited contribution both to personal and social education as an aspect of primary education and to what it has to offer pupils. The full understanding and development of PSE will be inexorably linked to the amount and quality of practice that is actually taking place in schools and individual classrooms.

The papers in this section are each concerned with a particular initiative in personal and social education in which their writers have been involved. They range from those concerned with the whole of a school's organisation and whole-school policies to initiatives taken in a single classroom. This section forms one of the book's central resources, as it offers insights into the development of PSE in practice.

11 Developing a structural social development programme in an inner city school

Joan Brier

In 1981 I was appointed headteacher of a large inner city first and middle school, designated as an Education Priority Area and recognised as an area of extreme deprivation. It rapidly became clear to me that class teachers, senior staff and support teachers were directing a high percentage of their time and energy to dealing with behaviour problems. Most staff meetings and informal staffroom discussions focused on the identification of problems and methods of containment, leaving little time or energy to consider conflict resolution or preventive measures.

The majority of behaviour problems involved a relatively large nucleus of disruptive pupils bringing out-of-classroom and out-of-school conflict and upsets into the classroom situation. Teachers expressed their concerns and frustrations about the demands of these particular pupils on their attention, which meant that the problems of withdrawn children and the education of all the children were in danger of being relegated to a secondary role. The problems we were experiencing were echoed wholly or in part by colleagues in schools in similar circumstances to ourselves.

Through discussion and classroom observation undertaken by school and support staff, we came to the conclusion that many of the common behaviours causing problems stemmed from poor socialisation. Most of the pupils who were involved had a limited range of behaviours and poor self-control skills, a combination which led to unacceptable and inappropriate classroom behaviour and frequently aggressive playground behaviours. A second factor which, we felt, contributed to attitudes to school was the cultural resistance in the local area towards persons or agencies who are perceived as representing authority. The school was regarded traditionally as an authoritarian institution by many parents and pupils and this had helped to generate something of a confrontational air in relationships between home and school. A number of staff expressed doubts that attitudes and behaviours could be changed; they felt that only impositional controls and negative sanctions would be effective in maintaining equilibrium in the school.

During the discussions involved in identification of the main problems there began to emerge varying degrees of agreement among staff that a less rigid and institutional organisation could 'take the heat' out of confrontation, without necessarily meaning that teachers lost control of the situation. Reorganisation of playground areas, exit routes, lunchtime arrangements, all contributed to the easing and softening of the 'sharp edges' in the running of the school. The involvement of parents with teachers, in attempts to resolve some of the acute problem behaviours, began to demonstrate that in a large number of cases (contrary to deep-seated expectations) the consultation exercise could result in the support of teachers by parents with a subsequent improvement in basic classroom behaviours of the children. The process of change had, in fact, started, and was followed by a steady 'opening' of the previously 'closed' regime.

Although fully committed to this opening of the school and convinced of the benefits to all those associated with it, I felt strongly that this change had to be effected slowly, sensitively and on a number of fronts, if true and effective change was to be achieved. Change of any kind can bring with it a high degree of threat to all concerned. To push too rapidly to a perceived end can, in actuality, achieve an opposite effect. This may be particularly so in a school where many children do not have the personal resources or the stability in their lives to enable them to cope with rapid change easily. Any new approach or strategy in a school cannot be made in isolation, but has to evolve through the wider context of the school philosophy.

Initially there were two main focuses in beginning the process of change. The first was the fostering of closer relationships between staff, pupils and parents; the second, organisational and environmental changes to enable these relationships to have a more supportive environment. These changes, while minor in some ways, were crucial in preparing the ground for in-depth changes of established attitudes. Improvement of the stark 50 year old building to make it more welcoming; regular communications and invitations to parents to unthreatening social events; an 'open-door' policy to both teachers and parents to discuss problems; all served to begin the movement towards the target of supportive and positive relationships between all parties involved in the development of the school. During this time there were endless staff discussions, frequently about the management of behaviour, as well as the normal 'nuts and bolts' of curriculum development and school organisation.

During these first two years the support teacher for children with adjustment difficulties became involved in helping teachers to develop their personal skills in the management of behaviour in the classroom – both that of individuals and of larger class groups. This was effected by individual counselling as necessary, and through in-service work. The teacher skills included the use of social awareness and social skills development games in the classroom (Brandes and Phillips, 1977); techniques for the management of behaviour through behaviour modification in the classroom; identification and targeting on particular behaviour areas with whole class groups within the classroom.

It was realised, however, that these steps, while necessary and to some degree successful, were purely a response to crisis. While perhaps the worst of the classroom behaviours were being modified and contained in a more acceptable and less stressful manner than previously, the basic attitudes and behaviours of the children were relatively unchanged, especially in the less structured playground and outside school behaviours.

An examination of the school's Punishment Records, from the 1930s up to the abolition of the use of corporal punishment by the LEA in 1981, revealed similar patterns of behaviour to those being currently experienced – and in similar proportions. It also showed that corporal punishment had little noticeable effect on the modification of unacceptable behaviour in the school. This picture of the apparent inevitability of the development of poor behaviour patterns was disquieting, but served to direct us to look for earlier and preventive intervention measures. To this end I requested from the LEA, and was granted, a one year secondment to study, and hopefully find answers to some of our problems.

The findings of a research programme by Shure and Spivak (funded by the US National Institute of Mental Health) which looked at the behaviour of inner city children, was found to have examined aspects of behaviour which paralleled our own situation. It appeared to give a logical and workable framework which was appropriate for adaptation to the British style of classroom organisation and teaching from the somewhat prescriptive US presentation. The basic premise of Shure and Spivak is that by teaching children *how* to think rather than *what* to think, they will advance their ability to think through and resolve real-life problems. They suggest that children displaying excessively impulsive or inhibited behaviours do not have an understanding or knowledge of possible alternative behaviours, whereas well-adjusted children demonstrate a wider range of alternatives. Extending children's thinking and thereby their 'behaviour vocabulary' offers them a wider range of behaviours from which to choose their action; they are thus helped to become effective in coping with the interpersonal relationships and events which they encounter daily.

A very modest and short-term examination of Interpersonal Cognitive Problem Solving, which I conducted in two primary schools with children aged five plus and six plus, appears to confirm Shure and Spivak's basic premise that the ability of children to conceptualise alternative solutions to interpersonal problems can be used as a predictor of behavioural adjustment. Although the results of my experiments could not be claimed as conclusive, due to the narrowness of the study, there were strong indications that inhibited children became more interactive in their relationships than they were prior to the programme. However, more impulsive/aggressive children, although able to generate and verbalise more alternative solutions than prior to the experiment, did not appear to generalise these solutions to their behaviour. This failure to generalise had been predicted due to the limited time span of the experiment.

In the study of Interpersonal Cognitive Problem Solving I also examined the viability and effectiveness of adapting the main framework of problem solving in interpersonal relationships to the British primary classroom organisation and styles of teaching. The conclusion drawn from this part of the study was that the problem-solving approach *is* viable, *is* adaptable to the British classroom and teaching styles, and could form the basis for positive classroom intervention.

The possibility of applying the framework across the age range, from five to twelve and across the curriculum had then to be addressed, and this was the task I took back to my own school to follow up. I felt it was important that any new approach to the social development of children in school should be applicable to existing curriculum areas for two main reasons. First, to add to the existing wide curriculum in the school would inevitably mean a sacrifice or diminution of some other area of learning and therefore would not be acceptable. Second, if the problem-solving principles are addressed through suitable existing curriculum areas then the effects are more likely to generalise to behaviour; a variety of presentation is more likely to aid children's understanding of the principles of problem solving, and there will be more varied reference points for teachers to help children to relate to real personal problematic events. Pellegrini and Urbain (1985) in their evaluation of the uses of Interpersonal Cognitive Problem Solving concluded that despite the methodological and evaluation problems pervading this approach, it appears to be effective both as a remediation and as a secondary prevention strategy. They suggest that it could also be efficacious as a primary prevention strategy. They acknowledge that the training schedules which exist may be disruptive in inner-city school setting where (presumably in references to US Schools) they see 'control rather than self-expression' as being the main approach to behaviour problems. However, we hope to be able to show that the more flexible organisation of the British Primary Classroom together with cross-curricular approaches will provide the 'Explicit guided practice in the problem-solving process in the child's real-life environment (which is) particularly critical for the generalisation of training effects' which Pellegrini and Urbain recommend. This leads them to support Kendall's (1977) argument that systematically applied behavioural contingencies may also be necessary to enhance the effectiveness of cognitive training programmes.

Through discussions with staff it was agreed that finding the optimum balance between the social and academic focus of the curriculum was crucial to the success of the children's development. While consensus was reached by staff that the social development and adjustment of the children is fundamental to their overall development and a vital precursor of successful learning, we were all clear that this could not be at the expense of all other areas of learning, and that the two aspects should be interrelated and complementary.

The basic framework of the problem-solving approach (Figure 11.1) adopted from Shure and Spivak's work has four main phases. These are developmental, in that the early stages are most appropriate to the early years and are prerequisite skills on which later stages are built, while the later stages are developmentally appropriate to the later years of the primary school.

Figure 11.1

Phase one – identification of feelings

The ability to be sensitive to one's own and to others' feelings is important to interpersonal relations at all ages.

Aim   to help children to learn that different people feel differently, feelings change and it is possible to identify this through listening, looking and talking.

i   recognition of feelings – happy, sad, angry
related feelings – excited, being bored, fear, embarrassed, aggressive, mean

ii   modes of recognition – language, non-verbal communication, situation causes, body language, reaction etc.

Phase two – cause and effect

Why because connection – an important pre-requisite skill in the development of consequential thinking.

Aim   to help children to develop an understanding of the concept of causality – the effect of one's behaviour on another and of others' behaviour on oneself.

i   the connection between why and because; reflecting on past events, eg *I did X, so he did Y.*

ii   might and maybe – terms important in hypothesising the potential consequences of our action eg *If I do X then she may do Y.*

iii   recognition that predicted consequences do not necessarily occur as predicted eg *If I hit him he might hit me back.*

Phase three – generation of alternative solutions

This element is the most significant in the development of social adjustment.

Aim   to help children to develop the ability to formulate a range of solutions to both real and hypothetical interpersonal problems.

i   through consideration of common interpersonal problems, the feelings involved, the causes and effects of the interaction, children are helped to generate a range of solutions.

ii   through consideration of hypothetical and less familiar interpersonal problems children are given opportunities to project a range of possible solutions.

Phase four – evaluation of solutions

The final element in the problem solving sequence. The most important element but also the most difficult.

Aim   to help children to use a range of criteria to evaluate a range of solutions to interpersonal problems.

i   by considering the relative merits of a range of solutions to interpersonal problems.

ii   by extending evaluation criteria from the predominant effectiveness criterion to include safety, fairness, feelings (of self and others) and whether the solution creates further problems.

iii   application of evaluation criteria to real-life experiences.

The problem-solving approach has been adopted as the basic framework for the whole school, which gives a workable unified approach and progression through the age range. In-service work with the staff on the basic principles of interpersonal problem solving has been undertaken to ensure a reasonably clear understanding by all those concerned in working with the children. At present we work to a rough rule of thumb guide as to the age appropriateness of the phases for teaching purposes.

Phase one	—	4+ to 6+ years	(F1 and F2)
Phase two	—	6+ to 8+ years	(F3 and F4)
Phase three	—	8+ to 10+ years	(M1 and M2)
Phase four	—	10+ to 12+ years	(M3 and M4)

This guide does not exclude the use of all the phases in any age group, but indicates the area of emphasis of teaching most appropriate. It is most likely that all the phases may be included when considering resolution of particular problems in school.

The problem-solving framework was accepted as the central core of our social development programme, together with a belief that the improvement of relationships in the classroom, the playground and at home is central to all successful learning and development. In workshop sessions the staff went on to identify:

128

1 The skills which children need to be effective in making positive relationships and which can be developed if they are addressed directly in the classroom setting.

2 Curriculum areas which lend themselves as vehicles for developing understanding of different aspects of social relationships, their application and the integrative possibilities between these areas.

3 The necessary infrastructure of organisation, observation, evaluation, planning and resources to support a successful programme.

Figure 11.2 illustrates how these elements interrelate. The present on-going task is to develop our own skills in utilising the identified areas of the curriculum in new ways and in collating materials and resources found to be suitable, practical and appropriate for use in developing curriculum areas we have identified so far.

During the present academic year the school has become involved in the School-Focused Secondment Project being run jointly by the local education authority and Sheffield City Polytechnic, in which one teacher from each of a number of primary schools has been seconded for one year to work on the development of curriculum in their own school. The secondee works part-time in study and part-time in schools on a whole staff project agreed prior to the secondment. The focus in our own school is on continuity within and between schools, with the main emphasis on the continuity of the social and organisational experiences and learning of children from nursery, through our own first and middle school, to the two secondary schools we feed. The project teacher has been involved in working with the three teams of teachers (early years team, transition team, upper team) in the identification of the social skills and curriculum areas which they consider appropriate to these age groups. Some of the techniques and approaches through which these social skills can be transmitted have been examined and demonstrated by members of our own staff, and other colleagues who have appropriate skills and experience, in enjoyable whole-staff workshops after school. These ideas are being developed and adapted as appropriate into the wider curriculum and organisation of the school.

The observations and evaluations carried out by the School-Focused Secondment teacher, particularly when involved with the transition team were illuminating. Although we had come a long way along the road towards our aims in the area of social develop-

Figure 11.2

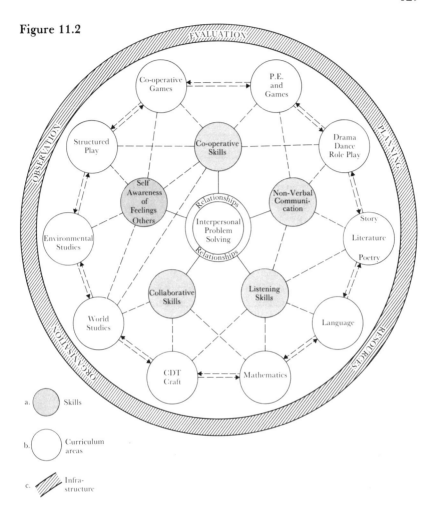

ment, there were obvious difficulties in developing related and co-ordinated curriculum initiatives.

After an in-service session with the whole staff in which we reflected on our joint progress over recent years, we looked to the future. Members of staff who had had some previous involvement in World Studies on an LEA course, suggested that this approach may give us the next appropriate stage of development.

The philosophy of World Studies, together with cooperative games and the social development programme, was seen as a

130

possible vehicle for the development of a broad curriculum embracing all aspects of the curriculum, including personal development. The affirmation, acceptance, self-awareness and personal value ideals of World Studies parallel many of the social skills we identified as being basic to the personal and interpersonal development of the child, and the What?, Why? and How? questions with which the World Studies philosophy challenges the curriculum were considered to be highly relevant to our present stage of development.

A further in-service session was arranged, in which staff posed questions and an advisory teacher involved in developing the LEA programme of world studies presented a rationale of the philosophy as well as answering the questions posed by staff. Following this an in-service programme for the school is being developed and will commence later this term.

We aim to continue the valuable observation and evaluation elements already in use and expect that by the end of the next academic year we will have a comprehensive set of guidelines through which new members of the school teams can easily integrate into this way of working and from which we can continue to grow to meet the changing needs of the children and of the wider society.

References

Brandes, D and Phillips, H, 1977 *Gamesters' Handbook* London: Hutchinson.

Kendal, P C, 1977 'On the efficacious use of verbal self-instructional procedures with children' in *Cognitive Ther Res*, *1* p 331–7.

Pellegrini and Urbain, 1985 'An evaluation of interpersonal cognitive problem solving training with children' in *Journal of Child Psychology and Psychiatry*, *26*(1).

Shure, M B and Spivak, G, 1979 'Interpersonal cognitive problem solving and primary prevention' in *Journal of Clinical Child Psychology* (2), p 89–94.

Shure, M B and Spivak, G, 1981 'A Mental Health Programme for Pre-School Children, Kindergarten Children and Mothers of Young Children: A Comprehensive Report.' National Institute of Mental Health, No. M H 20372.

12 Education for personal development: a whole-school approach
Tony Richardson

Part of the 'conventional wisdom' (Young, 1971) of the primary school since the mid-1960s has been the emphasis that practitioners and commentators have placed upon the development of children towards maturity through individual choice, pupil decision making, group work and self direction. Several researchers have illustrated, however, that this apparent liberal child-centredness was often a disguised form of social control (Sharp and Green, 1975; Hargreaves *et al*, 1975; Woods, 1979 and A Hargreaves, 1985). Moreover, although teaching methodologies such as group work are commonly supposed to be widespread in English primary schools, much of this 'group work' has mainly involved individual work within a group setting. As Galton and Simon (1980) have pointed out, some teachers claim to be employing group work as a major strategy, whilst actually organising teaching and learning for individual instruction. Nevertheless, a dominant feature of primary education remains an emphasis upon a child-centred ideology, including the ill-defined 'pastoral' role of the class teacher.

This paper argues that the key area of pupils' personal and social education should be explicitly structured into the organisation of teaching and learning, along with the intentional planning of 'pastoral' elements into the main curriculum work of the school. It is also suggested that the use by pupils of computerised curriculum databases, as 'tools of curriculum management' (Richardson, 1986) can enable children to begin to make sense of their own develop-ment – as learners and as people. The focus of this chapter, therefore, is upon the approaches being developed at one school to address the issues that arise from attempting to structure a pastoral and social dimension across the curriculum, through the development of pupil-based profiling and record systems, the introduction and development of small group work and the use by pupils of new technology.

Personal development and the curriculum

In our view, the personal development of pupils cannot and should not be seen as a separate part of the curriculum – nor as being the province of some sort of pastoral structure. Following Pring (1985), we see our pupils' personal development as an 'educational policy for the whole school and the curriculum as a whole'. For us this means that the organisation of the school and the processes of teaching and learning should be planned to encourage pupil autonomy, self and group reliance, responsibility, decision making and reflection. This means that the staff of the school need to consider in some detail how these kinds of attributes can be promoted at classroom level. However, a prerequisite of such planning is an agreement that the school is intending to provide opportunities for pupils which encourage autonomy as an educational goal.

A central aim of the school is systematically to involve pupils in planning and evaluating aspects of their work and progress. Since November 1984, the school has been introducing teaching strategies such as small group work, together with the use by pupils of internal record systems which support this aim. In our view, pupils need to have opportunities to develop and use abilities which enable them to operate without constant adult assistance. This means that the curriculum, resources and record-keeping systems of the school should be organised so that pupils can learn to make choices and decisions about aspects of their learning pathways. We believe that children need to learn to value their own work and achievements (as well as those of others) and to develop an awareness of what they can do. Thus, from about top infant level, pupils should have the opportunity to record what 'they think' they are able to do and relate this to their actual achievements, through the school's internal record system.

An important aspect of being able to plan and cooperate with others on tasks and to reflect upon learning, is the acquisition of the skills of group interaction. We are therefore making an attempt to structure the acquisition of such skills into the organisation of teaching and learning within the school. Thus, from an early age, pupils experience structured and unstructured group work in a variety of curriculum contexts. As pupils in our school progress and mature, the skills necessary for successful participation in group work are being made explicit to them in a way meaningful to their level of experience and understanding. For example, in our third and fourth year, children are encouraged to discuss, in pairs and groups, 'rules' which will enable the class to work in groups in English and mathematics sessions. In one class, the groups have produced lists of rules through group discussions and these have been prioritised by the whole class and displayed within the classroom. The important point is that these 'rules' have arisen from group discussion, they have been valued by both the teacher and the children and have been given high status by prominent display. In a similar way, all junior children have opportunities to learn, by active participation, how to share, how to organise, how to explain or prove and how to listen, through specific sessions concerned with social, moral, health and personal education.

Moreover, our infant classes have spent time discussing in pairs and in groups 'things which will make our class work better'. The children have generated very positive ideas about trying to encourage each other to: walk in sensibly from the playground; hang up each others' coats; work without disturbing each other. These points have again been displayed by the teacher on an individualised checklist, giving these child-produced rules high status.

Teachers throughout the school have worked sensitively with their pupils in establishing group work by building gradually upon paired activities to appropriate cooperative group tasks, matched closely to pupils' needs and experience. Currently, for example, a fourth-year junior class has established a 'mini-enterprise' scheme with the aim of producing a community newspaper. The task is a real one which has involved a group being responsible for finance, sales and accounts. They have opened an account at a local bank and negotiated a loan, costed the production of the paper and 'sold' over £40 worth of advertising space to local shops. Other groups control editorial aspects, assisting younger pupils with redrafting, production and distribution.

In all of the examples cited, the important point is that the pupils have been involved in the 'process' of learning to identify issues and how to handle and resolve them.

It is clear that when pupils are engaged in activities which can only be successfully achieved through cooperative group work, then the likelihood is that cooperation between children will result. As the children have increasing experience of these types of tasks and as the skills which underlie the tasks are made explicit to them, we have noted that pupils are able to address themselves to such activities more readily. The central aim of the use of pupil based records in mathematics is to provide the children with three key elements:

1 Details of what is expected of them as learners, in a form intelligible to them.
2 Opportunities for cooperation between pupils – as the whole group would be working on the same area and probably the same task.
3 Opportunities for pupils to review systematically what they have been doing, prior to meeting new work or engaging in consolidating activities.

As this process has developed it has become very clear that a crucial factor in the learning equation is the teachers' view of their own role. When the teacher is prepared to operate as a learning counsellor or aid to discussion – posing questions and raising issues – then the children have tended to learn to rely on themselves and each other rather than on the teacher. This does not negate the teacher's role, but rather enhances it. Instead of being over-concerned with controlling interaction in the classroom, the teacher becomes more able to focus on raising the quality of learning.

Group work, record keeping and pupil-oriented learning

Such structured group work is becoming an increasingly important aspect of curriculum development at the school. Through the medium of group work, children are increasingly being asked to plan elements of a section of their work or play; to engage in an activity with their group or individually; and then to review and reflect upon what they have done with an adult – often, but not necessarily, the teacher. It is our observation of children learning, that when they are given opportunities to think, plan and talk about their school tasks, motivation, enjoyment and understanding are substantially increased, as the work of Bruner (1973) and Tough (1977) suggests.

During the last two years we have made a start on making this 'plan-do-review' process more systematic and explicit. This is particularly the case in the curriculum areas of language and mathematics. In junior age classes, maths teaching centres upon particular concepts and these concept areas are broken down into a series of skills and activities. Each pupil has a record sheet which makes these concepts, skills and activities explicit through a series of 'I can do' or 'I understand' statements, which in turn are matched with book and page or resource references. Each sheet has a space for pupils and teachers to comment. Pupils are responsible for accessing their individual record sheets from filing cabinets adjacent to their class areas. Once they have located their record – which may have been used in a previous year when they first encountered the topic – they put it into a group ring binder, which also contains the maths records of other pupils in the group, separated by named file dividers. A vital element of the system is that the pupils 'manage' the records themselves. Clearly, if the class teacher were to spend time retrieving record sheets from filing cabinets and re-filing them in ring binders they wouldn't do much teaching! The value of the system is that it actively structures pupil involvement into an important curriculum management task, gives pupils real responsibility for that task and also enables them to acquire retrieval skills which are analogous to using a computerised disc filing system. The important point is that the pupils' status is enhanced by being given active responsibility for the organisation and management of their own record keeping.

During the time that these record sheets have been in use, and where the teachers' role has become one of 'consultant' or an aid to group discussion, we have found that pupils' views of mathematics have become very positive. Coupled with 'real' maths and practical work, this process of making the mathematics curriculum explicit to pupils and involving them in their own assessment as well as the planning of their future work, is one other way we are trying to enhance learning and raise expectations and pupil self-esteem.

New technology presents exciting, challenging and potentially revolutionary opportunities for teaching and learning. There are two main reasons for this. First, there is the use of the computer as an accessible information store. The mathematics and language concepts, skills and activities and resource references discussed above have now been put on to computer file. It is now possible for individual pupils or groups of pupils to obtain virtually instantaneous searches of large amounts of reference data and receive a printout which can be used for classroom planning. The computer also provides interesting possibilities for cross referencing between concept areas. For example, a child wishing to obtain information and references about, say, *time*, types this into the computer and receives a print out of book and page references. The pupil can then be encouraged to make a selection from everything that the school has to offer on *time* and may wish to select a piece of work on time and fractions. By typing in 'fractions' the pupil will not only receive information about time and fractions but also everything the school has on fractions, which may include work in other concept areas such as volume and capacity. Thus, use of the computer database can enable the children to engage in a series of highly sophisticated decisions and choices for their future work. This means that the children need to consider 'their own educational needs'. In other words, the use of the computer in this way can encourage self-analytical thinking (ie 'What do I need to know about time?') as well as promoting planning and decision making – and this, of course, supports the acquisition by pupils of the interpersonal skills we are aiming to engender.

The second important facet of the micro is its use as a means of organising interactive learning within groups of pupils. There is now some very good software available for the BBC micro which supports interesting and creative group work among primary pupils. Programs such as SPACEX, ADVENTURE ISLAND, SUBURBAN FOX, DRAGON WORLD and GRANNY'S GARDEN are all designed to encourage and promote problem solving and decision making within a multi-curricular framework. Such adventure/simulation game software provides a context for interaction between pupils and this context quickly becomes self-sustaining. Most of the 'work' is done, if not away from the computer, then without the need for constant keyboard use. Excitement and involvement generated by the situations presented on the screen is sustained and extended within the group context. It is here that the use of such materials has implications for teaching and the teacher's role.

The pupils talk a great deal when using such programs. They talk about and around the problems, analyse the situations they are presented with and are eager to try out solutions. When strategies are seen to fail, this 'failure' has an entirely different status from that experienced by pupils in other, more familiar, classroom settings – like getting sums wrong. This seems to be one of the keys to why the use of these programmes within groups leads to rapid learning and understanding, by very young children, of large amounts of information. The game context encourages the uninhibited use of speculation, trial, and assessment of what has failed or succeeded. This process is parallel to the 'plan-do-review' scheme which we are attempting to develop within the mathematics curriculum and indeed within the 'real' newspaper company. The crucially important link beween the two is that in both cases the pupil him or herself, has a degree of control over the learning situation – a degree of control stemming from decision making, which can often be absent within a more conventional pedagogic setting.

Implications

The use of computers in curriculum management and as part of the classroom learning context raises a number of issues for teaching and learning. The use of the computer and the other group activities described in this paper is fundamentally concerned with providing pupils with opportunities to use language to make sense of the processes of learning and their own development as learners and people. Bruner's work has shown us that language plays a vital role in thinking and learning. It is my contention that schools should be more concerned with making the *processes* of learning and decision making explicit to pupils, than with the transmission of arbitrarily selected knowledge. The impact of new technology means that people will increasingly need to know how to retrieve, handle and evaluate information. They will need to possess a repertoire of social/interactive and communicative skills, in order that sense can be made of such information. Primary schools are in a strong position to enable children to begin to acquire these personal and information handling skills. Such a shift in emphasis from knowledge itself to its manipulation has profound implications for the teacher's traditional role.

This traditional role, however enlightened, has been to decide upon the content and form of transmission of the curriculum. The pupil has therefore been forced into a dependent position. He or she has depended upon the teacher to define what counts as valuable knowledge. Moreover, the teacher has also regulated access to this knowledge, the pacing of work, the choices of resources available, the method of working and the evaluation of the learning processes taking place. The introduction of the micro-computer as a tool of curriculum management potentially undermines this relationship because it can give pupils direct access to the information they consider valuable. Hence the pupils will need to become self-reliant to a much greater extent and teachers will need to recognise that their task will be to promote and develop in their pupils the personal skills and qualities of self-reliance, interdependence and self-assessment.

To develop these kinds of qualities in pupils, teachers themselves need time and opportunities to develop. At our school, planning the curriculum and the discussion of professional work is given high status. Teachers need time to plan and think – without this, little real development work can take place. Teams of staff meet regularly – once a week at least – to discuss their work, to plan and review. These meetings start in school time and are organised on a 'quid pro quo' basis. As head I take half of the school for an end of day assembly and story while the junior staff have a curriculum meeting, which I join after dismissing the children. Meetings usually wind up at about 4.00 to 4.15 after an hour of discussion and planning. The infant and nursery teachers also meet in a similar way. Over a period, much productive discussion has taken place, covering all aspects of our work – including the developmental work described in this paper. Without time to think, the progress we have made during the last three years would have been impossible.

If schools are to properly address the issues made explicit in this paper and to have relevance for pupils' changing needs, in-service and curriculum initiatives will need to be introduced which take account of the uses of micro-computers as tools of curriculum management, rather than merely peripheral resources for the traditional curriculum. Moreover, teachers will need to examine the changes in their role necessary to facilitate and promote learning within this changing context, if they are to successfully integrate personal and social education into the main work of the school.

Acknowledgement

The work described in this chapter has been aided by a grant from the Schools Curriculum Development Committee. Solihull LEA has also provided support.

References

Bruner, J S, 1973 'Language as an instrument of thought' in Davies, A (ed) *Problems of Language and Learning* Heinemann.

Galton, M, Simon, B and Cross, P, 1980 *Inside the Primary Classroom* Routledge and Kegan Paul.

Hargreaves, A, 1985 'Motivation v Selection: A dilemma for records of personal achievement' in Lang, P and Marland, M (1985) *New Directions in Pastoral Care* Basil Blackwell.

Hargreaves, D, Hestor, S and Meller, F, 1975 *Deviance in Classrooms* Routledge and Kegan Paul.

Pring, R, 1985 *Personal Development* in Lang, P and Marland, M (1985) *op cit*.

Richardson, T, 1986 *Using Micros to Encourage Pupil Autonomy*, in *Education 3–13, 14*(1).

Sharp, R and Green, A, 1975 *Education and Social Control* Routledge and Kegan Paul.

Tough, J, 1971 *Talking and Learning* Ward Lock.

Young, M F D, 1971 *Knowledge and Control* Collier McMillan.

Woods, P, 1979 *The Divided School* Routledge and Kegan Paul.

13 Personal and social education: a report of two primary experiences in Nottinghamshire

John Berridge

The following two chapters record the experiences of two primary school teachers. The first is set in the context of a personal decision of an individual teacher to improve the learning environment by focusing on the children and their needs as people. The second, by Heather Rushton, is a record of a project undertaken by staff of a primary school in collaboration with a Classroom Support Service worker. Both teachers are self-effacing about their written accounts but, their modesty notwithstanding, they are making a successful rigorous and highly professional contribution to the current developments in personal and social education in Nottinghamshire primary schools.

The first teacher, Jane Needham, has now become a Classroom Support Service worker and is managing a second personal and social education project, this time involving a substantially increased number of primary schools. In addition a second, parallel project concerned with health and personal image is underway, a primary personal and social education residential course has taken place and further expansion of primary personal and social education in-service courses and other support is envisaged for the next academic year.

My work has, until recently, involved offering support to teachers in personal and social education and I am very conscious of the exponential expansion in interest and activity in PSE in primary schools during the last year, as is illustrated by the response of the support services. I am delighted to report that primary school teachers seem to be universally concerned with process. Knowledge and content have been subordinated by a desire to develop skills, to promote self-esteem, and to enhance personal relationships. These impressions have been substantiated by recent in-service events at which primary school teachers have been devising definitions and identifying aims and objectives. More often than not it has been possible to remove the words 'personal and social' leaving the word 'education'. Personal and social education seems to be a brand leader, identifying and exemplifying those aspects of education which are of significant importance by focusing on cross curriculum issues and the climate in which children learn most effectively.

The debates are causing teachers to re-examine their own relationships and to reconsider the role models they present. The nature of schools as institutions and the implicit social learning the institution promotes is being scrutinised with a view to positive change taking place. Modes of management and their consultative and democratic procedures are being recognised as a crucial part of the means by which teachers develop and deploy their social skills. Indeed the parallels between the development of teachers, and of children as people are becoming evident. Personal growth is being recognised as a shared experience. Early skill development in co-operative group work is seen to be vital if positive personal relationships are to be established in the classroom. Evidence of infant classes or even nurseries giving attention to the issues is increasingly common.

All of these developments have been enhanced when it has been possible to give some support to schools where it counts – in the classroom. This has long been recognised as a crucial part of teacher development in Nottinghamshire. During the last two or three years attention has been given to the development of an educational support service which can not only be responsive to teachers' needs but also involve them directly in the supportive processes which will enable them to reflect on their own practice. At the heart of the theoretical propositions which underpin the work is the notion of action research.

Through the process of action research the Nottinghamshire Education Support Services uses its combined resources to develop and extend the learning opportunities which teachers plan for children. The needs of children are identified and matched to the professional needs of teachers. Achievable plans of action to enhance existing skills, knowledge and understandings are clarified. Support is given in the practice of teaching styles and learning methods in the classroom and in the review of understandings about how effective teaching and learning occurs. Progress is monitored and assessed

142

with a view to providing data to inform further developments in classroom practice.

Figure 13.1 describes the process:

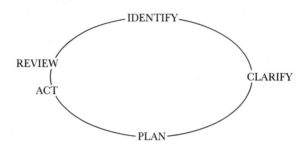

The Nottinghamshire Education Support Service is organised in six sections:

1 *Classroom support service* To support school-based programmes of development against annually agreed policies and to work alongside teachers on programmes of school-based curriculum development.

2 *Dance and drama support service* To work with teachers in schools to develop understanding and skills in areas of dance and drama education and to support the work of practical section 11 sessions.

3 *Music support service* To support teachers in their schools and classrooms in the development of curriculum music, to provide specialist tuition and to support the work of practical section 11 sessions.

4 *Off-site resources support service* To manage the development and integration of various resource sites and facilities, to ensure the delivery of programmes to meet curriculum and professional development needs.

5 *Section 11 support service* To deliver English as a Second Language teaching programmes to children, to provide accessible multi-cultural resources which will support the Authority's programme for the development of multicultural education. To work with communities on the development of supplementary schools and to work alongside teachers on programmes of school-based curriculum development.

6 *Special needs support service* To provide support and development for teachers in schools in order to enhance their skills and understanding of pupils with special educational needs. To provide support both on and off the school site for pupils with particular learning needs or behavioural problems, to provide support for parents of children with special learning needs, and to develop off – and on – site special resources and accommodation.

Support is therefore available for those teachers and schools who want to make developments. The mechanisms by which teachers influence the curriculum are theoretically available. The LEA is currently making resources available and encouraging schools to plan for development. The schools are having to engage in discussions to decide priorities; the professional development funded by the LEA is expected to bear a relationship to those identified priorities. Power and resources have been delivered to schools. If personal and social education features in their priorities, schools now have the wherewithal to make the developments happen. Teachers are being empowered. They are expected to make decisions. Some will have to develop the skills. How is this different for children? Should children not have access to a similar decision-making process with regard to their own learning? (Prescribed curriculum allowing, of course!)

14 An approach to personal and social education in the primary school or how one city schoolteacher tried to make sense of her job

Jane Needham

For the past five years I have been teaching in a large and lively inner-city primary school, containing a varied mix of people. About 40% of the families are Asian (mostly Moslem) and there are a few Afro-Caribbean families, as well as English working-class and middle-class professional families. Throughout this time I have worked with six to eight-year-old children and each year have set about trying to provide appropriate learning situations for each child. I have also tried to provide a sense of unity among the wide range of social backgrounds, personalities, intellectual abilities and behaviour that the children present and the varying parental expectations.

In order to do this I have had to do some careful thinking about my priorities as an educator, and this has resulted in the belief that my concern to develop the skills necessary for successful oracy, reading, writing and numeracy should not override the promotion of the children's happiness, their belief in themselves and their ability to relate to each other. It is the development of the whole person, myself included, that is important.

I have tried to provide a classroom environment which is an 'OK' place to be and in which children have the space to be themselves. I have tried to encourage a sense of togetherness among the children in an atmosphere of cooperation, trust and empathy. With this has come the realisation that young children can learn a great deal from each other in an atmosphere of mutual interdependence, rather than one which revolves totally around the teacher as the giver of all things. Any competition that exists should be with oneself rather than with others – 'Is this the best I can do?' rather than 'Is mine better than anyone else's?'

The emphasis has been on learning rather than teaching and my role as teacher has focused on being an organiser of learning situations. By these I mean situations which are exciting and rewarding and which provide a realistic match to the children's abilities, but also those which are carefully thought out so that they encourage the development of personal and social skills. It is the learning process that is all-important and given this emphasis my own teaching style has, I think, become increasingly varied.

The actual choice of classroom projects needs careful consideration, bearing in mind the necessity of providing an overall well-balanced curriculum together with the incorporation of those projects which naturally lend themselves to the development and understanding of the self and empathy with others. Projects I have favoured for the latter have been those based on relationships, eg family, friends, ourselves; those based on child-centred activities, eg games, mazes; those enabling a more global approach, eg festivals, different types of food; and literature-based projects using appropriate books.

In what follows I have tried to pick out the key points in the process I endeavour to put into action.

Flexible groupings

Groups are organised so that all the children have the opportunity of working and playing with each other rather than keeping with one particular group all the time. Sometimes the groups are chosen by me, sometimes by the children and sometimes through random sets (eg all the children with the same colour shoes/hair/eyes). Sometimes the choice of activity will determine the membership of the group. I try and keep one of the groupings fairly constant for a time so that the children can build up working relationships and the membership of these groups is carefully considered so that there is an even balance as regards sex, race and existing friendships.

Positive feedback

It is important to provide an audience for the children's achievements so that their work has a sense of purpose. The nature of these feedback situations varies greatly – from 20 minutes or so at the beginning or end of a session, looking at what each other has done, to actively teaching the children to value each other's work. For example, I asked the children to read someone else's work and write a positive book review about it. One little girl ended her review with 'It's an exciting story for bedtimes and it is one of those books where you want to see the end'.

On other occasions I have linked up with another class in the school to share weekly achievements and concerns, no matter how small. I have found that the value of this type of sharing lies not only in giving the children the opportunity to appraise each other, but also in providing a situation in which they need to express themselves in the clearest way, explaining what they have done and how or why they did it. I feel that the children's work is enriched through ideas being shared and also through the desire to produce something that is worthy of sharing.

During one year my class and I were involved in a link with another school. Initially this was planned by another teacher and myself as an experiment to investigate the presence of any stereotyped attitudes among our children. It began with a swapping of photographs in which the children had the chance to choose how to present themselves to each other, wearing favourite clothes/special hats, holding favourite possessions, with different facial expressions and gestures and so on. Gradually, special things happened; the children reached out to each other in words and pictures, writing letters, cooking and sewing presents for each other, planning and preparing surprises, learning to give and to receive.

I also think it is important to give the children the opportunity to evaluate and appraise their own work. I have used several simple ideas to facilitate this. One of the most effective was to draw a simple cartoon face with an empty speech bubble, at the end of a piece of work. The child fills in the spaces with words and/or pictures to express how they feel about what they have done. I always try to think of positive comments to write on children's work, and to make them meaningful to the particular child and appropriate to the particular context. I might ask the child which bit of the story he/she thinks is the best as well as picking out which part I like. I may sometimes use this written comment to encourage the child to explore another aspect of his/her work. Sometimes the children write back asking me questions, sometimes they discuss their comments with a friend or parent, sometimes we talk them through.

I often use more specific evaluation sheets. In one, the children complete unfinished sentences, such as *Today I feel* . . .; *Something I'm good at is* . . .; *Something I'd like to be good at is*. . . . The children sometimes ask me to fill in the same sheets and we share what we think and feel in this way.

I have also asked the children to draw a map or a maze showing what has happened to them in their lives so far, the ups and downs, the dead ends, the roundabouts. They chose appropriate colours for associated feelings and wrote on personal comments. In this way some of the children were able to express their feelings about what they see as the important events of their lives. They pinpointed events like starting school, the arrival of brothers and sisters, accidents and illnesses, parents splitting up, good holidays and making good friends. When the maze or map was complete the individual child explained what he/she had done to someone else.

Class/group cooperative activities

Class and group activities have taken many forms, from full coopera-tive games to cooperative group projects – making books, models, pictures, or simply working on a problem or an idea together. In each of the activities, everyone involved plays a part in bringing about the end product or solution. This is followed by a discussion and sometimes we will make a zig-zag book in which everyone involved has the chance to describe and reflect on their part in the process and any difficulties encountered. Science work, too, presents opportunities for small groups of children to work together to carry out different parts of an experiment and then to pool and compare results before coming to a conclusion. In this way we carried out experiments to find out the optimum conditions for growing turf. Using our conclusions we set up the appropriate conditions and made and mowed a miniature turf maze. At the end of last term we made a class jigsaw puzzle. It started as a large outline drawing done by one of the children of the Joybaloo creature from the book *Ned and the Joybaloo* by Hiawyn Oram and Satoshi Kitamura. I cut the picture into jigsaw-shaped pieces which we shared out. Each child involved had to decorate his/her piece with the appropriate details and patterns and this necessitated finding and matching it up with other people's pieces so that the whole picture was correctly formed. It proved to be a difficult but rewarding activity.

In other group activities the end product is for the benefit of the whole class, as when making a book or a board game to be used by everyone. I also used paired activities eg paired reading partners, or one child writing a story to fit the interests and reading abilities of another, or two children writing a story together, sharing out the task and working with a joint purpose.

Rolling activities

With 'rolling' activities the intention is for one group's work to act as the stimulus for another. For example, one group may collect specific information from the class, like the type of pets kept at home. This information is then passed on to another group who organise it into different graph forms which are, in turn, passed on to another group to be interpreted. The children are learning to share. A project on families began with the whole class brainstorming ideas for questions that they might ask their grandparents about their upbringing. A group of children then went to visit one child's grandmother and asked questions about her childhood in Pakistan. The information they gained was written up and was passed on to other children to read. These children then had to answer comprehension type questions on the text.

In another useful rolling activity I ask one child to write the beginning of a story. He or she passes it on to another who reads and develops it, then passes it on again and so on around several children. I also use a version of the 'consequences' game for creative writing/picture making/affirmation work. These activities help children to share, to take turns and to value the contribution that others can make to their own ideas.

Providing opportunities for children to make their own decisions

Many opportunities for decision making arise from everyday classroom organisation – simply asking the children to make decisions and to sort out jobs rather than me, the teacher, always delegating. Planning for such opportunities can also be more complex; in one scheme, three other teachers and myself set aside a period of time each week for our children to get together and organise activities to present to the rest of the group. The session became the high spot of the week for some children as they learnt to choose and present activities that were fun to share and watch as well as fun to do. They impressed us with the variety and quality of the activities that they organised ranging from Indian dancing and the Can Can to quizzes, telling jokes and French skipping demonstrations. The children took full responsibility for everything they did, both as performers and in learning to be part of a positive audience. Even the shyest of children became involved and parents were sometimes invited to attend. One of the children once asked me what I would do if no children prepared any activities to perform. This never happened. There was always too much.

Activities that encourage self-expression

I feel it is important to give the children the time and space to express their thoughts, ideas and feelings through a variety of creative activities, especially paint, clay, fabrics, puppets, poetry, drama etc. We have had lots of fun with these. More structured activities have included making footprint mazes; exploding class-made ginger beer and using the experience as a stimulous for writing poetry; and designing and making Santa's castle in box model form and in cake (and eating it!).

Role play situations

I have found role play a valuable way of encouraging the children to put themselves into other people's shoes and to explore different ways of thinking and behaving, finding alternative solutions to problems. For example, in looking at playground problems we have explored things like: how to join in a game; how to refuse entry into a game without causing upset; how to resolve playground conflicts without always asking the teacher on duty to intervene. We have also looked at the possible causes of the conflicts to try and prevent them from happening again.

Use of photographs

I do a lot of work using photographs. I take photographs of the children performing different activities in and around school and the

150

children involved use them to make class and individual books. Photographs of other children in the school, past and present, and magazine photographs depicting people of different ages, social/cultural backgrounds and different sexes performing similar activities can be photocopied and used for projection work using speech and thought bubbles, or to make jigsaw puzzles and games. Somehow the use of photographs makes the conversations come alive. We have real conversations about real people and events and this also leads to more vivid and expressive writing.

Listening to children and valuing their comments

I believe that it is vital to set aside time for children to listen and to be listened to. I sometimes use structured listening activities and games, as well as a great deal of open discussion. I have found the use of the tape-recorder to be invaluable here, enabling me to provide transcripts of the conversations we have so that the children can read and talk about each other's thoughts and ideas. The following is an extract from a class book on 'Peace'.

Instead of violence

Child L 'We should discuss things and say what we think and say some of that's right and some of that's wrong to make it equal: so. We should both agree, so it seems like it should be and we should be able to say what we think is wrong.'
Child A 'We should have a bit each.'
Child K 'We should sort of vote and if the people don't want that to happen we should discuss it and make it all fair. Gangs in the playground are wrong. Gangs are what started wars.'

Inevitably every primary school teacher is a teacher of personal and social education, not just at allocated times but at all times of each day, explicitly and implicitly. Everything you do as a teacher comes under the gaze of those eyes you encourage to observe, is heard by those ears you encourage to listen, is analysed by the mind you encourage to evaluate, and can be interpreted and challenged by those voices you encourage to ask questions. The relationships you form, not just with the children but with their friends and their parents, their brothers and sisters, all add pieces to the picture of the child's view of him/herself and the world around him/her. The most daunting fact of all is the wide gap between the cooperative environment that I, as a teacher, try to create and the unfair world outside. Maybe I should do more to promote an intolerance of unfairness!

15 A primary school personal and social education curriculum development project

Heather Rushton

The school joined the PSE project formally in September 1984 although initial contacts with the Curriculum Development Support Service were made in July 1984. As a school we feel that we must do as much as possible to equip our children with the skills and knowledge to understand the nature of society; to become competent participating citizens in the community; and to make informed choices in order to enjoy a healthy life to the full.

It has not always been easy to define our focus and we are still working on our understanding of personal and social education within our school. The following are some of the messages and issues that the work has raised (in no order of priority).

Sexism	Hidden curriculum
Self-concept	Media
Motivation	Abilities
Responsibility for decision making	Language
Community	Racism
Attitudes	Organisation
Relationships	Non-verbal communication
Cooperation	

Defining a focus was difficult at first, although for a considerable time prior to September 1984 we had been examining our curriculum in the context of a multicultural society and developing anti-racist attitudes. A relatively small number of incidents had occurred within our school, chiefly name-calling, and we were concerned that dealing with these individual occurrences was not in itself a particularly constructive approach in developing healthier attitudes in our children. After a series of discussions, we recognised the importance of the concept of 'self': the way in which our children see themselves and the ideas they have of themselves were clearly significant in determining how they behaved in a variety of circumstances. This pointed to the question of whether the experiences we offer at school support or undermine pupils' belief in themselves as valuable and valued persons.

Project teachers worked with two classes on a half-day basis examining a variety of ways in which cooperative learning could be effective. I was fortunate in having the support of a Curriculum Development worker in my classroom from May to July 1985. The on-going topic during that time was Class 4 itself.

By using games, role play, discussion groups, group work and encouraging communication (where there was little) we aimed to help the class consider others and to get together. Figure 15.1(a–c) shows the development of activities chosen to support these aims. At first the situations encouraged a fairly superficial examination of the positive attributes of each child (Figure 15.1a). This was extended to cooperating and sharing with others – and more internalised learning (Figure 15.1b). Finally, having grown in their ability to communicate feelings, it was hoped that children would increase their ability to listen and share (Figure 15.1c). I should say at this point it was expected that these aims would not be realised in such a short period of time.

The experience of having an observer was at first nerve-racking but the sensitive and constructive support offered raised a number of questions about my own provision for the needs of my children and encouraged a positive view of attitudes, achievements and abilities. It provided an opportunity for my own professional development; clarifying ideas, expectations and attitudes (my own especially,

Figure 15.1a

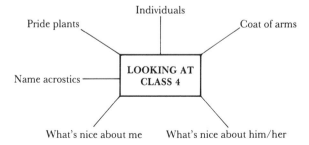

154

Figure 15.1b

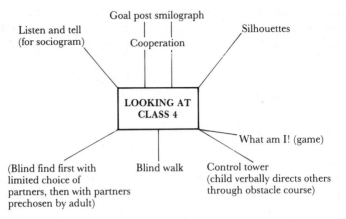

Figure 15.1c *Communication*

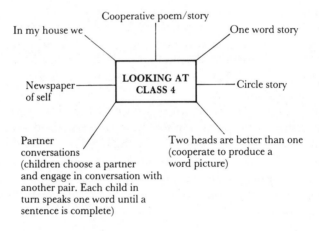

through on-the-spot reflections) and, most importantly, provoking a conscious awareness of what had been intuitive classroom practice.

At the beginning of September 1985 I had the opportunity to become a support teacher in my school. I found the position very beneficial and gained considerably in confidence by working closely with another member of staff; through this I learned a great deal about reinforcing the confidence of colleagues. I was able to apply the conclusions of my observation and evaluation to my own classroom practice, preparation, teaching, dealing with other members of staff and, most importantly, to my relationships with the children. All staff fortunate enough to experience this role held the same positive view. Involvement of the whole school staff was sought in order to examine issues which were raised and evaluate the work undertaken during the term. As a result of this we were able to identify and draw out certain classroom strategies employed and found to be successful in our school:

Environmental considerations
- examine, question physical situation of the classroom
- examine group mix in terms of personalities, gender, ability
- use all additional help available within school ie Terri, Anita, Helen, Chris Sz, Sally
- keep disruptive/unsettled children close to teacher to enable the child to spend part of every day engaged in positive activity
- create specific areas within classroom to encourage small group interactions
- how are learning experiences organised?
- examine communications – How well are children prepared?

Social skills
- give children particular responsibilities
- encourage positive peer support
- encourage children to be responsible to and for themselves
- examine appropriateness of work
- examine home background/cooperation
- set easily-achievable aims, gradually building to a situation or socially acceptable code of behaviour
- pair activities and/or 2 v 1.

Developing attitudes
- encourage positive attitudes and activities
- develop relationships between child/things, activities, people
- negative approach – ignore unreasonable behaviour, encourage positive attitudes
- discover as much about child's home background, routine, role of parent(s)
- reasoning – explain teacher's role
- place emphasis on the child

- through discussion, discover source of problem
- examine subject matter
- discover root of poor self-image
- direct work towards problem child.

Communication skills
- *talk* to child (rather than lecturing) ask the child to account for action
- encourage reflection
- encourage parental interest and cooperation
- involve parents as much as possible in school
- use praise and reassurance
- involve any outside support agencies appropriate to problem
- non-verbal communication
- reason with children about code of acceptable attitudes.

It was felt that a wider consideration of the implication of the influence of home was required at this stage. The need to encourage parental support for the attitudes and concepts we were trying to promote in school was considered to be essential for our work to be successful. This has been attempted in many ways; parents invited into school to work in a classroom with staff, cooking, creative activities, school visits, swimming etc. A 'good food day' was organised which aimed to promote good food and healthy eating habits in our children and parents. The parents were invited to spend the whole day with us and we hoped not only to display healthy attitudes towards food but also to provide an opportunity for parents to feel and see the ethos of our school in action. A 'fun day' is also organised each year, as an alternative to the traditional competitive school sports day. As a school we are convinced of the value of learning through play. As well as providing time for uninterrupted spontaneous experimental play in our classrooms, we also feel there is a place for adult intervention. To aid parental understanding of the importance of the play a nursery nurse ran sessions for parents, showing the equipment and discussing reasons behind the work. In this way we provided an opportunity to discuss play in the community and gave practical ideas for play at home.

As the project in school developed, the aims spread to encourage awareness of others' differences, personalities and cultures and to consider racist attitudes in the classroom. We used resources from the Mobile Unit for Development Education and Afro-Caribbean Education resources. In addition a M.U.N.D.I. worker assisted in the classroom.

Another interesting development was the drama support scheme, set up under the guidance of the drama inspector. Many classes and members of staff have developed 'experiential drama strategies' with help from the drama support teacher. Through role play, staff and children alike have been able to reflect upon the concept of self and to develop the beginnings of an understanding of others.

During the period of personal and social education support, staff discussions took several forms, including workshops, feedback sessions (from the supporter and the supported) and development sessions relating to overall principles and methods. From these discussions the importance of personal and social education in

Figure 15.2

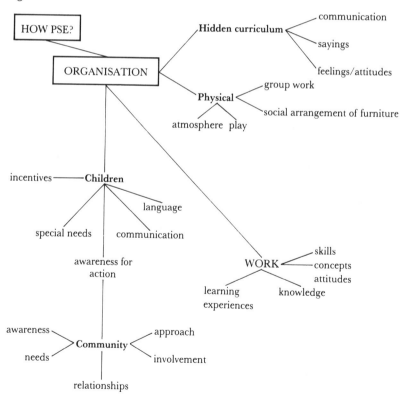

school has become evident and staff have recognised key issues in the nature of the process and how it should be carried out. Some of the priorities within each area are shown in Figure 15.2.

As we continue with our work in personal and social education we become increasingly aware of the 'hidden curriculum' – the hidden messages communicated to and from the children. Once aware of the hidden criteria, we realised that we need to take control over the messages given and received, in order to promote more positive ones. As indicated in Figure 15.3 emphasis is directed more towards organisation, with special consideration given to the hidden curriculum and physical factors in the classroom. Of paramount importance are the needs of the children and, through them, of the wider community.

Figure 15.3

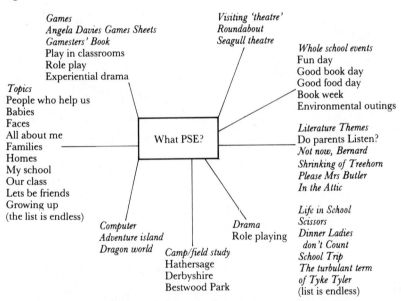

As we have encouraged children to respond to and reflect on their own roles in society, we have become aware of the need to make personal and social education a more conscious theme across the curriculum. Some of the areas in which we are making efforts to fulfil this need are shown in Figure 15.3. There are, of course, many more areas and as time goes on these become apparent across the curriculum. We are still left with many unanswered questions and continue as a staff to promote and reflect on PSE within our school. We are keen to share and discuss the resources and ideas we have used in tackling these issues with other primary schools and look forward to this in the near future.

16 Personal, social and moral education in the infants school: a practical approach

Sylvia Braddy

How my interest in PSME arose

In 1985 I was a member of staff of an infant school in Trafford, Greater Manchester, which was one of three schools on one campus; the other two schools being a corresponding junior school and a Roman Catholic primary school. The area was one of social deprivation, with high unemployment, broken homes and drug abuse. As a result of the educational problems created by the environment the LEA was awarded an Educational Support Grant (Category F – Improving the quality of education provided in selected urban primary schools). A two-year project was organised by the LEA in such a way that one member of staff was released from each of the three schools for a term and a half to study an area of the curriculum and become a curriculum consultant to the school. I was one of the first group of three teachers to be released to look at PSME. As a team we visited schools, researched the subject, attended courses and collated resources and strategies. Individually we worked alongside colleagues in our own schools, improving their expertise in PSME and drawing up a policy document with them. The information, strategies and resources we collated as a team are now being implemented in the schools on the campus, in other schools in Trafford and elsewhere.

Sylvia Braddy has been teaching infants over a period of 30 years in schools in the North East and North West of England and now teaches in Inner London. She points out that her classroom is no different from any other infant classroom, that there is no overnight transformation with PSME but it adds a new dimension and meaning to school life.

She wishes to acknowledge her gratitude to Nessy Lindsay and Marie Robertson who shared in an initial project on PSME and expresses appreciation to Brian Wakeman for his encouragement and support.

Given the opportunity to reflect on my career as a teacher of four to seven year olds, covering a period of 30 years, I was able to see clearly that my philosophy (like that of most teachers) embraced the values underlying PSME. Many of the aims which I already had for my classroom practice have become appropriate aims for PSME, others have been added because I want PSME to be explicit as well as part of the hidden curriculum. Looking at the personal, social and moral well-being of my children some of my aims are:

Personal
- to enable each child to feel valued, respected and cared for, helping to develop a positive self-image
- to increase self-awareness
- to enhance self-esteem
- to enable each child to be aware of his/her feelings and to express them
- to enable each child to experience success
- to create a secure atmosphere where each child can learn to cope with failure

Social
- to encourage cooperation, sharing, caring
- to encourage mutual respect
- to encourage children to listen to each other
- to encourage children to be friendly to each other and welcoming to newcomers
- to help childen appreciate and accept differences between each other – sex, race, creed

Moral
- to provide opportunities for children to make choices in everyday situations
- to develop strategies with children for problem solving
- to develop techniques with children for resolving conflict situations
- to encourage the children to be aware of their own intentions and the intentions of others
- to provide opportunities for children to exercise responsibility and trust

I believe that the whole atmosphere and organisation of my class is of paramount importance to PSME. The same is true for the whole school. The following questions help to focus attention on the atmosphere of the school.

How do we endeavour to make the school welcoming?
As members of staff (teaching and non-teaching) how do we support one another?
In what ways do we enable the children to welcome visitors and extend hospitality?
How do we involve parents and the community in school activities?
How do we define acceptable/unacceptable behaviour?
What is the school's policy on rewards and sanctions?
What account do we take of the home ethos?
In what ways do we encourage the children to be aware of the world of nature and the environment?
How do we enable the children to be aware of the needs of others at home, in school, in the community and wider world?

Practical activities

What then do I do in the day-to-day classroom situation to achieve the aims which have been set out? How do I encourage self-awareness, enhance self-esteem and encourage a positive self-concept? How do I achieve a feeling of community where there is mutual respect and where children can begin to solve their own problems? Often these areas overlap so in the following descriptions I will seek to cover them all in some way. Much of what is recorded here is common practice to most teachers but it is good to reflect on what we are doing and define our terms.

Enchancing self-esteem

I am very much aware that young children are greatly influenced by the adults with whom they come into contact, first parents and family, then teachers. These 'significant others' play an important part in the formation of a child's self-concept. I try to provide a secure framework where each child feels wanted, respected and useful. When children are valued they are more inclined to value each other.

At the beginning of the day I make sure that each child is welcomed, giving them a special greeting as they come through the door. I use their name, say how good it is to see them and try to touch them in some way – on the shoulder or hand or ruffle their hair – using an affectionate gesture. I use the children's names frequently and ask that the children do the same and do not refer to each other as 'him' or 'her', 'she' or 'he'. I try not to use 'put down' statements eg 'I haven't time now', 'You aren't trying, are you?'. I discourage the children from using unkind statements about each other which are sometimes heard in the classroom and playground. I ask them to try to find good things to say about each other, encouraging a positive attitude to their relationships. I try to be a good listener and show interest in the children's conversation even when time is at a premium.

I use affirmation as much as possible, Patrick Whittaker (1984) in *The Learning Process* describes affirmation as 'positively communicating to others those aspects about them which please and satisfy us'. So I use affirmation and praise accompanied by caring gestures whenever possible. I praise children whom I recognise as having low self-esteem, for the minimum of achievement; we often 'down tools' and clap individuals or a group who have maybe made a fantastic model, finished a reading book, tidied up well, etc.

I find as many occasions as possible to affirm and praise the good in children whose behaviour is frequently unacceptable. Instead of saying *'don't* do ...' I would say *'try* not to do ...'. I provide opportunities for these children to help, giving them responsibility so they can feel good about themselves and be aware of their own worth, to counteract some of the negative responses they receive. I generally allocate responsibility on a rota basis so that all the children are aware that the organisation is 'fair' and everyone has a chance.

I try to provide as many opportunities as possible for the children to make choices, for example choosing activities in play situations, maths and language activities, etc. When they have finished a task I encourage them to choose another one without asking. Often they need the security of a further suggestion, but after persisting with this method some children begin to say 'I've finished my ... can I do ... now?', which is very encouraging. The children choose each other to take part in singing/number games (I check that all children get a turn). Enabling children to make simple choices at an early age in a safe environment can be the foundation for making more important choices later.

Cooperation

Building a cooperative supportive atmosphere is important when children ultimately look at ways of problem solving and conflict resolution. However, children have difficulty in establishing relationships with each other and making friends if they do not have a good self-image or high self-esteem. It is important to have cooperative activities where children can work together towards a goal. This happens frequently in play situations where they have opportunity to share, or a chance to put themselves in another role (mother, father, baby, shopkeeper, etc) and become aware of the circumstances and feelings of others. Singing and music-making provide other effective social activities. Singing games are particularly good with younger children and can often enhance self-esteem when children are chosen to suggest actions or be in the middle and the centre of attention. Visiting the park, library, museum, etc, cooking in small groups, all add to the sense of belonging to the group.

At the end of this section there is a list of some games and activities which are useful for enhancing self-esteem and building a cooperative atmosphere.

Problem solving and conflict resolution

Often poor self-image is at the root of many conflicts; if children and adults do not feel positive about themselves it is very difficult for them to feel positive about others. If we can establish a spirit of affirmation and a sharing, supportive community, conflict can be reduced. In the area of problem solving and conflict resolution research has shown that the most effective way of dealing with this is to use classroom situations as they arise. An alternative is to use role play, which I shall expand on later. Whenever possible I use conflicts which arise in the classroom as a learning situation. When a conflict arises I stop the group or the class and we discover together what is happening. Then I ask the children for suggestions as to how this conflict can be resolved. For instance, four children were playing where there should only have been three, so one would have to leave the group. Some of the children's suggestions were: the one who draws a short straw; the last one to come should go; Tom (who came first) should go because he played last time. After discussion an amicable decision was reached. I find that after a few of these brainstorming sessions some children get the idea and can start sorting situations out for themselves.

There are certain phrases which we all use with the object of preventing conflict; I try to ensure that the children use them and of course I try to use them myself. Most of these are common courtesies – 'Please can I join in?' 'Please can I borrow . . .?' (instead of just taking) and making sure the borrowed object is returned, 'Have you finished with . . . please'. Some children get the idea and I've heard them encouraging others to 'ask properly'.

Another phrase which I encourage children to use if someone is annoying them is 'Don't do that please, I don't like it'. When children are on the receiving end of this remark they are quite taken aback and often stop whatever they were doing. Parents also tell me they hear their children using it and one parent was the recipient of the remark! Other helpful suggestions like these can be found in *A Manual on Nonviolence and Children* (Judson, 1977). These techniques are not to be relied on alone but help children and adults to think creatively about their actions.

I try to be firm but caring in my attitudes towards discipline, at the same time keeping a flexible, reflective attitude. We have specific guidelines and ground rules for our classroom which the children help to formulate. Young children need models and principles to guide them, but they also need to know that their model, in this case their teacher, is consistent and fair. I always try to give reasons for asking for a certain kind of behaviour, eg 'Please don't do that because . . .', so that the children get the idea that there are reasons behind requests.

It is my intention then to 'provide a secure framework within which children's personal identity can develop and where they feel wanted, respected and useful' (Downey and Kelly, 1978), I aim to create an environment where we can affirm one another, cooperate with each other and help to resolve our own and each other's problems creatively.

Some useful activities

Circle activities can help to enhance self esteem; establish a feeling of community; and develop listening and speaking skills.

The children and teacher sit in a circle so that everyone can see each other and take part equally. Simple ground rules should be that everyone has a turn if they want one and that everyone is listened to and respects others' contributions. The activity should be kept moving to maintain interest.

Begin with a common phrase, eg

> *My good news is* . . . (a good news circle)
> *My favourite food is* . . . (toy, game, story, TV programme, etc)
> *Hello, my name is* . . . (when there are new children or visitors)
> *I can hear* . . . (a listening circle – after a period of silence)

Feelings, experiences, ideas and information can all be shared in this way, and children enjoy making their own suggestions for a 'circle'.

Cooperative activities include:

- cooperative games of all kinds
- outside visits
- preparing for visitors in school
- celebrating birthdays and festivals
- class assemblies
- singing and music-making
- puppetry
- cooking and baking
- cooperative pictures and models (young children can work in pairs, older children in groups)

Drama, role play and puppetry are particularly useful in the areas of conflict resolution and problem solving, in addition to techniques already mentioned. Often children who are shy find it easier to express themselves and their feelings through puppetry. Appropriate stories can be used for this purpose (eg The Little Red Hen) or classroom situations. Alternative solutions to problems can be dramatised, then discussed.

More ideas and activities can be found in *Winners All* (Pax Christi,

1980); *Tinderbox Assembly Book* (Barratt, 1982); *The Friendly Classroom for a Small Planet* (Prutzman *et al*, 1978).

Stories, books and poems can be directly linked with personal, social and moral education in many ways. They can form the basis for discussion about:

- feelings, *The Day Grandma Died* (Selby, 1975)
- cooperation, eg *It's Your Turn Roger* (Gretz, 1985)
- caring and sharing, eg *Dogger* (Hughes, 1977)
- making choices, eg *Would you rather?* (Burningham, 1978)
- appreciation of the environment, eg *Dinosaurs and all that Rubbish* (Foreman, 1972)

The children's reactions

What do the children make of all these activities? How do they respond? I have been aware of shy, rather withdrawn children growing in confidence. Children who did not feel able to join in circle activities later joined in. Children ask, 'Can we have a . . . circle?' or say 'We need to have a "hello" circle' when we have a visitor. I see children being much more cooperative, willing to share and trying to befriend others. Some children display a great deal of sensitivity in their dealings with their peers, even at five and six years old. I was thrilled by the insight of one five year old; we were trying to sort out a fight between two of his friends and John said 'I think it's just a toy fight Mrs Braddy'. I'm sure he was right and he was beginning to see his friends' intentions. It is very rewarding to see children responding to praise and affirmation, particularly if their behaviour is frequently unacceptable, maybe because their self-esteem is low. I sometimes see children with poor motivation who are underachieving respond to 'You're good at this aren't you?'. The picture is not all rosy: there are still children who don't want to share; the fights still go on; the games and activities don't always work . . . but it is reassuring to look at the successes and keep on trying. Above all we have lots of fun working and playing together to build our community.

PSME across the curriculum

I have described how important it is for PSME to be identified as a separate area of the curriculum, as well as being part of the ethos of the school. When it is also found across the curriculum its presentation can be varied and this adds to its effectiveness. The following outline suggests a few areas of content to be explored. PSME can also be part of a thematic approach.

Language
- developing listening and talking skills
- making books, eg *All About Me*
- stories and poems
- drama and role play

Mathematics
- practical activities in groups
- solving problems as class or group
- making graphs using information collected from class
- place in a set
- comparisons: same, different, taller, shorter

Music
- cooperative music-making and singing
- songs expressing feelings

Art and craft
- working together on pictures, models, painting
- puppet making
- self-expression and creativity

PE
- sheer enjoyment of movement
- awareness of own body movement, strengths and weaknesses
- individual creativity and achievement
- cooperation with a group
- cooperative games
- fun and happiness in games

Science
- senses
- growing seeds, caring for plants
- caring for animals and insects
- caring for surroundings – home, school, neighbourhood

Health education
- finding out about our bodies
- looking after ourselves – good diet, sleep, exercise

RE
- myself, myself and others, myself and the natural world
- celebrating religious festivals in a multi-faith society.

Why bother with PSME?

The reader may wonder if it is worth the effort to look at yet another area of curriculum and find time for more activities in an already busy school day. It appears to me, however, that there is an obvious need. The following headings from reports in *The Times Educational Supplement* over the past three years would support this

Pupils' social skills found lacking
Growth of disruptive behaviour at primary levels
Praise more, blame less, report tells teachers

There is a government initiative at present to improve standards in schools. Research referred to in *100 Ways to Enhance Self-Concept in the Classroom* (Canfield and Wells, 1976) indicates a link between improved self-concept and academic attainment, so that any programme to improve self-image may enable children to achieve their potential, not only in self-awareness but also academically. We need to find as many ways as possible to work in partnership with parents and others in helping children achieve their potential, PSME provides an ideal opportunity.

We need not look far to be aware of vandalism and lack of respect for the individual, so the emphasis PSME places on respect for people and surroundings would be a step towards an improved society.

What values underlie PSME?

In considering the underlying values of PSME I am looking at my own values, principles and beliefs as well as those of the school, because these permeate all that we do. My example, who I am, my own attitudes and behaviour towards the whole school community, all influence the children.

My values are based on religious beliefs as a Christian, acknowledging the Fatherhood of God, but every teacher must work out their own values for themselves. I have a basic love of humankind, believing everyone to be of equal worth. I value cohesion, so I am motivated to bring about peaceful settlements to all kinds of misunderstandings between individuals and groups.

Children come to school with values and standards which they have already absorbed 'moral learning, the development of values and attitudes begins at birth and is fed from many sources' (Downey and Kelly, 1978). It is on this foundation that PSME would build, embracing the values of the children, the school community and the individual teacher.

In conclusion I would like to describe the 'ideal' school, where PSME is an integral part of the life. This school is a place central to the life of the community where:

- there is a relaxed and welcoming atmosphere;
- children feel secure, loved and cared for;
- children are enabled to achieve their potential;
- children are happy, enjoying each others' company and finding ways of solving their own problems;
- children show consideration for the feelings of others;
- there is a feeling of mutuality between adults and children;
- children are having fun and find joy in learning;
- all members of staff, teaching and support, work in partnership;
- teaching staff support each other, share ideas and expertise and enhance each others' self esteem;
- all members of the school community show respect for the world around them.

High ideals maybe, but certainly a challenge!

References

Barrett, S, 1982 *The Tinder-box Assembly Book* London: A and C Black.
Canfield, J and Wells, H, 1976 *100 Ways to Enhance Self-Concept in the Classroom* Englewood Cliffs: Prentice Hall.
Downey, M and Kelly, A V, 1978 *Moral Education Theory and Practice* London: Harper and Row.
Judson, S, 1977 *A Manual on Non Violence and Children* Philadelphia: New Society Publishers.
Pax Christi, 1980 *Winners All* London: Pax Christi.
Prutzman, P *et al*, 1978 *The Friendly Classroom for a Small Planet* Wayne New Jersey: Avery Publishing Group.
Whittaker, P, 1984 *The Learning Process* York: World Studies Teacher Training Centre.

Books for children

Burningham, J, 1978 *Would you rather . . .* London: Jonathan Cape.
Foreman, Michael, 1974 *Dinosaurs and all that rubbish* Harmondsworth: Puffin Books.
Gretz, S, 1986 *It's your turn, Roger* London: Picture Lions.
Hughes, S, 1979 *Dogger* London: Picture Lions.
Selby, J, 1975 *The day Grandma died* London: Church Information Office.

SECTION FOUR
Approaches

Ideas about the way that PSE or aspects of it should be undertaken and understood will be something that many teachers will see as an essential resource, especially as the demands on their time increase and multiply.

How can personal and social education be promoted? The approaches found in this section are all concerned with this question, though they vary considerably in terms of their breadth and scope. The papers by Patsy Wagner and Arthur Wooster are concerned with the development of a specific approach within a particular context. Pam Stoate and John Thacker are again concerned with an approach that has direct practical implications but which is based on the theory and methodology of one of the most significant current approaches to personal and social education. The approaches with which Andrew Pollard and Delwyn Tattum are concerned are very different, not so much dealing with promoting action as with providing ways of understanding it. Each writer presents a theoretical approach which, they argue, can increase our understanding of the context in which PSE operates. Doug Harwood and Peter Lang's papers are general reviews, Lang is concerned with some of the implications for PSE of approaches to guidance found in Canada, while Harwood provides a detailed and illuminating review of a key dimension of the methodology of personal and social education.

17 Developing cooperative learning in the primary school

Patsy Wagner

This short paper describes how a project to develop cooperative learning was set up in a primary school with a class of children aged between six and eight years; it was initiated by the school's Educational Psychologist together with teachers working in the school. The project was carried out over two and a half terms with the Educational Psychologist involved initially in one session per week of INSET and collaborative planning with the teachers. The teachers were involved in one further session a week of classroom-focused work which developed out of the INSET and planning session.

The techniques and approaches used were based on active learning methods and geared to the class teacher's own aims, routines and organisation. Activities were developed following observation (and enquiry) of the children in the classroom and of the learning experiences on offer. The aim was to develop cooperative learning experiences based on the customary curriculum offering in the class, rather than to set up a separate learning offer.

Background to the project – the 'general needs' approach

This project arose from a series of workshop sessions run by the school's Educational Psychologist with a cluster of primary schools. (The sessions stopped prematurely because of teacher action which made meetings after school problematic.) The focus of those workshops was 'general needs', an approach taken to counter the tendency to allocate to particular individuals a 'special needs' label (with all the negative concomitants of the labelling process).

The 'special needs' label is usually based on a deficit model – that is to say, a deficit is perceived in some area of functioning, for example, in social skills, learning or study skills, or communication skills. In such cases the child has frequently already been labelled as 'aggressive' or 'disruptive', 'slow learner', 'withdrawn' etc – the 'special needs' label, it seems, is seen as less value-laden, probably because it tries to focus on what the child's *needs* are. But often the end result of the allocation of a special needs label is a tendency to individualise programmes in a way that can deprive children of cooperative learning experiences and of a range of role models for learning.

A 'general needs' approach was put forward to redress the tendency towards separating out the learning experiences of some children in a way that might be counter-productive, *and* to establish the principle that social skills, study skills and communication skills are needed by all children. These needs are best addressed through a whole-school approach which is a structured and explicit aspect of the learning on offer to all children. Of course, some children may need more extended support to develop these skills, but by taking a general needs approach these children may be helped through extension work in a mixed ability setting without being singled out through individualised programmes which may insulate them from the enrichment of the full mainstream curriculum.

It was noted by the author and confirmed by the teachers at this school (and others), that most primary schools seemed to use incidental learning as an approach to those aspects of skills, experience and knowledge that might cluster under a pastoral curriculum (including personal and social education) more than they used any pre-planned programme of activities. So, for example, in a typical infants class, if two children got into a fight over using the home corner, then this incident would be used by the teacher as an opportunity to teach the individuals concerned, and the class, about sharing, turn taking, and conflict resolution. Hence the learning opportunities for the children in this area which we might call social skills, depended on things 'going wrong' and there seemed fewer opportunities for exploring and developing skills in a more proactive style.

How the project was set up

The project described here took place in one of the schools which had been involved in the workshop sessions. The headteacher of that school was keen for the general needs approach to develop further in his school and was concerned to support any work that could be done in the area of social skills. One class teacher from a team in the junior part of the school asked for his class to be the focus of the project. Two other teachers were also involved, one a special needs teacher already in the school, and the other a special needs teacher attached to the School Psychological Service. None of these teachers had worked before in any explicit ways on aspects of the pastoral curriculum (other than the previous workshop sessions).

It was agreed that for the project to develop there would need to be time for observation and work in class with the pupils, and a need for INSET sessions for the teachers to help them develop the knowledge, skills and experience to work confidently in the area of social skills. The project took up two sessions a week, one in class involving the three teachers, and one in-service session in school time, with the teachers and the school's Educational Psychologist.

The Educational Psychologist was involved in leading the INSET session. This session took place initially on a weekly basis and later fortnightly. The Educational Psychologist's role was to facilitate the exploration of ideas, skills and approaches in the area of social skills development, and to help in the discussion and analysis of classroom observation and activities and in the planning of further activities in a continuing process of development.

The particular focus of the project was determined by the class teacher who had put himself and his class forward – he was concerned that the class members were constantly falling out in vehement, angry and aggressive ways over sharing materials and working in groups. He felt that they were excessively reliant on him for resolving their conflicts. The aim was to develop cooperative learning in a class group that seemed at the moment to be incapable of working in that way. It was, therefore, very much concerned with the social skills of the classroom.

The project itself

Initially the teachers felt puzzled about how to translate ideas about social skills into action in order to achieve their aim of developing cooperative learning skills. Particular individuals in the class seemed to dominate their thinking at this stage. These individuals in the class remained salient characters in the group, but gradually, through their observations, the teachers were able to see more patterning in the interactions of the groups, and to spot the build-up in situations leading to conflict in the groups. From this perspective they were able to divert and defuse conflict and help the children learn how to avoid it or cope with it.

An important stage was reached when the teachers decided that they needed to find out more about the social skills that the children might *have* rather than merely focusing on those they might *lack*. Their starting point had been that these children generally seemed to be lacking cooperative and conflict resolution skills, but their detailed observations revealed that the children were in fact showing more cooperative behaviour than they had thought was the case. They decided, therefore, to investigate the skills the children had by taking some of the situations they had observed as producing conflict in class and then interviewing children in pairs about how they might resolve a 'hypothetical' situation based on one of the observed situations.

The situations the children were asked about were:

1 *You are singing to yourself, the person next to you tells you to shut up because your voice is awful and you are driving them mad.*
2 *Someone picks up something horrible from the ground (eg a squashed slug) and runs to you and tries to put it in your face.*
3 *Someone says something silly about you or calls you by a name you don't like (eg 'Smelly').*
4 *Someone grabs something that you are using.*
5 *You are cleaning up while someone else is just watching you.*

By their responses to questions about what they might do in these situations the children showed that there was a wide range of strategies available within the class group for resolving conflict. For example, some children, when faced with such a situation of potential conflict, tended to use strategies of avoidance and withdrawal; others tended to use physical symmetrical behaviours (responding in like fashion). Some tended to use statements which were verbally escalating – retaliatory, or threatening; others tended to use strategies which were defusing – reasoning or asserting. Some used strategies of appealing to others to help – peers in the room, for example; others tended to appeal to authority figures for help – teachers or older peers present, or older relatives or parents not present; others still tended to appeal to the other person's concern about punishment and the consequences of rule breaking as a strategy. Some would use combinations of these strategies. The striking point was the children seemed to develop a preferred strategy and then, mainly, to stick with that.

This led the teachers to conclude that if the children could be encouraged to learn from each other by exploring the range of strategies they had available within the group in relation to situations that they might have to deal with in school, then they would have a wider range of options to choose from when facing a conflict. Having reached these conclusions the teachers felt more able to plan and structure activities with this aim and to recognise the value of using techniques of 'active' group work with pupils of this age (rather than the approach to 'group work' which had been used hitherto, which tended to put children in small working groups and then gave them *individualised* tasks to work on).

Group learning was seen as a useful approach in most areas of classroom-based learning in this school and consequently the activities that were used varied a great deal in their content. What follows is a selection of the activities that were used.

Drama

Some pupils grouped together to create a drama through cooperative work, planning a plot and improvising on a theme which was based on a myth. This involved cooperative selection of story, theme and characters and development of the drama from that starting point. Another group of pupils used a situation from a popular TV drama and worked cooperatively to choose and explore the situation that they wished to work from.

Mathematics

One group of pupils worked cooperatively to make a number frieze for display in class, making decisions together about who would do what and with whom so that the tasks were carried out jointly, rather than each pupil working in the group but individually on a 'bit' of the overall task.

Another group of pupils worked collaboratively on number concepts using logi-blocks – sharing the equipment and problem solving together. In this activity (as in the others) collaboration was built in by the way the tasks were set up by the teacher – the children could only complete the tasks successfully by sharing equipment and ideas about solving the problem they had been set.

Language
One group worked cooperatively over sequencing pictures which were then coloured and displayed. The pictures were handed out to each participant so that the children had to find a way of discovering what the 'whole' (whole story) might be by sharing the 'parts' (the pictures). They then had to work cooperatively to put the story together and after that to decide how they were going to colour it and how they were going to decide on the colours they would use for the different components of the picture (thinking about consistency across pictures etc), and then to work on how they were going to display it.

One group made a story by matching sentences to pictures, in a similar fashion to that described above, which they then illustrated and displayed. Another group worked on self-description, which they achieved through collaborative rather than individual work; they then shared their products in pairs with the whole group.

None of these activities is particularly earth-shattering in itself and many primary schools will already be carrying out similar activities with groups of pupils. But in some schools these so called 'group tasks' are in fact carried out *individually* by children in groups. In these cases they cannot truly be called group tasks and they have little to do with cooperative learning. In fact they frequently lead to increased conflict and competition over materials and resources between children who are grouped in this way. Some teachers might argue that this conflict and competition provides the opportunities that they need in order to teach the children about cooperation and sharing. But creating conflict (however inadvertently) seems an unnecessarily negative, and, I suspect, counter-productive way of achieving these aims. Indeed, the success of this project is most probably highly related to the use of common classroom activities with which the teachers involved were familiar. The difference was in the way the teachers were using them, with a clear collaborative aim built in to the way they were organised and presented to the children.

Strategies to help the children to learn to work more independently in their groups, using each other more as sources of help when that was appropriate, were also developed. This resulted from observations made by the teachers of classroom processes which revealed that conflicts in class also arose when children were waiting for the class teacher to give them help. The teachers then discussed their observations with the children and helped them to explore other sources of help ie other pupils, and when and how to seek this. The conflict caused in these occasions decreased dramatically following this session.

The approach used led, therefore, to a range of considerations about classroom process and management as well as to developing specific activities to promote cooperative learning.

Evaluation

In a project such as this evaluation is an on-going process rather than a 'once and for all post-test'. However as part of the evaluation of the children's use of the skills that were being developed (to work cooperatively and productively in groups and to resolve any difficulties over work without the intervention of a teacher – when that was appropriate), a particular observation was carried out after about a term. This observation took place over an hour and a quarter, between morning break and lunchtime. The classteacher left the group with a series of activities which, it was felt, each group could manage without teacher intervention. One of the project teachers sat just outside the bay (the open-plan classroom) observing the pupils as unobtrusively as possible for that period. During that time the children worked cooperatively and productively on group tasks with no adult intervention required. So for well over an hour this class of young children (six to eight years) successfully and cooperatively worked together, changed tasks, and packed away in a completely self-directed manner.

Developments from the project

The project started half-way through the autumn term; at Easter the School Psychological Service project teacher left and the class teacher and special needs teacher continued together developing activities from observations in a similar style. Since then the project has moved on to the next stage: the special needs teacher is now viewed as a teacher in the school who has skills in helping other staff problem solve over the cooperative and collaborative aspects of classroom-based group learning ie the social skills of the classroom. A major part of this assistance is observation of classroom process as a basis for discussion with the class teacher. This then leads to working out collaborative group learning activities based on the teacher's usual activities, routines and classroom organisation.

The Educational Psychologist who was involved in setting up the project now meets with the special needs teacher on a monthly basis for consultation and support; review meetings with the head and special needs teacher are planned to take place on a termly basis.

Conclusions

The project described above suggests that:

1 Primary schools' view that they provide a more integrated curriculum may not lead to them covering social skills learning in an explicit fashion.
2 Leaving social skills to opportunistic and incidental learning is unhelpful and probably inefficient.
3 Social skills learning activities (of the classroom) that are effective are those that are planned into the learning offer and take place in the classroom.
4 Most teachers will already have the skills and the appropriate learning contexts needed to develop effective social skills programmes, but they may not be using them in a deliberate and pre-planned fashion with this aim in mind.
5 Effective INSET projects match the organisation of the school, the classroom and the individual teacher and should, therefore, be negotiated offers at the levels of both the school *and* of the individual teacher.
6 The effective INSET provider is one who facilitates a process which helps teachers to define their aims on the basis of *their* immediate classroom concerns, and to develop and try out ideas in a continuous process along the lines of – observation – feedback – ideas – activities as intervention – observation – ideas etc. This could as readily be done by an in-school colleague with the interest and skills to do this.

7 INSET that is effective, in the sense of becoming a part of the school, derives from the school being helped to identify its *own* INSET needs (rather than the school being offered INSET which may not address the schools' felt needs). Continuation of a particular project over time will depend on the degree to which it evolves with the schools' developing needs and its organisation.

8 An approach which focuses on strengths and interests and taps into parts of the system which are interested in development and change is likely to be more effective than one which focuses on deficits and which attempts to innovate 'uphill'.

18 Application of developmental group work principles to personal and social education in primary and middle schools

Pam Stoate and John Thacker

Since the Plowden Report (1967), working in small groups has become commonplace within the primary classroom. The stress throughout the report was upon the values of individual work and groups were seen as the best compromise in achieving individualisation of learning and teaching within the time available. Social benefits were also claimed, such as pupils learning to get along together, to help one another and to realise their own strengths and weaknesses as well as those of others.

However, research by Galton, Simon and Croll (1980), who looked at grouping practices in the age range 8–11 years, has confirmed that seating in groups is common in most classrooms but that, with few exceptions, the pupils then work largely alone, as individuals. Bennett (1985) sees the 'reality of groups as currently organised as a physical juxtaposition of individual pupils operating without a clear purpose or adequate management'.

Over the past three years we have been involved in a project which aimed to look at the possibility of taking a more rigorous form of group work to younger children as a means of contributing to their personal and social education. We had had experience of developmental group work which evolved from the work of Dr Leslie Button, who had older adolescents in mind. The essentials of the work as Button saw them were:

a that members of supportive groups should engage in mutual help and concern;
b that individual people, with the support of their peers, should be at the centre of their own development;

c that the work should be inspired by caring, concern, and a responsibility in relationships.

d that the work should be developmental in the sense that there will be some kind of deliberate and sequential structure that enables individuals and groups to chart their own personal exploration and development, and to be helped to move along by self-conscious and manageable steps.

(Button, 1985, p 9)

Button (1981) emphasised individual development within the small group. The purpose of such groups, as he saw it, was to increase the speed and intensity of the work by for instance, enabling more people to be at the centre of attention at any one time. He saw these small supportive groups as continuing, at a personal level, the exploration that is initiated as a whole-class activity as well as providing a place to reflect on the implications of these experiences for individual group members. For example, a class discussion on the meaning of friendship would be followed by the children examining their own friendship patterns in their support groups.

The support group acts, too, as a platform from which to venture out into new areas of experience. It can provide an opportunity for coping with strangers, engaging positively with adults, managing authority feelings and making a contribution to family life. For example, police officers, health workers or parents might be invited into school with the children taking responsibility for receiving them into their small groups, and talking with them.

Our intention for the project was first to give a group of middle school teachers a thorough training in the basic Button methodology before exploring with them the possibility of taking the work to younger children. The teachers who became involved were all good, experienced teachers of the post-Plowden tradition who were already using groups, in the sense of children working alongside each other rather than in this planned developmental sense. For many of these teachers the new way of working suggested by Button was found to require a fresh approach to children, to groups and to teaching since the skills necessary to initiate this kind of work are not yet part of the normal training experience of the teacher.

The training which they experienced involved them first in undertaking the same programme that they would be expected to lead with the children, including the use of small support groups as described by Button. One of the important reasons for this is to help the teachers understand how the issues raised in their own lives can be of profit for their own understanding of personal and social matters, but also how such issues can be difficult and require careful handling. This promotes a sensitivity to the impact on the children and also helps to develop skills of handling personal situations which are not necessarily part of a teacher's training.

It is difficult to isolate these skills. However, at a later stage, the following list was produced corporately by the team to try and identify some of the dimensions which seem to be important in our practice.

1 There is a need for: a clear structure and good preparation by the teacher, coupled with a sensitivity to what are the real concerns of the children so that these might form part of the work; an openness to what might emerge; a recognition that this is a human situation and that learning is done by whole people who may bring to and take from any situation a wide variety of learnings.

2 The teaching style should be economical in the sense of teacher talk. Instructions and prompts have to be clearly worked out so that the teacher does not dominate the class but rather provides the space, time and opportunity for children to think, listen, speak, respond and act themselves.

3 The teacher should aim to create a sense of involvement for all, with an invitational style which allows people to choose whether and in what way to be involved. This involves a sensitivity to the pace and intensity of the work, to allow children to join in a way helpful to them. Part of this is an acceptance of children 'where they are' rather than where another might think they 'should' be.

4 All of this requires that the teacher accepts a high level of responsibility and makes it vital that they have a clear sense of their own values.

The teachers acquired confidence in their ability to use these skills by initially having the opportunity on the course, over a number of days, to try them out in a team-teaching situation. This was carried out in a school not their own. They then returned to their own classes and consolidated this learning. The teachers were then in a good position to be able to investigate what contribution the work could make to personal and social education with primary age children. For example, early work in the project suggested a very mixed reaction to small support groups from the younger children. Unlike adolescents, for whom peer group is a strong influence, seven and eight year olds are still largely influenced by the family and peer groups are only just becoming well defined and reasonably stable. However, our overall conclusions after three years are that the small support groups have a real part to play in providing an area for younger children to receive and give support and to reflect on, learn and practise personal and social skills. Group formation needs to be carefully considered, with the children themselves involved in the decision making and with a conscious effort to encourage mixed sex groupings.

Another feature of developmental group work is that it is enquiry-based. In Button's words, this aims at

helping young people to explore their own situations, the social forces that influence their behaviour and state of mind, and the alternatives open to them . . . This is not to say that they will do this uninfluenced or unaided, but the tutor's role is to feed their own self-discovery and not to pre-empt it. We are much more influenced by what we discover for ourselves than by what we are told, and this is particularly true of matters that influence our personal attitudes and behaviour.

(Button, 1981)

The idea of this type of action research has taken on a very wide set of meanings within the project. It has ranged from the children asking themselves questions privately, in their heads, through to fully-fledged investigations involving questionnaires. For example, one first-year middle school class investigated the needs of the first school children who were due to transfer at the end of the term. They then devised an induction programme for these children, based on their findings.

In order to illustrate the reactions of the children to the whole programme here are the views of some eight and nine year olds after one year of developmental group work:

It helps you when you come from the first school.
It helps you get to know people and talk more freely.
I'm not all that lonely now.

We can share things more.
You can share your happiness and sadness and worries.
It has given me much more confidence – the conversations and the small groups.
I've definitely got more friends and I feel a lot easier with people.
It helps you to mix more. (boys/girls)
It doesn't feel funny to go and ask a boy if he wants to do something instead of just girls.
It helps you to understand people and to understand that people like different things that you don't like and to know we're all different.
You learn to make allowances for people.
I always found it hard to speak in front of the class. Now I am much more confident.
It has made our class much happier and better behaved.
It should be on the timetable in every school.
It's good to know that when you look around for someone to play with outside you can think to yourself – I chatted to her in the 'Wednesday special', I could go and talk to her and not be on my own.

This last comment refers to the fact that much of the work has been done at a particular time each week or at least in a time and space devoted to developmental group work. This has proved to have a number of advantages. At the beginning, it provided a clear space and structure for the teachers to practise their new teaching approaches with the children. This allowed a gradualist approach which permitted both teachers and children to explore these changes in some security. Over time the project teachers have felt able to change their teaching style in other parts of the curriculum, bringing a more child-centred approach to their work. As the work has proceeded the 'special time' has increasingly been seen as advantageous in allowing a space when attention can be paid specifically to personal and social issues in their own right as part of the curriculum. In addition, this provides a context for reflection and examination of how individuals view themselves in the classroom. This enables them to explore, develop and change, if necessary, the ways in which members of the class live and work together. Such work at this time is seen to influence other parts of the day by improving the working relationships between the children so that they are able to work more effectively when the prime focus of attention is, say, work in mathematics.

This is not to say that the rest of the curriculum does not also feed the personal and social development of the child. Clearly it does and the intellectual, aesthetic, physical, moral and spiritual experiences provided by the whole school experience are vital. However, there does seem to be an advantage in providing a time and space when these issues can be raised into full consciousness, issues of trust and support focused on and nurtured, and the skills of social relationships reflected on and practised. This also provides a backdrop to other work when the main focus is the mastery of some other intellectual task and helps to maintain the children in a harmonious working atmosphere. Increasingly the special time is seen as having extremely permeable boundaries which allow for more careful examination of issues concerning class life, and for enquiries to be designed and mounted – which can then be taken into other areas of class life for further exploration. This core time, above all, provides an opportunity for personal and social issues to be brought into clear focus and this is appreciated by both teachers and children on the project.

The developmental group work approach adopted by this project grounds such an exploration of personal and social issues in the real life experience of the children, in their daily lives inside and outside the classroom. This view of education has a long tradition in the child-centred approaches but there is always a question of where the proper balance lies for the school, between its public, social function and what is more appropriately dealt with within the family and other contexts. This is partly a question of individual freedom. Children have no choice in whether they attend school and the prime justification for this curtailment of present freedom is the later freedom of choice which this permits.

Developmental group work helps prepare children for full and responsible adult roles by offering them an opportunity to explore crucial areas of personal functioning and relationships. The style of the work is invitational and not coercive, and space is given to allow people to opt out of activities which they find difficult. The values underlying the work respect the importance of the person, child or adult, as a real part of their own educational process.

To conclude, here are the comments of a second year teacher whose class comprised some children who had spent the previous year doing developmental group work and some who hadn't met the work at all. She saw the differences between the two groups as being:

Communication – developmental group work children seemed more able to:

(*a*)   express their real feelings;

(*b*)   discuss sensitive issues openly;

(*c*)   talk about potentially embarrassing issues sensibly and seriously.

Sensitivity – children seemed more:

(*a*)   aware of the needs of others;

(*b*)   willing to try to meet these needs;

(*c*)   able to cope with difficult or disturbing behaviour in others;

(*d*)   appreciative of each other's efforts.

Cooperation – children seemed more:

(*a*)   willing to help each other;

(*b*)   prepared to put group or class needs before their own;

(*c*)   prepared to work with children outside their particular friendship group.

Responsibility – developmental group work children seemed more:

(*a*)   able to take a responsible attitude in and out of class;

(*b*)   willing to own up or apologise;

(*c*)   prepared to take positive action in situations where children were upset or damage had occurred;

(*d*)   willing to help with everyday chores without being asked or reminded.

References

Bennett, N, 1985 'Interaction and Achievement in Classroom Groups' in Bennett, N and Desforges, C, *Recent Advances in Classroom Research*, British Journal of Educational Psychology, Monograph, Series 2. Scottish Academic Press.

Button, L, 1981 *Group Tutoring for the Form Teacher* Volume 1: The Lower School, Hodder and Stoughton.

Button, L, 1985 'A Living Force' in *Network* p 4–9.

Galton, M, Simon, B, and Croll, P, 1980 *Inside the primary classroom* Routledge and Kegan Paul.

Plowden, Baroness, 1967 *Children and their Primary Schools: A Report of the Central Advisory Council for Education* (The Plowden Report) HMSO.

19 Some Canadian approaches to elementary school guidance

Peter Lang

Guidance and the psycho-social needs of all children

The guidance function focuses on the developmental needs of students. These needs arise from the demands and pressures of society, as well as from the nature of the growing and developing human being. At *every* stage of a child's development such basic human needs include

- the need for acceptance and a sense of belonging; the need to feel accepted as a worthwhile member and to have meaningful (ie effective) participation in the group;
- the need for a sense of one's own developing competence and power to have an effect on one's environment;
- the need for a sense of significance, self-respect and self-esteem;
- the need for attention, respect, affection, and acceptance from adults;
- the need for security and structure;
- the need to reach one's potential through the development of personal capacities and talents;
- the need for goal-setting, planning, and the activity to achieve personal goals.

In addition, it is well known that individuals progress through developmental stages. With respect to the school system these stages are those of the early years, the middle years and the senior high school. Guidance programmes must be congruent with the developmental characteristics and needs of children at each of these levels.

(Ministry of Education, Manitoba, 1987)

Under a slightly different heading the list of needs above would not seem out of place as part of a set of guidelines for the development of personal and social education in the English primary school. In fact they were produced as part of a consultative document concerned with the revitalising of the provision of guidance in one of the Canadian provinces.

For several years I have been working on a comparison of the provision of guidance in England and Canada (Lang and Young, 1985; Lang, 1987). Underlying the research I have undertaken is the following hypothesis:

> Superficially then it would appear that though some very general notions of broad based guidance inform aspects of both the British and Canadian Educational systems, at a more specific level, and particularly in terms of their articulation and practice, there is very little common ground. However the assumption that underlies this paper is that though this may well have been the case at one stage, in the last few years there have been a number of changes which are likely to have resulted in the current divergence being more apparent than real. My suggestion is that there has been a recent convergence in the thinking which informs approaches to guidance and also its actual practice in Canada and the United Kingdom.
>
> (Lang, 1988)

Though the research has been small-scale and limited, it has generally tended to confirm the hypothesis. Some of these areas of convergence are as follows:

1 An increasing move towards offering support for students not only in coping with problems and crisis but also in positively tackling developmental tasks.
2 A move toward working through preventative, proactive methods rather than curative, reactive responses.
3 A move to working through groups as opposed to with individuals (though working through the group may be seen as the most appropriate way of reaching the individual) and a greater emphasis on the importance of the relationships within the groups in which the students are placed.
4 A move away from the situation where most guidance is delivered through a limited number of specialists to a situation in which it is delivered through programmes in which a wider range of

individuals are involved and where the specialist role is an increasingly supportive and facilitating one.

5 An examination of documents and programmes relating to pastoral care and personal and social education in England and guidance in Canada demonstrated significant correspondence between the aims which informed both modes of delivery. This particularly applied to the area of positive developmental aims. For example, in both countries most sets of aims analysed included the development of: feelings of self-worth and self-esteem; the ability to relate effectively to others, both as individuals and in groups; effective decision making and independent personal management skills; effective interpersonal communications skills; the ability to explore and respond to personal and social issues; the ability to respond proactively to choices and challenges, particularly in terms of career; the ability to identify sources of support.

So far my research has been particularly concerned with a comparison between aspects of Secondary/High School thinking and practice. If the comparisons that I have drawn between England and Canada, so far, are to be extended to the primary/elementary sphere one important factor must be noted. Though the trends I have described can be identified from kindergarden to Senior High School in Canada they are only clearly apparent at secondary level in England. In Canada the area of 'guidance' is seen to apply equally to all stages of education (see the quotation from Manitoba at the opening of this paper) and as a result the provision of guidance at school board and provincial level is at least in theory as much concerned with elementary (primary) as with high school (secondary). In England, on the other hand, though there is some tacit acceptance of their relevance by some primary schools and by LEAs, the provision of pastoral care and personal and social education are generally seen as secondary issues, by most LEAs, policy makers and teacher trainers. This, of course, is a situation that this book is concerned to challenge.

In England, attention to the 'affective' dimension of pupils' education at primary level is not a conscious policy in most areas and schools (although this book includes some notable exceptions); in Canada it is much more likely to be so. Clearly, given this situation, there are likely to be some insights to be gained by those concerned with PSE in English primary schools from a consideration of elementary school guidance in Canada.

The key personnel in the provision of elementary school guidance in Canada are *counsellors*. They are usually organised at a school board level (school boards being roughly equivalent to LEAs) and are usually directed by a *coordinator of guidance*. There are, of course, many variations throughout Canada; guidance management roles vary both in their nature and number as do the roles of the counsellors. High schools usually have one or more counsellors, often with one counsellor appointed as head of guidance for the school. Elementary counsellors usually work in four to six elementary schools. In some areas only those with full-time postgraduate training in counselling are employed; in other areas qualified teachers can serve as counsellors with no further qualification.

Among different guidance services, and indeed within individual ones, there are varying views of what the proper role and functions of such a service should be. Indeed these differences reflect the moves that have brought about the 'convergences' discussed earlier. The nature of the tension that exists in some services is well expressed in the following extract from a position paper on elementary guidance produced by the Scarborough Board of Education in Ontario.

Elementary guidance in Scarborough has been experiencing the identity crisis felt by most educational guidance services in North America. For many years, it was seen as a 'support service' for students in crisis. More recently, many have come to view guidance as a 'program,' developmental in structure, to be directed to *all* students. These divergent philosophies and the range of views between have left counsellors, principals and teachers in some confusion and frustration about the aims of guidance and the specific role of the counsellor . . .

. . . Throughout the history of guidance, its goals have frequently been viewed as different from the mainstream of educational programs. For example, counsellors have been seen as concerned only with the career preparation of students or with the behavioural modification of maladjusted individuals. As ideas about guidance and classroom teaching have evolved, it has become apparent that there is considerable overlapping of goals and that counsellors and teachers are members of a team whose aim is to maximise individual potential.

(Scarborough Board of Education, 1987)

The knowledge of teachers and educationalists within a particular education system tends to be confined to that particular system. Though they may have some general ideas about other systems, these tend to be very general and stereotypical. In England, this professional tunnel vision is not surprising given the professional preoccupations of teachers and the lack of information (the *Times Educational Supplement* devotes at most two of its pages to news from overseas). This limited vision is perhaps particularly the case in relation to the way different countries approach the affective dimension of education. This may in part be due to the fact that in many countries precise information as to what is happening is not readily available, as Dockrell has observed

Of the 32 countries represented at the 8th World Congress of the World Association for Education, ranging alphabetically from Argentina to Zimbabwe at least 30 assumed that education had a role in the development of personality. Yet there is a marked Anglo-Saxon reluctance to be concerned with research in this area. At the last meeting of the American Educational Research Association I looked for sessions which were concerned with affective or social development. There were some in the index but none of those sessions saw affective development as anything other than a peripheral issue as it related to some important concern.

(Dockrell, 1987)

In my view, this situation is an unfortunate one. A level of knowledge and understanding which is confined to the education system in which you work is limiting and might even be described as impoverished. In the rest of this paper I shall endeavour to illustrate the potential value of the ideas and insights that may be gained by looking at the approach to affective education of other systems. I shall do this through a brief consideration of some aspects of the Canadian approach to guidance at the elementary level, coupled with discussion of their possible implications for the development of personal and social education in English primary schools.

196

It must be recognised that the view of Canadian elementary school guidance presented here is likely to be a somewhat idealised one. Just as there is a gap between the rhetoric of pastoral care and personal and social education in England, guidance in Canada has its own rhetoric which, equally, is not always reflected in practice. It is also true that the quality of guidance provision varies considerably between provinces (as does resourcing). Further there are considerable variations between individual school boards. A particular problem is the fact that counsellors often find themselves spending more time on administration than on performing the tasks they are supposed to carry out. (There are interesting parallels to be drawn here with the administrative orientation of the Pastoral systems of some English secondary schools.)

It is evident from the results that a large portion of counsellor time is being used to perform tasks which are neither related to priority roles and functions nor to societal needs and problems.
(Task force report, Burnaby School District, 1985)

Across Canada, elementary school counsellors are invariably overworked. Typically they are responsible for four to five schools, each with diverse populations of children from a multiplicity of backgrounds and with as diverse needs. In some provinces, compulsory guidance curriculum has been mandated requiring counsellors to teach in a variety of classrooms and/or consult with teachers who are unfamiliar with the content and delivery of the material. The number of children requiring counselling intervention continues to rise. And always there is the paper work.
(Studd, 1987)

Conservations with elementary counsellors from most parts of Canada have indicated that many are very concerned to find ways of concentrating on what they perceive to be the key aspects of their work. For the majority of these counsellors, this work is increasingly proactive and developmental in emphasis. They see their sphere of work as being in elementary schools rather than in a central office. Though the majority tend to stress the importance of the expert counselling support they feel they can offer, they also emphasise their role in programme development and delivery, particularly in facilitating the development of skills throughout the school that will ensure that all pupils receive the full benefits of such a programme. These counsellors were all convinced that their existence ensured that guidance in the elementary school had a higher profile, was given greater priority and was, most importantly, more effective, than would have been the case had their roles not existed.

Where elementary guidance services are fully developed and effective it is arguable that the quality of elementary pupils' affective education and support will be better than is currently the case in the average English primary school. The following example illustrates this point. It is a programme from a paper presented recently in the Canadian journal *Guidance and Counselling* in an issue focusing on elementary school guidance. The paper was concerned with the effective marketing of elementary school guidance. Where the strictures of the suggested ideal programme were even approximated to, the quality of affective education in the elementary school concerned would be high.

The ideal Guidance Program

Elementary school guidance
An elementary school Guidance program is necessary to complement the services of principals and teaching staff. The Program must be under the direction of a suitably trained counsellor to whom teachers, parents, students and others concerned with a student's welfare have ready access.

Aims of elementary school guidance program
The elementary school guidance program should:
* teach children to accept responsibility for their own behaviour;
* develop in children an understanding and acceptance of one's self and others;
* identify children with special needs related to learning, behaviour and interpersonal relations, which affect their social and educational growth;
* teach children how to take decisions, solve problems, communicate and relate to each other;
* teach children how to acquire and use information which is essential to their career awareness and development;

* assist principals, teachers, parents and students in locating and using suitable school and community resources.

All of these aims are of equal importance.

The total program for elementary schools

A total elementary school guidance program designed to meet these aims will enable every child to:
* have access to counselling
* learn such group skills as communication and interpersonal skills
* have an awareness and understanding of the world of work
* learn and practise problem solving and decision making skills
* receive help in adjusting to new situations, and
* learn acceptable, appropriate and responsible behaviour.

A total elementary school guidance program will include the following services and activities:
* individual and group counselling
* providing information
* consultation with parents, school staff members, and other significant adults in a child's life
* referral to and consultation with those concerned with the special needs of the child
* interpretation of achievement test results
* classroom instruction
* providing orientation programs for students entering or leaving the school
* secondary school liaison
* group work program which includes the teaching of communication, decision making techniques and interpersonal relations
* career awareness programs
* in-service programs and
* evaluation of guidance program.

(Morrison, 1987)

There is certainly a rhetorical aspect to an idealised programme of this sort; but in Canada it is quite common for issues relating to the affective education and support of elementary pupils to be consciously articulated in this way. Anyone concerned with primary education in England will be well aware that there are currently few parallels to this situation here.

Equally there are a number of examples where school boards have developed, or are in the process of developing, very comprehensive programmes of elementary guidance – for example Scarborough School Board in Ontario has recently embarked on an initiative to reorientate and revitalise its guidance.

Philosophy

As previously stated, the field of Guidance has undergone many changes since its origin, and there presently exist a number of different philosophies about the aims of guidance and the most suitable strategies for its delivery. The CEDSS review recommended that the Scarborough Board of Education articulate a well-defined *philosophy* of guidance to provide the framework for the program. The recent Scarborough studies, together with release of *Guidance 84*, have led the Student and Community Services Department to propose the following principles for guidance, JK–12:

1 The guidance program should reach all students through a continuous, cumulative program from elementary to high school.
2 The program should focus on many aspects of the student's growth (eg personal, social, educational, career).
3 The program should emphasise preventative and positive approaches to helping students while providing crisis intervention as required.
4 The guidance program should involve the efforts of the entire school staff.
5 In co-operation with the principal, the counsellor should assume a leadership role in a team effort of teachers and specialists.

The developmental guidance model K–8

A team approach

The implementation of a developmental model for elementary guidance requires a team effort by counsellors, principals and teachers. This should not be seen as creating additional

200

responsibilities or curriculum pressures for school staff; because of the considerable overlap between guidance objectives and the goals of education, guidance is already an integral part of Scarborough's classrooms. A major portion of guidance objectives are readily integrated into existing curricula, while guidance counsellors deliver specialised educational and career planning information.

The delineation of responsibilities of staff in regard to guidance should result in: a) removal of frustration caused by confusion over role and responsibilities b) the fostering of a team approach to guidance delivery c) a heightened awareness of principals and teachers as to their commitment to achieving the affective goals of education and d) the encouragement of educators in this pursuit by assuring them of the Scarborough Board's dedication to affective teaching.

(Scarborough Board of Education, 1987)

Burnaby, a relatively small school district in British Columbia, employs seven elementary school counsellors. All of these counsellors have undertaken two years of full-time postgraduate professional training to MA level. They are strongly encouraged to act as facilitators, assisting schools to implement programmes of positive developmental guidance.

The type of initiatives and approaches described above are by no means uncommon at all levels within Canadian elementary guidance. What is being suggested is that, as a result of this, the affective dimension of education will be more often consciously considered in Canadian elementary schools, and seen as a greater priority than in their English counterparts.

During my work in Canada I have found that the existence of a nationwide educational concern with elementary school guidance has had other significant results. A number of centres exist, providing courses and producing material to support and develop affective education at that level. Notable amongst such centres is 'the Values Education Centre' in Scarborough, Ontario. At another level, a catalogue produced by 'The Guidance Centre' at the University of Toronto, contains a substantial section under the heading *Personal and social growth*. Within this section a wide range of Canadian and American materials are described, including two major programmes for elementary pupils: *Towards affective develop-*

ment and *Developing understanding of self and others*. The point here is that, unlike England, Canada has a wide range of material available with which teachers can work. Most university departments of Counselling Psychology in Canada have a significant concern for elementary guidance, running courses for counsellors and teachers, and promoting research and the development of practice.

One particularly interesting development in Canada has been that of 'peer counselling'. This is currently being developed at all levels of schooling. In relation to this at the elementary level, in a training manual for teachers and counsellors Trevor Cole states

> Trying to be an elementary school counsellor in five different schools is a pretty formidable task. There is very little doubt that public education is entering a period of rapid change. The results of these changes are increased demands placed upon teachers and administrators to meet the needs of their students. As class sizes increase, so do class problems, ie less time to spend with individual students, discipline and behaviour problems, extra supervision and a lack of time to deal with students developing social skills.
>
> As a counsellor, I look towards a goal of guidance for all children, and the thought that all children may need counselling at some time during their elementary years.
>
> The introduction of Peer Counselling in schools benefits administration, teachers, students and parents. Peer Counselling is a vital extension of the counselling and guidance service.
>
> Peer influence is looked on by many as a negative force which has to be constantly monitored by adults. Peer influence need not be a negative force. By using peers as a resource to provide assistance to other students, we are able to create a caring and supportive environment.
>
> (Cole, 1986)

The notion of Peer Counselling is one which could well make a valuable contribution to education in personal and social development in English primary schools.

Conclusion

The purpose of this paper has not been to uncritically extol the virtues of the Canadian approach to elementary guidance, suggesting that it is in every way superior to PSE in English primary schools. What has been suggested is that it is valuable to look at alternative approaches from those of one's own system, and that where this has been done, in relation to Canadian elementary guidance, it has been found that there are elements of this approach which have particular strengths and from which something can be learnt. Some of these strengths are

• the mandatory provision of elementary guidance at provincial level (school boards have an obligation to provide it);
• the existence of specialised guidance teams at school board level to fulfil this mandate;
• the appointment of a number of well-trained elementary counsellors to these teams in many school boards. These counsellors serve to heighten awareness about, and facilitate the development of, affective education in schools.
• the specialised support offered by these counsellors to the pupils in their elementary school;
• that in Canada, as a result of the points above and other factors, concern for the affective education of elementary/primary pupils has a much higher profile than in England.

References

Burnaby School District, 1985 *Counselling Services: Roles, Expectations, Directions, a Task Force Report*.

Cole, T, 1986 *Kids Helping Kids: a Training Manual for Elementary Teachers and Counsellors* The Peer Counselling project, Victoria.

Dockrell, B, 1987 'The Assessment of Children's affective Characteristics' in *British Educational Research Journal*, *13*(1).

Lang, P and Young, R, 1985 'Pastoral Care in English Schools: a Canadian Perspective' in *Canadian Counsellor*, *19*(3&4).

Lang, P, 1987 'Pastoral Care in English schools: Applications to Canadian Educational and Counselling Practice' in *Guidance and Counselling*, *2*(5), University of Toronto.

Lang, P, 1988 'Whole School Guidance Curriculums' in *Guidance and Counselling*, 4(1), University of Toronto.

Ministry of Education, Manitoba Curriculum Development and Implementation Branch, 1987 *Task force on Guidance Consultation paper* Manitoba Ministry of Education.

Morrison, C, 1987 'Marketing Guidance in Elementary Schools' in *Guidance and Counselling*, 2(5), University of Toronto.

Scarborough Board of Education, 1987 *Position Paper on Elementary Guidance*.

Studd, D, 1987 *'Editorial'* Guidance and Counselling, 2(5), University of Toronto.

20 Social skills training in the primary school

Arthur Wooster

I hate myself. Sometimes I wish I could throw myself in the dustbin!
This outburst from an eight-year-old sprang from his experiences in the worst class in school. 'The most difficult children I have ever known', said their first-year teacher. She handed them on with relief. They would not cooperate, lacked motivation, and swore at one another. They disliked each other and were disliked by teachers, supervisors and other children.

The class members obviously lacked social skills. Their training had been poor. In their EPA school they had met six teachers in the last term of infant school. Of the 26 children, ten came from broken homes, six were itinerants. It was easy to dismiss the problems of these under-achieving, unpleasant children as beyond solution. So many factors could be blamed.

Their new teacher did not waste time blaming. She saw that the children were experiencing difficulties which needed to be put right before they could give their full attention to school work. They were too frightened to work at full power. Much of their energy was spent on attack and defence. To reclaim that energy it was necessary to reduce the threat. The children must stop their unhelpful actions and behave in a friendly way. They must learn *social skills*.

A socially skilled person is one who can deal with others in such a way that they respond positively and in a way that is helpful. It requires skill to work toward your goals in such a way that others will be more helpful than unhelpful; to do that the child must have learned to make good guesses about the best way to treat others, and also learn to adapt to what is seen to be the needs of the present situation. It is necessary to know how to begin and how to break off meetings, how to keep an interaction positive by the use of your body and your language. It is necessary to be very aware of the other person and to respond to or make allowances for their wishes and intentions.

The class teacher knew about social skills training. She was taking a course designed for pastoral care teachers at the local university (Nottingham), and was beginning her second year of part-time study. The course was an experiential – that is, practical – introduction to such areas as counselling, communication and group dynamics. There were few lectures and a great deal of face-to-face work in pairs and in small and large groups, where skills were identified and practised.

Drawing on her training the teacher began to help the class to build self-awareness, confidence and a sense of responsibility. She did this by being very concrete and specific, she was a practical, rather traditional person, and her aims reflected this. She identified very specific skills and strategies which the children needed to learn in order to cooperate successfully.

These skills include listening to one another, fitting in movements and activities with those of others, and taking part in social behaviours that will help the group to get along together and stay together in enjoyable interaction. The children did not know how to make and keep friends. Their teacher was sure that once they had learned to do so, and built a positive, supportive climate of trust in their classroom, much more of their energy would be set free for the task of learning in traditional areas. First they must learn how to learn.

The awareness essential to learning how to learn was developed by the use of experiential activities. These involved the children in movement, language or other symbolic activity, and prompted them to reflect on their own experience. Exercises pin-pointed aspects of social skill and gave a frame within which to practise them. Occasions which were shared in the classroom were used to illustrate the relevance of what had been learned to the wider setting.

Members of the class shared experiences regularly in small groups, beginning with light, less-demanding situations, and analysing them together. The children became used to sharing their views in public, at first in pairs, then fours and gradually in larger groups. Group sizes increased and topics deepened as time passed. The children became aware of the need to treat confidences supportively, without cross-examining the speaker or reacting unhelpfully through embarrassment. They learned to be open and genuine with one another.

The training in social skills took place when the teacher saw that the time, place and children involved were right. It could not be done to a fixed plan, but depended upon the teacher's exercise of her art. *Circletime* (Ballard, 1975) became the anchor activity of the class. This activity uses structures, or topics, which the children discuss; it offers the opportunity to practise the inter-personal skills of listening and sharing and at the same time to develop self-awareness. An important advantage is that in the circle everyone is visible to everyone else.

Circletime meetings take five minutes at first, with each child responding briefly to such supplied topics as: *A time I felt really happy*; *A time I felt really scared*; *A time when I was lost*; *A time I felt really angry*. The rules are: *Everyone who wants to, gets a turn; everyone who takes a turn, gets listened to*. Sharing is quick, everyone listens to the speaker and one volunteer then tells what they understood the speaker to say. There is no further comment, question or discussion. Skills of sharing are modelled and practised. Immediate evidence of being heard is given in a restatement which includes reference to any feelings expressed.

The circletime model gives priority to the speaker's need to be listened to. Responses are deliberately limited so that the listeners may stay focused upon the speaker, whose views are clarified by the volunteer respondent for the group's benefit, without stealing the focus away. The speaker can nod agreement with the summary offered, or call for a second attempt. After this try the focus moves to the next speaker.

The technique of *brainstorming* extends the experience of sharing, with everyone who wishes to speak being heard. This technique, de Bono (1970) suggests, offers a setting for the use of lateral thinking; it is a group activity which does not require teacher intervention. It is a valuable summary of the humanistic principles of experiential learning. A topic which has been indicated by some recent inter-action in the classroom could be reviewed by the class, for example, a row between members could be used to promote learning about anger and its positive and negative features. The teacher might, after a brief warm-up activity, write up *Anger is . . .* and record every response class members offer. *Give another name for anger* would extend the list; *When I am angry, my body feels . . .* brings out another important aspect. Members are encouraged to make the list as long as possible, to build on each others' ideas, and to be adventurous. Every contribution is recorded without comment.

Following a brief discussion the pupils might then look at the topic from another aspect. In one activity small groups of six members drew around the body of one of their number, on a strip of wallpaper. Then, without talking, the six spent a few minutes crayoning on the outline to show symbolically how anger is experienced. Locating the situation in which the feeling was met and identifying the parts of the body in which it was felt helped to link word and experience. This exercise made the link very individual for each child.

This kind of exercise goes beyond the cognitive. It offers an opportunity to take a risk and, when you find your view accepted, is encouragement to do more. The pupil can risk exposing more of his or her thoughts, views and feelings; the individual reveals himself or herself and comes to know others better as they do the same. Respect for others and their differences grows. As trust between members rises ideas flow more freely in the atmosphere of reduced threat, task performance improves because of this and enjoyment builds.

The use of fantasy and guided imagery helps the class make and share personal statements. Used when a certain level of reliability has been developed and explored, even a simple exercise such as building an 'ideal room' in your imagination as you sit with closed eyes for two minutes, and then discussing it with a partner for five minutes, can be a scene for revealing more of your personal tastes and attitudes and becoming known as an individual. Fantasy can be used to build calm or restore it. Spend three minutes seeing in your mind's eye a wind-tossed lake at daybreak, as the sky brightens, the sun appears, the temperature rises, the wind falls, the noise of the branches subsides and birds and insects begin to make themselves heard whilst the sun sparkles from the calm lake . . . This, and similar imaginative exercises can produce a significant change of mood.

As the children learn to identify and own their behaviour, alternative ways of interacting are discussed. The next step is to begin to work towards self-chosen change – to set goals and plan to achieve them. This process of goal setting can be encouraged by working on short-range goals to be achieved within the class meetings. In this way trios can help one another examine goals and consider alternative routes to the desired end. Goals will need to be such that others can see whether or not they have been achieved. This teaches the need for concreteness and realism – *Will I know if I have achieved it? How? When do I want to have done this? Where? With whom? Who will help me check or revise my plans?* Personal journals, not necessarily shared with anyone – including the teacher, can help the learner see how much has been learned about taking charge of her own life over a period of time.

Gradually, through work of the kind described above the children learned to use each other as consultants. In circletime they raised their own problems, seeking advice and practical help. In a public situation they practised communication skills, attending to the thoughts and feelings of others, checking their understanding of what they had heard with the speaker and coming to appreciate the need to express themselves carefully, fully and objectively. Non-verbal aspects of communication were highlighted along with sense-training (Castillo, 1974; Simon and O'Rourke, 1977) and physical education activities which built body awareness and self-concept (Colwell, 1975).

Improved reading and self-concept

The fruits of improved relationships showed in both the academic and social areas of school life. Reading ability rose sharply in two terms. The average reader in the class rose from being in the bottom 30% to being able to read at the level of the top 30% by national standards (Wooster and Carson, 1982). At the beginning of the programme the children were generally unhappy about their achievements, their behaviour, appearance and popularity; after two terms they expressed normal feelings about these aspects of their self-picture.

An outsider's view was provided by a visiting journalist who spent an afternoon with the class. The children were told of her visit and arranged a programme. 'I watched a class where cooperation, sensitivity towards each other's needs and responsibility for one's own, seemed a natural part of the activities', she wrote (Hagedorn, 1980). She saw the children working in pairs, talking of their homes, their friends, their likes and dislikes; moving into groups where they listened to one another and showed that they had heard and checked that they had understood. They were working on the social skills involved in attending to a speaker: showing that they had listened and encouraging further discussion if the speaker wished to go on. As they did this they were both showing and experiencing trust in interaction.

Advantages for poor readers

The value of social skills training when it is used to build a positive learning climate was shown when two further classes were encouraged to see and discuss how they got on together. In each class the teacher drew on his or her experience to decide when to introduce an exercise or suggest a topic for examination in circletime. The class discussed at the beginning of this article was experiencing a range of difficulties, these two were not. However when the results of reading tests given at the beginning and end of the two-term programme are compared it is clear that children who began as average or below average readers improved at a level unlikely to be due to chance. Compared with children in two untrained classes the average gain of six points was three times as great. In the untrained group, which improved on average, some children had gained quite a lot, some had fallen back. In the trained group, all children had remained stable or made gains. To a teacher this must imply a happier class who had met a better learning experience.

This evidence supports the view that the effect of social skills training is most marked in those who need it most. It is worth remembering that the trained groups did not receive any extra training in reading skills – simply they were a little freer to learn. This was shown by a marked increase in the willingness to acknowledge responsibility for their shortcomings – a first step in motivation and an indication of the improvement in self-discipline (Wooster, 1986).

A marked improvement in the social climate – a rise in the friendliness shown to one another – can be brought about quite quickly. An example is the study reported by Wooster *et al* (1986). A class of 12 slow-learning children in a special school were taught social skills in a series of structured activities for one day each week over ten weeks. These activities and a discussion of the methodology, rationale and underlying philosophy have been fully reported in a handbook designed for classroom use (Leech and Wooster, 1986). The aim was to help the children understand and voluntarily undertake the socially skilful behaviour which is typical of friends. Friends show a high degree of liking for one another, respect each other, confide things of personal importance and spend time together. The children identified, discussed, wrote about, drew, modelled, imagined, learned and demonstrated the basic steps of friendly behaviour.

At the end of the training period the children showed a significant increase in liking and friendship on several measures. Attendance improved, at first on the training day, then every day, and this held over the following term, as did the increased friendliness. Their class teacher found the children more interested in school.

Teaching social skills

Why don't we teach children how to make skilful contacts with people? We could help them to avoid repeating mistakes in dealing with others; to reflect and learn from what they hear, see, think and feel in their dealings with people. We could help them to pick out what was skilled and productive in an interaction and avoid what was not. So why do we leave the process of building trusting relationships to trial and error learning?

One reason for our neglect, Sapon-Shevin (1986) suggests, is the emphasis Piaget and his followers put on what they saw as the egocentricity of the junior child. If you believe that the young child is too self-centred you will not try to train him or her in social skills. If your teaching is aimed at such abstractions as 'teaching the whole child' you will tend to avoid clearly-defined and concrete goals. Providing such goals and strategies for reaching them might help many teachers.

A further reason for the neglect of social skills is the popular myth that improved social relations can only be achieved, at the cost of academic achievement. Arguments have been advanced in this article to dispute this view. A linked claim is that competition produces motivation and that children achieve more in competitive settings. This is not a reason for avoiding training in skills of cooperation. Adam Curle (1973) has formed the sad conclusion that '. . . the world's largest industry, which has the greatest opportunity to sow in our minds and those of our children the seeds of peace, justice and equality . . . sows more the seeds of destruction'.

We can set about establishing cooperative and friendly behaviour in a systematic way. Cooperative behaviour can be promoted through exercises, games and stories and by teaching children to review their own behaviour. Not all activities are suitable. Some games – structured, rule-bound interactions – do not, when analysed, encourage the social behaviour a teacher would wish to see on other occasions. Some require teasing, taunting, grabbing, snatching scarce objects, monopolising attractive objects, excluding others, or using physical force to pull, push or strike. However, exercises can encourage working together and provide experience which the child can pick out in discussion and employ to make plans for anticipated situations.

The teacher must help the learner develop trust in teachers and other children, for without trust the learner will not venture out into the unknown areas of potential experience. New problems will not be tackled and old problems will not be tackled in new ways. If the learner is not helped to trust others how can he or she come to trust him or herself? Social skills training can give the child realistic experiences on which to base trust.

References

Ballard, J, 1975 *Circlebook* Amherst, Mass: Mandala.
Castillo, G A, 1974 *Left-Handed Teaching* New York: Praeger.
Colwell, L C, 1975 *Jump to Learn* San Diego: Pennant.
Curle, A, 1973 *Education for Liberation* London: Tavistock.
de Bono, E, 1970 *Lateral Thinking* London: Ward Lock Educational.
Hagedorn, J, 1980 'Learning to Live With Trust' in *Junior Education*, December.
Leech, N and Wooster, A D, 1986 *Personal and Social Skills* Exeter: Religious and Moral Education Press.
Sapon-Shevin, M, 1986 'Teaching Cooperation' in Cartledge, G and Milburn, J F (eds) *Teaching Social Skills to Children* Oxford: Pergamon Press.
Simon, S B and O'Rourke, R D, 1977 *Developing Values with Exceptional Children* Englewood Cliffs, N.J.: Prentice-Hall.
Wooster, A D, 1986 'Social Skills Training and Reading Gain' in *Educational Research*, *28*(1) p 68–71.
Wooster, A D and Carson, A 1982 'Improving Reading and Self-Concept through Communication and Social Skills Training' in *British Journal of Guidance and Counselling*, *10*(1) p 83–7.
Wooster, A, Leech, N and Hall, E, 1986 'Personal and Social Education in the Special School' in *Pastoral Care in Education*, *4*(3) p 210–15.

21   Social education is interaction

Delwyn P. Tattum

Personal and social education in the primary school is regarded by most teachers as an implicit, taken-for-granted part of the daily interactions of teacher and pupils – it is caught rather than taught. How many schools have a social education syllabus? How many teachers have consciously thought about their aims and objectives in the area of personal and social education? But to be critical of schools and teachers is to simplify the issue, for I believe that few initial teacher training courses have adequately prepared their students for this aspect of school social life. Part of the problem stems from the lack of an approach which enables tutors to conceptualise the central concerns in a systematic way. With these views in mind, Symbolic Interactionism (SI) is offered as an approach which can be adopted by teacher trainers, on both pre- and in-service courses, to focus on the central questions involved in the purposes and practices of personal and social education. What is offered therefore has to do with the *process* of personal and social education rather than the *product*. It is an analysis of the processes by which a child develops a world-view as he or she also learns a self-view.

SI is more a constellation of concepts than a tightly integrated body of theory, and in this paper I propose to briefly deal with the core of ideas which revolve around the process of socialisation and to diagrammatically present the wider constellation of concepts; in a more applied section, I will consider an important stage in personal and social education, namely, starting school.

The interactionist view of socialisation involves the following elements:

1 It is an *ongoing* process;
2 It is a *reciprocal process* based on social interaction between active partners;
3 It is a *life-long process* as the individual enters different social situations – some more critical than others;

4 It is a *cumulative process* as each individual does not begin afresh in each new situation but builds on previous knowledge, that is, he or she takes into each new situation a set of previous social learning. We are not all that free today from what we experienced yesterday!

(Tattum and Tattum, 1988)

Before the child arrives at school a great deal of socialisation has occurred through the main agency of the family. Also, socialisation in school is more than just formal education, for it includes the acquisition of values, beliefs, attitudes, habits and skills essential for survival in the complicated process of living in an advanced industrial society. A function of the school is to socialise children into the ways of society, but before this function can be successfully achieved teachers must also socialise the children into the ways of the school, that is, into pupilhood. The importance of a successful introduction into the new role will be evident to all teachers, but none will be more acutely aware than the front line troops of reception classes. There is more to starting school than reaching a certain chronological age, it means a new status, new challenges, threats to self-image, personal assessment, and so on. Starting school requires behavioural changes, but also much deeper personal changes before a much wider social audience. Thus socialisation means the transmission and acquisition of language, social roles, morality, culture, personality and, most relevant for this paper, identity – gender, racial and occupational, or, as in our case, *pupilhood*.

Evolution has produced an organism with a potential for human behaviour, but that potential is not realised unless a person engages in social interaction, as studies of feral children have shown. Therefore, in order to understand how each of us acquires a self, we must focus on the problem of socialisation – biology is not enough (Kando, 1977). Within the process childhood is usually dealt with under *primary* socialisation and subsequent inductions into new sections of society, like the school, come under *secondary* socialisation. Primary socialisation is the *sine qua non* for the successful integration of new members into society and for the successful continuity of society. The primary interactants in most cases are parents, and children not only take on their parents' identities but also their social world. That world is given as inevitable and absolute, and the internalisation of its ways is both cognitive and affective. However, doubts, questioning and reinterpretation occur as individuals enter into new institutions, cultures and alliances, for these are the concomitants of the life-long process of *secondary* socialisation; the primary school is often the child's first real experience of alternatives and contradictions.

An essential tenet of SI is that social experience is unique. The approach holds that the individual acquires a unique social self through the universe of social experiences in which he engages, and also through the creative reflexivity by which he gives meaning to his social environment. Rather than seeing socialisation as a constraining straitjacket, SI conceives of it as a blueprint to be interpreted, for it lays stress on the adaptation of the individual to the various social situations he meets – like starting school. The concept is still about fitting individuals and society together, but the emphasis is on the individual's learning, and includes the learning of behaviour appropriate to the various other individuals or groups encountered throughout life.

Fundamental human questions are 'Who am I?', 'What kind of person am I?' and 'Why am I me?'. These questions and attempted answers have no meaning outside social interaction; in Mead's words 'the self is social', emphasising the growing self-awareness of the child of *himself* as he experiences interaction with others in an ever widening circle of social contacts. Mead defines self as 'that which can be object to itself, that which is reflexive ie which can be both subject and object'. This means that the human being can be the object of his own actions just as he can act towards other persons. He can analyse and criticise his own behaviour and its motives. Similarly, he can modify his actions in the light of self indications as he reviews his action and its effect on himself and others. Interactive life is a constant flow of self-indications, through 'internal conversation' human action becomes both purposive and creative. It is creative when an individual faces a new situation, and purposive as the individual takes into account consciously held purposes, plans and knowledge. In other words, through 'reflexivity' human beings are acting and not merely responding organisms. This idea is dramatically conveyed by Berger in the following extract.

For a moment we see ourselves as puppets indeed. But then we grasp a decisive difference between the puppet theatre and our own drama. Unlike the puppets, we have the possibility of stopping in our movements, looking up and perceiving the machinery by which we have been moved. In this act lies the first step towards freedom.

(Berger, 1966)

The reflexive self incorporates two ideas: first, that people have a view of themselves and that they evaluate this self-view; second, that this self-view is based upon, and can ultimately only survive within, certain sets of relationships. This means that self is not seen as some immutably fixed entity, but as constantly changing and precarious. Each person develops, over time, an enduring central core which is less immediately vulnerable, but both aspects are socially derived. Changes in identity can thus result from changes in a person's position in society – his progress (or lack of it) from one status to another. Our identities (or views of ourselves) are constantly under threat, most especially in person changing institutions such as schools. An extreme view of this position is that 'teaching is an assault on the self, and resistance to it can be explained as unwillingness to upset one's inner status quo'(Geer, 1968).

As indicated in Figure 21.1, the genesis and development of self is found in social relationships, 'it is not initially there at birth but arises in the process of social experience and activity' (Mead, 1956). In his exploration of self Mead concentrated on the process of social interaction by which the individual's consciousness of self emerges, which, to Mead, is indicative of the existence of *mind*, that is, the capacity to respond to one's self as others respond to it. The child acquires self-conception through communication in social interaction, for example, through the relationship with parents, teachers and other children. Much of this learning takes place in the family setting where parents are usually the 'significant others' with whom the child interacts. The child quickly learns that by influencing the feelings of his parents he is able to control in some part what happens to himself. This self-learning process Cooley (1902) named the 'looking-glass self', a concept which describes the self as our imagination of our appearance to others, their judgement of us, and our consequent feelings. There are few things more relevant to a child than how people react to him; it is not surprising, therefore, that the reflections of himself in the eyes of significant others play a crucial part in the self-concepts a child acquires. From observing the

216

Figure 21.1 *Personal and social education is interaction*

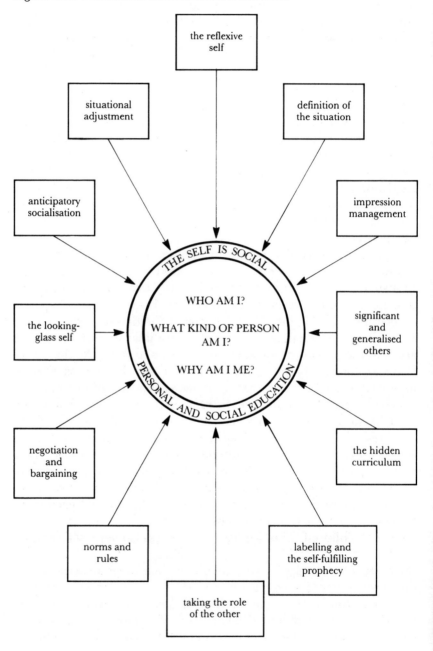

reactions and responses of others to our presentation of self we learn to become the kinds of persons we are – kind, thoughtful, poor at sums, a good reader, and so on.

The central mechanism in an infant's progress towards self-consciousness is symbolic communication. Lower animals communicate with each other by what Mead called a 'conversation of gestures' – a gesture is a social act which stimulates a direct automatic and non-reflective response from another animal. Humans are unique in that they respond to one another on the basis of the intentions or meanings of gestures, for example, the gesture of shaking a fist becomes a symbol to be interpreted. Human society is based on shared meanings and common understanding, whereby each individual is able to respond to his own symbolic gesture, thus holding to the same interpretation as do other persons. The most important category of symbols is language, where the sound conveys the image.

A person's verbal development cannot take place outside a social group, and it reflects the specific group and culture – consider Bernstein's restricted and elaborated codes. Language in large part structures thought and many writers have emphasised the insep-arability of thought and language (Vygotsky, 1962) – although that is not to claim that they are identical. Nevertheless, the ability to think abstractly does fully depend on language, and language, by deter-mining how and what a person thinks, also greatly determines what a person becomes. It is 'partly responsible for a person's self-concept, identity, personality, attitudes, social and emotional adjustment, in sum his *self*'. (Kando, 1977). The idea that the speaker can put himself in the position of the other person and view the situation from his perspective is called 'taking the role of the other', as the speaker not only reflexively interprets the meaning of his words in his own mind but seeks to actively imagine their inter-pretation by others. As teachers we must be able to put ourselves in the child's shoes to appreciate learning and behaviour problems. For their part, children need to develop a capacity to take account of the needs of others as well as their own feelings.

We each have a repertoire of perspectives which enable us to take on different roles, and with each role-taking we project ourselves into the situation and imagine how we would feel – the better we are able to do this the more we are capable of seeing the other person's point of view. Equally important, it also means we begin to see ourselves as others see us – we become object to ourselves. This action is difficult for young children, especially as it occurs in many teacher-pupil interactions. For some pupils it is a problem of adopting the pupil role; as the role is not part of the child's self-awareness he is unable (or unwilling in the case of older pupils) to acknowledge the role of the teacher with whom it is reciprocally linked. In the process of learning our own role we must learn the role of other(s) opposite whom we role play – in learning the role of a daughter or son a child must also learn what it means to be parent. A child role-playing at teacher is a good example – although their caricature is usually stricter than Dickens's character Whackford Squeers!

Mead distinguished between *play* and the *game*. The child imitates the role of specific significant others when playing at being mother, teacher, nurse, spaceman etc, and in this way he learns to understand the importance of particular social roles. In the *game* the concept is taken a stage further – in any organised game each player must learn the roles of all other participants in terms of his own performance and of his rule-governed interactions with the other players' roles. That is, he must take systematic account of the attitudes of the others and synthesise them into what is called the role of *the generalised other*. In this way the individual is constructing his own social identity on the basis of his understanding and predictions of others' actions. Each of us belongs to many social groups, from the family to school, peer groups or clubs, and ultimately to society itself. We each identify with different significant and generalised others, and they, in turn, provide us with perspectives – or our ordered view of life. Together they are sources of values, beliefs, attitudes and norms, in other words they are also mechanisms for social control. As the child takes to himself the culture of the group he progresses from 'Teacher said it's wrong' to 'I know it's wrong'.

Finally, the dialectic relationship between society and the individual is encapsulated by Mead in the dual and reflexive nature of the self as expressed in the concepts of the 'I' and the 'ME'. He writes that 'the self is essentially a social process going on with these two distinguishable phases', and in so doing is referring to two parts of self-interaction rather than two parts of the personality.

The I is the response of the organism to the attitudes of others; the ME is the organised set of attitudes which one himself

assumes. The attitudes of the others constitute the organised
ME, and the one reacts towards that as an I.

(Mead, 1956)

The ME is the conventional, habitual individual, composed of an
organised set of attitudes which the individual has learned as a
member of the group. It stands for the roles which have over time
been internalised by the individual – without the ME the individual
could not be a member of the social group(s). The I, on the other
hand, is the initial, spontaneous aspect of human experience, it is the
self acting in the present. The ME is the socialised aspect which
directs and regulates behaviour along socially prescribed lines,
whilst the I is creative and innovative – both are essential to the full
expression of self, for in their dialectic interplay they mutually
determine one another, as neither represents the total self.

In this brief introduction to the core elements of SI it has not been
possible to deal with all the concepts applicable to a course on PSE
and in the second part of the paper I shall apply some of the other
concepts to the critical adaptation a child has to make when starting
school.

Starting school

In part one I emphasised the social self to the neglect of the social
context, but in this section I wish to argue that the social situation,
and the person's subjective definition of it, is of greater importance
for the understanding of the self and its behaviour than social
background and personality characteristics. Transition from home
to school can be upsetting, even traumatic, for a child. The child
leaves a warm, intimate, familiar place for a large, confusing, strange
place; how well that transition is effected can determine the child's
acceptance of school and all that it offers and represents.

During life we make many *situational adjustments*, most very small,
but some major ones, like getting married, going to college or
starting work, becoming a parent, entering hospital. For a child,
starting school is probably the most challenging adjustment (see
Figure 21.2). Linked with the concept of situational adjustment are
anticipatory socialisation and *status passage*. For the child the new
status is becoming a pupil. Pupilhood is a special status within

220

Figure 21.2 *Starting school*

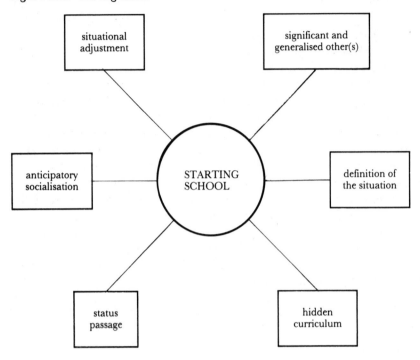

childhood, a status our society compulsorily bestows on all its new members. We do not have a choice whether or not to go to school and so a successful adjustment is essential. In school the age and sex statuses which operate in the home and in society generally are *confirmed* by teachers' behaviour and school organisation, but a new status is *conferred*, that of ability/achievement, as evaluation is a fundamental feature of pupilhood. (This is a point I shall return to later.)

Linked to the smoothness of status passage is anticipatory social-isation, the process whereby an individual adopts the attitudes of a group to which he does not yet belong – the professional socialisa-tion of teachers is an illustration. The more effectively it is carried out the smoother the transition into the new status. Some children learn about school from older children in the family, but some form of pre-school education is undoubtedly the best method of preparation.

The importance of the provision of nursery-type education lies not so much in lasting academic gains but in personal and social advantages. It prepares children for full-time schooling by gradually adjusting them to being with other children, responding to relative strangers who have charge of them, and experiencing being in an orderly, controlled environment.

Since the Plowden Report (1967) the importance of parental involvement has been highlighted and given official recognition. The provisions of the Education Acts of 1980, 1981 and 1986 allow parental views considerable weight and so successful home-school links have become more formally sanctioned. First contacts between home and school need to be handled sensitively and thoughtfully to assist the transition stage and also to lay secure foundations for future parental involvement. The methods adopted by schools will vary but are likely to include one or more of the following:

1 Parents are invited to visit the school in the term prior to admission – often at an informal gathering to acquaint parents with the organisation of the school, to get to know the head-teacher, class teacher and each other.
2 On the first day parents are invited to stay with the children in the classroom, but the visit is kept relatively short so that the children are not overwhelmed or over-tired and leave happy and settled.
3 Some headteachers or nursery/reception class teachers make home visits to new entrants.
4 An extension of this contact to be found in some LEAs is the appointment of home/school liaison teachers whose role is to prepare parents and children for the transition. In examples 3 and 4 it is a good idea for the contact to take information booklets, story books and a specially prepared pack of learning materials.
5 Many schools adopt a staggered admission system over a week and operate vertical grouping or family grouping where older children help the new ones settle in and provide good models.
6 Another interesting introduction in a small number of schools is to use any spare room as a parents' room, where they can meet and talk to the class teacher and work together should they be involved as volunteer helpers.

Teachers and lower infants seek to make their classrooms warm, friendly and secure places; they present themselves as surrogate parents who care, are approachable and supportive when needed.

But a classroom is also a very busy, active place into which the teacher must bring some order and it is in response to this contextual demand that teachers exercise their authority and children are expected to comply. The initiative in classroom interaction rests with the teacher and one only has to observe a reception class at the beginning and end of a term to appreciate the amount of social learning that has taken place. The problem of social adjustment is the problem of finding a role, and the *definition of the situation* determines one's role. The dual socialising aims of the primary school referred to earlier held that socialisation into the ritualised formal organisation represented by the authority of teachers is a paramount necessity. The experienced teacher who faces a new class faces a semi-defined situation, but for the child in school for the first time the total situation will be unfamiliar and confusing. Many teachers maintain that the first few days and weeks of school are the time to establish and make secure their dominance. Elsewhere (Tattum, 1986), I have discussed the idea of consistency management, maintaining that children work better in a context that is secure and stable; they prefer to know what is required of them, to be occupied, and to be treated fairly. The twin concerns of consistency and coherence are important in the creation of a well-managed classroom that is task-oriented, and is predictable in that children know what is expected of them and are clear about the consequences of not conforming to expectations.

To achieve consistency teachers need to concentrate on four broad themes, namely,

1 Detailed *planning and preparation* – which extends beyond subject matter, activities and materials and gives due attention to pupil groups, basic rules and procedures, appropriate consequences and other organisational features.
2 Careful teaching of *rules and procedures* – these may be conduct rules (governing entering and leaving the room, talking and shouting out, movement, the distribution and collection of materials and so on) and work habits (neatness, effort, sharing but not copying, competition, public assessment and so on).
3 Frequent *monitoring of pupil behaviour* to prevent problems from arising. In early encounters, consistency on the part of the teacher enables pupils to learn that their action will result in consequences or rewards.

4 Coherent *communication of instructions and information* to reduce confusion. This also means that a teacher circulates amongst the children, makes individual contact with as many of the class as possible, and so communicates involvement and awareness.

But situations are fluid and so if a teacher is to retain control she must renew her definition from moment to moment; children, regardless of age, will seek to impose their own definition of the situation to their own advantage. Classrooms are complex places which provide an arena where children learn to come to terms with new significant others and begin to develop a social awareness of what it means to be a member of a group with alternative and conflicting needs, demands, attitudes, norms etc. Waller (1932) has argued that conflicting definitions of the situation held by teachers and pupils are the basis of all discipline problems, writing that classrooms are in 'perilous states of equilibrium'. The above concept stems from W Thomas' dictum, 'If men define situations as real, then they are real in their consequences'. This has led interactionists to see social action as a product of the situation and the actor's definition of it. This does not mean, however, that each situation has to be defined anew and in a vacuum; situations have histories, and predefinitions of the situation arise from institutional requirements and philosophies of education, and in turn serve to buttress the predominance of the teacher's definition of the situation, containing as they do sanctions of varying degrees of formality and influence, from loss of privileges to being sent to the head.

The 'hidden curriculum' is one of those catch-all phrases so popular in education; it is elaborate, pervasive, and yet, ambiguous. I shall resist an attempt to define it and focus on some aspects particularly applicable to the child starting school. That children come to terms with the hidden curriculum is essential for their personal survival and success as pupils, because failure to do so will result in failure in the formal curriculum too. Central features of the hidden curriculum can be viewed as a variant on the '3Rs' namely, *rules*, *ritual* and *routine*. These are the social control mechanisms used most 'overtly' to regularise behaviour along adult prescribed lines. Rituals and routines occur in filing into school, sitting in set places, the daily work pattern, morning assembly and many others. Rules are even more expansive and complex systems for children to learn. Elsewhere (Tattum, 1982), I have drawn up a five-fold categorisation:

Legal/quasi-legal rules
Organisational rules
Contextual rules
Personal rules
Relational rules

It is not possible to discuss each of the five categories in this paper but I shall combine the last three with a consideration of Hargreaves *et al*'s (1975) five themes of talk, movement, time, teacher-pupil relationships, and pupil-pupil relationships. Each theme contains a wide range of rules. Some are common to most teachers – such as not talking when teacher is talking; others are more individual – such as the level of noise permissible, or talking to your neighbour. Within the rule system in a classroom children will test the teacher out as they explore the social parameters of acceptable behaviour. Relational rules regulate the interpersonal interactions between teacher and pupil, and pupil and pupil (as applied by teacher). As teachers check the behaviour of pupils, they expect unquestioned compliance – a query, hesitancy, or gesture of dissent, by word or action, can be interpreted as a challenge to teacher authority. Obedience, politeness and respect are the essential rules that teachers hold.

> Rules of action cover acts of defiance, refusal to cooperate, rudeness and disrespect, dishonesty, physical violence, or threat of it. Rules of word would extend to answering back, giving cheek, arguing or dissenting, abuse, swearing, and mouthing off. Teachers reduce pupil-pupil relational rules to consideration and care – no bullying, physical or verbal abuse, theft, cheating, or copying.
>
> (Tattum, 1982)

Jackson (1968) deals in detail with the hidden curriculum and summarises the context of classroom learning for children as coping with pressures from teacher and other children. First of all, he writes, life in classrooms is learning to 'live in crowds', involving delay, denial, interruption, and distraction. As a preparation for life it teaches a child how to tolerate frustration, boredom and passivity. Learning to accept the public assessment of others – teachers and fellow pupils – is Jackson's second factor. The young child soon discovers that success and failure are going to be measured in precise terms and schools employ a wide array of rewards and punishments in this evaluation. But children are not passive participants in this process and Holt (1969) describes how children devise preservation of self strategies, early experiences of learning the social gamesmanship practised by adults as a way of deceiving one another. These strategies are:

- looking attentive rather than actually attending
- acting docile to avoid punishment
- playing the game of 'right-answerism'
- acting stupid as a way of opting out of the pressure to learn.

Jackson also writes that 'the fact of unequal power is a third feature of classroom life to which students must become accustomed'. No matter how inviting teachers make their classrooms, they exercise power to teach punctuality, attentiveness, compliance and restraint.

In summary, starting school can be both exciting and distressing for the young child as he seeks to adjust to the demands of the new social context and the quality and quantity of relationships. The only activity which occupies a greater proportion of a child's day is sleep (although television must be a close third) and schooling continues for at least 11 years. In secondary school many teenagers become disaffected as they reject the pupil status. Have the seeds of that disaffection been sown in the primary school? Can we do more to help young children develop positive self-images as learners and social selves that are positive and healthy?

References

Berger, P L, 1966 *Invitation to Sociology – A Humanistic Perspective* Harmondsworth: Penguin Books.
Cooley, C H, 1902 *Human Nature and the Social Order* New York: Charles Scribner.
Geer, B, 1968 'Teaching' in Sills, D S (ed) *International Encyclopedia of the Social Sciences*, *15* New York: Free Press.
HMSO, 1967 *Children and their Primary Schools* (The Plowden Report) London: HMSO.
Kando, T M, 1977 *Social Interaction* Saint Louis: C V Mosley Co.

226

Lindesmith, A R, Strauss, A L and Denzin, N K, 1977 *Social Psychology* New York: Holt, Rinehart and Winston.

Mead, G H, 1956 in Strauss, A (ed) *On Social Psychology: Selected Papers* Chicago: University of Chicago Press.

Shipman, M D, 1972 *Childhood – a sociological perspective* Windsor: NFER.

Tattum, D P (ed) 1986 *Management of Disruptive Pupil Behaviour in Schools* Chichester: Wiley.

Tattum, D P and Tattum, E (forthcoming) *Social Education and Personal Development in Primary Schools*.

Waller, W, 1932 *The Sociology of Teaching* New York: Wiley.

22 Rule-frame and relationships
Andrew Pollard

One of the most important issues in personal and social education concerns the development, within each individual child, of social awareness regarding themselves in relation to others. Children are active learners in this process and among the most important influences on them are the provision, action and guidance which they experience, interpret and respond to at school. As teachers, we thus have opportunities and responsibilities to develop the social climate of our classrooms so that the atmosphere is as favourable as possible to the children's development of personal and social awareness.

In one sense this is simply to reaffirm the importance of 'good relationships' in primary school practice. However, it also provides an opportunity to analyse the issues more deeply and to try to identify some of the underlying elements which facilitate or compromise such relationships. The development of suitable conceptual tools is, it can be argued, an essential part of such reflective practice (Schon, 1983; Woods, 1985).

In this brief paper I try to develop a concept which is intended to be helpful in describing and analysing the social climate within a school or classroom, and which might be used in processes of review and evaluation or when policy options are being considered. I have called the concept 'rule-frame' and perhaps the best way to introduce its meaning is through an example.

Rule-frame in an infant school

A few years ago I was deputy head of an open-plan infant school. Relationships among staff and children seemed to be fairly good but, nevertheless, the children often became rather 'high' at certain times and in some parts of the school. This tended to affect the atmosphere in the school as a whole. It also seemed to lead the children to exhibit less care than was otherwise normal – regarding both other children and their school work.

I produced an analysis of this which was intended for discussion at a staff meeting and, in an embryonic way, this analysis used several of the concepts which I want to discuss in this paper. An edited version of this discussion document follows.

Points for discussion

Problem: a tendency towards a rather noisy and high school atmosphere which does not seem to be conducive to careful and high quality thought or considerate relationships.

Analysis: I think this is produced by a generally low degree of 'rule-frame' for many settings and phases. The children sometimes think that they can get away with a bit too much! These understandings seem to be taken for granted but we could try to change them.

This cannot be done by confrontation. Rather, we ought to aim to use our concerted influence to initiate and negotiate new understandings which might be more interpersonally constructive. In addition, we ought to be more positive regarding the curriculum and look at various organisational issues which could also contribute to creating a more consistently productive atmosphere.

A In order to improve the quality of the curriculum and activities which we offer for the children we could

- *Coordinate the curriculum more* The aim here would be to provide a more collective sense of school direction and purpose. This would enable sharing of ideas, materials, exhibitions, stimuli, educational visits. It would require planning well in advance and ought also to improve progression through the school.

- *Introduce a more child-centred start to the day* Things which children bring in, experiences they have had, etc. could then be used immediately. Each classroom could be prepared so that stimuli for art, craft, topic work could be taken up directly.

- *Provide more play apparatus* – particularly on the playground, so that better alternatives to chasing, fighting, teasing are offered.

- *Reconsider policies for wet playtimes/dinnertimes* Leaving the children unsupervised or weakly supervised seems bound to create difficulties.
- *Stress 'sharing and caring'* in a series of assemblies and apply the theme to the school.

B In order to improve our organisation so that we produce smooth transitions between phases and settings and provide more stable routines we could

- Organise hall and assembly times to come at start or end of work session only.
- Hold assembly in central areas (shoes have to be changed to enter hall).
- Develop more controlled exits from classrooms – especially with dinner ladies. Coordinate policies of all staff on child movement in the open area.
- Ensure that all staff are in the classrooms at the start of sessions.
- Develop more regular and predictable daily school routines where possible – eg hall times, the same every day for each class?
- Minimise interruptions to classroom sessions for administration etc.

Four reasons behind these prescriptions:

1 To introduce more consistent and clear-cut rules for behaviour and work at various times and places as a first step in negotiating new taken-for-granted understandings about them.
2 To motivate the children more and provide incentives for collective involvement and compliance.
3 To provide more secure routines for stability.
4 To eliminate disruptions to teaching/learning sessions as far as possible.

Looking back at this document now is an interesting experience. Perhaps the most important impression for me is to see the links between my concerns to maintain order and control, to develop the curriculum and children's learning and to increase the quality of the interpersonal climate of the school. There are tensions and dilemmas here but at the nub of these concerns are the issues of expectations and of the way in which behaviour is 'framed'. How did the children expect themselves and others to behave in different situations and what were the effects of those expectations? What could we, as a group of staff, do about it? In fact this document itself was not discussed with my colleagues – perhaps I thought it to be provocative. Yet the issues it began to raise are of enormous importance to school life. Indeed, I would argue that the expectations and atmosphere of a school provide a type of infrastructure – without them a great deal would be impossible to do. The ways such rules are created, 'framed' and interpreted is thus of the greatest possible significance.

Schools and social morality

Personal and social education seems to me to involve, among other things, the development of what we might call a sense of social morality. In social contexts and in interaction with others, children learn how to conduct themselves. Of course, children can be seen as acting strategically in order to cope with particular situations, but it should not be forgotten that part of acting in such ways requires the interpretation of social conventions and expectations and of appropriateness. In a school context the overall climate – or institutional bias as I have preferred to call it (Pollard, 1985) – may encompass sets of rules about behaviour which permeate through school life, as suggested in the example above. In a sense, and following Durkheim, when such a coherent and accepted institutional bias exists, it represents the dominance of a type of collective solidarity over individualism. Each participant in school life then regulates their actions in the light of their sense of the prevailing social understandings. This is not a static situation, though; individuals also negotiate, perhaps on the basis of deeply held values and interests, to develop new understandings.

A similar analysis can be made at classroom level. Here the concept which, in my view, best describes the social climate and nature of teacher-child relationships is that of 'working consensus'. Teachers and children are seen as being engaged in continuous processes of negotiation. They each act strategically to cope with the difficulties which are routinely faced in classrooms but, in addition, there is a phenomenon of interpersonal exchange. Both teachers and children recognise that the other has the power to threaten their classroom survival if provoked. A working consensus, in which each recognises the legitimate interests of the other, may thus be negotiated and, in many instances, 'good relationships' and a positive classroom climate becomes established. Less positive types of truce are also possible.

The main point of the present argument is that a working consensus defines and legitimates a type of collective solidarity and moral order for the classroom. Further, it is on the basis of the understandings reached between teachers and children that the classroom sense of order, standards and justice is established.

Turning directly to the concept of rule-frame, I would suggest that such a concept can be related both to the working consensus at classroom level and to the institutional bias at whole-school level. In each case it describes the nature of social understandings about behaviour which have been produced by the negotiations of the participants. Such social understandings are contextually dynamic and this is where the concept of rule-frame is particularly useful. Understandings and 'appropriate' behaviour can be seen as varying in patterned ways, over time, setting and activity and also with regard to the people who are involved. 'Rule-frame' provides one way of analysing such variations.

Criteria for analysing rule-frame

There are several dimensions which can be applied to describe rule-frame but perhaps the most important one is that of 'strength'. If the rule-frame is strong then actions are clearly circumscribed by social expectations. If the rule-frame is weak then more individualised actions are possible. Teachers can often control the strength of rule-frame through their actions when using their position to initiate and lead. For instance, differences resulting from the presentation of emphatic instructions compared with casual requests would normally be clear.

A second dimension of rule-frame concerns its content. This encompasses the meaning of the understandings themselves and is likely to take into account such factors as time, space, movement, activity, noise level and standard of work. At a whole-school level the content of rules is most clearly seen through assemblies.

232

Closely related to content is breadth. This reflects the range and comprehensiveness of understandings which have become established. This can vary. For instance, it is not at all unusual for a class or school to run very smoothly in all 'normal' situations, only to be thrown out of gear by something unusual – a visit outside the school, a classroom crisis, a fire-drill.

A fourth dimension of rule-frame is that of consistency. This relates to the degree of variation in the strength of content of rule-frame over time. Consistency might be expected in the same situations over a period of time – certainly a lack of predictability is likely to be viewed negatively by children. Consistency can also be studied as rule-frame varies during sequences in the phases and episodes of teaching/learning sessions. A session may move dramatically between periods in which behaviour is highly circumscribed and those in which 'anything goes', or it may, at the other pole, reflect a relatively calm seamlessness in behavioural expectation.

The fifth, and final, criterion which, I would suggest, can be usefully applied to analyse rule-frame, is that of legitimacy. This is of the utmost importance, for it provides a clear indicator of the degree and quality of teacher-child exchange in the establishment of behavioural understandings. After all, it is quite possible to conceive of a set of classroom rules being imposed by a powerful teacher which children have little option other than to accept. In such a case the working consensus would reflect the power differential but would lack a negotiated moral foundation. It is thus possible for the rules and the rule-frame in operation in particular situations to be perfectly understood by children but for them to be resented and contested. When rules are regarded as 'unfair' then their legitimacy is low. Where there has been open negotiation and rules are based on a recognition of the interests of the other then understandings will be 'shared' and the legitimacy of rules, and of particular levels of rule-frame, will be higher. The degree of legitimacy of rule-frame reveals the degree of acceptance of the content and application of rules.

We thus have five criteria which might be applied to the analysis of rules and rule-frame over time:

Strength
Content

233

Breadth
Consistency
Legitimacy

I would suggest that at both school and classroom levels the nature of rules and the patterns in variation of rule-frame over time are of considerable significance for personal and social education. In a sense they describe the tacit moral curriculum which is offered to the children by example and through direct experience, rather than the social curriculum that is overtly projected by explicit prescription and advice. The analysis begins to describe the form by which interpersonal relationships in school and classroom life are actually lived and practised. If the strength, content, breadth, consistency and legitimacy of rules and conventions within a school or classroom are weak and limited, then the children may experience relatively incoherent, unclear – and possibly threatening – examples of inter-personal relations. It seems likely that in such circumstances the children's personal and social awareness will develop in directions which are relatively defensive, individualistic and insular. In contrast, I would suggest that the existence of a clear, comprehensive and openly negotiated institutional bias and/or working consensus is likely to produce a much more positive climate for personal and social development.

Conclusion

Personal and social education is often discussed as if it constitutes a curriculum area. In many secondary schools it even appears on timetables and published schemes of work are available. In a primary school context such an approach seems to me to objectify and demean a set of issues which have always been central to the stated aims and personal commitments of many of those who teach young children. However, it is fair to say that such ideals have not always been thought through and actual provision and practice sometimes falls well short of realising them. Perhaps such problems arise partly because of the difficulties in conceptualising and analysing such tacit, ephemeral and interpersonally complex issues – hence this attempt to develop the concept of rule-frame. It is offered here in the hope that it might provide one way for reflective teachers to analyse an important aspect of the more 'hidden' and tacit everyday contexts through which, by example and experience, personal and social education takes place.

References

Pollard, A, 1985 *The Social World of the Primary School* London: Cassell.

Pollard, A, forthcoming 'Relationships, rules and control in primary classrooms' in Cullingford, C (ed) *The Role of the Primary Teacher* London: Robert Royce.

Schon, D, 1983 *The Reflective Practitioner* London: Temple Smith.

Woods, P E, 1985 'Sociology, ethnography and teacher practice' in *Teaching and Teacher Education*, *1*(1).

23 Personal and social education through cooperative and developmental group work in the primary school: questions for research and development

Doug Harwood

It seems important that any book which aims to help teachers reflect upon the nature of personal and social education and pastoral care in the primary school should devote some space to looking at class-room methodology. In this context, the emergence of cooperative or collaborative group work as a key strategy has been perhaps the most significant development during the last decade. This approach, particularly in the form referred to as 'developmental group work' has been prominent amongst recent initiatives to develop personal and social education in secondary schools, following the pioneering work of Button (1981) and the *Active Tutorial Work Project* (Baldwin and Wells, 1979–84). Although originally intended for use in tutorial time, attempts have been made more recently to extend these strategies to other areas of the curriculum.[1]

Despite their secondary pedigree, these innovations are being increasingly adopted by primary teachers. ATW training has already been pioneered in 40 primary schools and a growing number of LEAs are implementing the approach with this age-level, sometimes supported by the education departments of colleges and universities (Thacker, 1985; Stoate and Thacker, this volume). It is both right and responsible that primary teachers should be initially cautious about attempts to foist secondary practices upon younger

[1] The *Active Tutorial Work* project changed its name to the *Active Learning* project, in order to communicate this broadening of the application of its strategies.

age groups. The purpose of this paper is to address those questions likely to be raised by the sceptical primary teacher:

What is meant by cooperative group work, especially in the form referred to as developmental group work?

What, if anything, do these recent secondary initiatives add to what is already practised in primary schools?

Are these approaches effective in furthering children's learning, especially at primary age?

What questions does the strategy raise for future research and development?

What is meant by cooperative group work?

In its simplest form, cooperative or collaborative group work involves 'pupils (being) placed in groups (of 2–6) and given a joint task to be undertaken through cooperation' (Yeomans, 1983). The teacher is not usually present in the group, although he or she may visit the pupils in order to monitor progress. The group is therefore self-directing, with information, ideas, skills and feedback generated mainly by the children through their own research and discussion.

One problem with the very simplicity of this definition is that it disguises the potential variety of the strategy in practice. Good and Brophy (1987) have outlined the many types of organisational and incentive structures that can be identified under the umbrella label of cooperative group work. Pupils can be organised to pursue either 'group' goals (in which they cooperate to create a common group product) or individual goals (in which they help one another to fulfil personal objectives through 'peer-tutoring' etc). The pupils may be given either 'differentiated roles', in which 'different students perform different tasks' on behalf of the group, or 'undifferentiated roles', in which 'each student has the same task'. The groups may or may not operate in the context of explicit incentives or rewards, where either individuals or teams compete for marks or grades. There may be differences in the degree to which individual members are made accountable to the rest of the group. Clearly, cooperative group work comes in many guises, and involves the teacher in deciding between a number of alternative possibilities.

How does 'developmental group work' relate to these organisational variables? Some idea of its distinctive flavour is described in qualitative terms by Stoate and Thacker (Chapter 18). In addition some of its chief characteristics have been revealed by the analysis of

15 tape-recorded, secondary school lessons and five published VTR extracts, each using ATW or Button-type strategies,[2] as follows:

1 The pupils usually work independently of the teacher in either pairs or small groups on a series of tasks or questions identified and controlled by the teacher. In none of the lessons observed, did the pupils themselves choose tasks or methods of working. This process was regularly punctuated by teacher-led plenaries, in which all the pupils discussed their findings together.
2 There was an equal balance between group and individual goals. Usually these two types of objective implicitly coalesced so that they were the same for both individual and group learning.
3 In most lessons, all the pupils had the same task and were therefore not given separate roles. Only in activities such as 'preparing for a visitor' and in games and simulations, were the pupils occasionally given differentiated roles.
4 Pupils were only made accountable to the rest of the group in situations where they had been given these 'specialist' roles. Even here, the accountability was usually loosely and informally applied. How much or how little the pupils contributed to the group was usually for them to decide individually. It was clear, however, that the group itself was accountable to the teacher in the plenary sessions.
5 In the great majority of lessons there were no additional incentives, beyond the implicit expectation that the task should be completed satisfactorily.

In conclusion, although it involves a broad and eclectic range of different workshop activities, 'developmental group work' can be

[2] The VTR extracts were:
i 'A Way of Learning' by the Active Learning Project, St Martin's College, Lancaster;
ii 'Small Group Discussion in the Classroom', Health Education Council;
iii 'Developmental Work in Tutorial Groups', ILEA
    (a) First and second year pupils participating in a range of structured tutorial activities
    (b) First and second year pupils receiving visitors in a classroom
    (c) Using developmental group work techniques to explore the issue of drugs in education with teachers.
(A paper: Harwood, D L, *The nature of teacher-pupil interactions in Active Tutorial Work*, is in preparation.)

identified as a particular type of cooperative group work, characterised mainly by a coalescence of personal and group goals; with
mainly undifferentiated and shared pupil-roles; a virtual absence of
individual accountability or incentive structures and quite a high
level of direction from the teacher in identifying a sequence of
questions, issues and activities.

How far is this strategy already practised in primary schools?

One limitation with regard to this question, is that only the general
implementation of cooperative group work in primary schools can
be described. So far none of the research has differentiated between
the different types of organisation available. There are no separate
data on 'developmental group work'.

First impressions might suggest that there is nothing particularly
new in the approach, as far as the primary school is concerned. In
her review of the origins of cooperative group work, Tann (1980) has
been able to trace its roots back to the beginnings of the progressive
movement in American and British primary schools, especially
through its close association with Deweyan values, ie child-
centredness, democratic relationships, respect for the individual,
discovery and discussion. However, there was no evidence about the
extent of implementation until the Plowden Report (1967), which
gave support in the following terms:

> in this way children learn to get along together, help one
> another and realise their own strengths and weaknesses as well
> as those of others . . . (they) . . . make their meaning clearer to
> themselves by having to explain it to others (and) benefit from
> being caught up in the thrust and counter-thrust of conversa-
> tion in a small group of children similar to themselves.

Plowden encouraged the view that cooperative group work was
already being widely adopted in the primary schools of the 1960s.
When asked what relative proportion of time should be given
respectively to 'class instruction', 'group teaching' and 'individual
work', teachers replied that 'group teaching' should be the main
priority. Unfortunately, there were no systematic observations to

cross-check the impressions derived from these teachers' opinions and self-reports. It was not until the 1970s that a series of classroom-based research reports began to suggest that, in reality, cooperative group work was infrequently practised (Bealing, 1972; Boydell, 1975; Bennett, 1976, 1978; HMI, 1978; Galton, Simon and Croll, 1980). The ORACLE Study, based upon the systematic observation of teacher and pupil behaviour in 58 classrooms, found that:

> although pupils are normally seated in groups . . . in practice it seems most pupils are normally engaged in their own individual tasks. Co-operative groupwork, where pupils co-operate together to solve a problem, construct a model, etc, was found to be very rare. Many pupils never experience it at all.
>
> (Simon, 1980)

The ORACLE findings thus highlighted the distinction between 'grouping', which teachers use as their main method of organising children and 'group work', where children actually work together cooperatively. Galton (1981) concluded that cooperative group work was 'a neglected art'.

Of course, the ORACLE research is now almost 10 years old. Since its publication, a growing number of workshop techniques supporting collaborative groupwork have been made available to the primary teacher, through such initiatives as ATW, the Health Education Project and the World Studies Project.[3] The picture may be very different now. However, even the most recent surveys continue to confirm the ORACLE findings. Barker-Lunn (1984) found that cooperative group work ranked only fourteenth in the order of frequency of classroom activities reported by the teachers themselves and that 'for the most part, groupwork involved each member working individually'. Mortimore et al (1986) reported that 'collaborative work . . . was not frequently seen, although there was a slight increase as pupils moved up the school'. In conclusion, it would seem that cooperative group work is not yet widely practised in primary schools although there does need to be a regular mapping of the situation to keep up with developments. Remember-

---

[3] For example: Rees, Sue (1986), *Health Education: Drugs and the Primary School Child*, Tacade/Health Education Council. Schools Council/ Rowntree World Studies 8–13 Project, St Martin's College, Lancaster.

ing the mythologies that were sometimes constructed to describe the Plowden classroom, we should be continually vigilant about the possibilities of a mismatch between rhetoric and reality. Systematic observation is a necessary corrective.

Is cooperative group work effective in furthering children's learning, especially at primary age-levels?

The previous section has indicated that the adoption of recent secondary initiatives involving cooperative and developmental group work would probably add significantly to what is currently practised in primary schools. Certainly teachers of young children have been under increasing pressure to implement changes in this direction (HMI, 1982). Yeomans (1983) has summarised the theoretical claims for cooperative group work, as follows:

(a) that the very process of learning through groupwork can be a rewarding and valuable experience;
(b) that groupwork enables children of all abilities to learn more in their academic subjects, by exploring ideas, constructing knowledge together, clarifying meanings, etc;
(c) that working in groups helps children in their personal development, especially in regard to self-confidence and independence ... social skills are also developed as commitment to the group grows, and with it feelings of empathy, consideration for others and the acceptance of joint responsibility;
(d) the processes involved in the collaboration are seen as valuable learning experiences in themselves.

How far can we be sure that children, especially of primary age, will benefit in the ways suggested? One of the problems of assessing the research is that a variety of forms of organisation and educational objective can be subsumed under the 'collaborative group work' label. In addition to the alternatives already discussed, the method can be used for 'low level' learning, such as recall of information and literal comprehension; or for the 'high level' learning of concepts and ideas, the analysis of problems, judgement and evaluation; or for the development of general procedural and social skills. The work can be closely structured by the teacher through the use of key questions and targets, as is often the case with 'developmental groupwork', or it can be entirely open-ended. It can take place in a context of competition for rewards between the participating groups or individuals, or it can be organised so that all groups are contributing cooperatively towards some larger project.

Against such a complex background, it is not surprising that in their recent reviews of the American and British literature, both Yeomans (1983) and Bennett (1985) have expressed doubts about the quality and reliability of the current research evidence. Moreover none of this research has attempted to evaluate 'developmental group work' as a special type. Nevertheless, Yeomans has argued that the following tentative conclusions can be justified for cooperative group work in general.

Academic achievement

1 Cooperative learning techniques are no worse than traditional techniques, and in many cases they are significantly better.
2 For low-level learning performance, such as recall of information and literal comprehension, cooperative learning techniques appear to be more effective than traditional techniques to the degree that they use:
 a a structured, focused, schedule of instruction;
 b individual accountability for performance among group members;
 c a well-defined group reward system, including rewards or recognition for successful groups.

(It should be noted that these results were obtained mainly from the system of peer-tutoring, which bears little resemblance to the developmental approach to cooperative group work under discussion in this paper. In fact the method retains 'many fundamental features of traditional whole class instruction'.)

3 For high level cognitive learning, such as identification of concepts, analysis of problems, judgement and evaluation, it is strongly claimed that less directed techniques involving greater pupil autonomy and collaboration, and participation

in decision-making, may be more effective than traditional individualised learning. Much more evidence is required to substantiate this particular claim.

Personal and social development
1 Cooperative learning techniques have strong and consistent effects on relationships between pupils of different ethnic backgrounds.
2 Mutual concern among pupils is increased regardless of the structure used.
3 There is some indication that self-confidence and self-esteem are improved.
4 Pupils in classes using co-operative learning generally report increased liking of school.

Finally, Yeomans reported encouragingly, that

The American evidence suggests that co-operative groupwork is more effective than either traditional class teaching or competitive group work, using peer-tutoring techniques based on rewards, for both academic achievement and social development.

Despite these positive general conclusions, there still remain some important questions: Do all individuals necessarily benefit from the cooperative group work experience? Do all pupils find cooperative group work rewarding and valuable? Does group work disproportionately benefit the already articulate and extrovert? Does it favour the high as opposed to low achievers? Will some pupils be disadvantaged if too much time is devoted to such work?

Slavin (1983), whilst accepting that cooperative groups are superior to individuals in problem solving, warns that in the process some children may actually achieve or learn nothing, because of the dominance of other members of the group. He concludes that, at the level of individual learning, cooperative groups may prove detrimental.

In his review of earlier studies, Bennett (1985) has also found differences in achievement between those giving and those receiving help. In the case of the former, there is a positive relationship between giving help and achievement, but there is no such correlation for those receiving help. Since high ability children are the main sources of help, it follows that it is these children who seem to benefit most from cooperative group work. The learning of average and low ability children may therefore be put at risk in some cooperative group work settings.

The research conclusions described so far have made no reference to the influence of age-level upon the effectiveness of cooperative group work. Yet this is of crucial importance to the primary teacher. In this context, the general view emerging from the research is one of caution. Both Bennett (1985) and Good and Brophy (1987) agree that the method 'may be less relevant and more difficult to implement for teachers working with primary grade students'. Peterson *et al* (quoted in Bennett, 1985) go further in suggesting that 'pupils as young as seven or eight are unlikely to have the social or cognitive skills necessary to work effectively in small groups'. Children apparently made appropriate responses to requests in only half the cases and the process of receiving answers and explanations from other children was not related to achievement. There is other research, which supports this position. Boydell (1975) concluded that 'it might be more difficult than is generally supposed to set up the group conditions envisaged in the Plowden Report' and stated that 'observed sex bias militates against group discussions involving boys and girls'. On the other hand, both of these reports were based mainly upon quantitative analysis, 'rather than on the content and quality of the answers and explanations offered' (Bennett, 1985).

Even those studies which have analysed transcripts of children's self-directed discussions more qualitatively, however, have sometimes revealed negative findings. Roth (1983), although finding that three-quarters of the talk was task-related, also discovered that most of this was of 'low order', 'not all responses were correct' and 'explanations were rare'. Tann (1981) analysed 96 examples of problem-solving discussions in cooperative groups, with children aged 10+ and 11+. Each session lasted 20 minutes and was fully transcribed. She was able to identify some of the constraints which hindered group cooperation. Although the groups often provided solutions and displayed evidence of satisfaction, analysis of the interaction revealed many problems, such as the general lack of questioning; of risk taking, especially by girls; the number of silent members; the amount of fooling around by low-ability older boys.

Tann concluded that the composition of the groups was an important factor for successful group work.

Tann (1981) also collected data on pupils' attitudes to cooperative group work through the use of open-ended, written feedback. The responses revealed 'a wide divergence between pupils' attitude to group work and the potential that research suggests exists in this mode of learning'. Pupils reported 'that they did not feel that they were in a learning situation'. Another cause for concern was that, despite owning a high level of enjoyment from the activity, the majority felt that they had gained nothing. In a similar way, detailed analysis of transcripts by the Ford Teaching Project (1975) also revealed that the internal dynamics of cooperative group work, especially the rivalry between some members, could sometimes hinder work.

Clearly, cooperative group work is no panacea and needs to be implemented with caution. However, not all the research reports of work with younger children have been so negative. Stauffer (1969) used collaborative group work successfully with six and seven year old children learning to read. Tough (1977) found that even nursery and infant children were able to hold exploratory discussions. Biott (1984) demonstrated, through transcript evidence, that older primary children could use quite sophisticated procedural and thinking skills in cooperative group work settings. Finally in their chapter in this volume, Stoate and Thacker provide illustrations from pupil feedback and teacher observations of some of the positive outcomes of 'developmental group work' with middle school children.

Research into cooperative methods is relatively undeveloped at present. The limited evidence available at present suggests that there are potential gains for some children, possibly a majority. However, it is also apparent that there are sufficient grounds for caution to dissuade teachers from attempting to introduce collaborative group work across too broad a curriculum front too quickly, especially with younger children. Instead there should be a phased introduction in specific parts of the curriculum, accompanied by some training in cooperative methods for the children themselves. Almost all the research, including case studies, has been carried out with experimental groups, in which the methods still had novelty value for both pupils and teachers (Good and Brophy, 1987). This could have had two opposing effects. On the one hand, the freshness of the approach could inflate the level of positive response. Alternatively, the lack of experience of participants could depress the outcomes, both in terms of quality of process and level of achievement.

Question for future research and development

Cooperative group work is clearly at an early formative stage of development, with many issues requiring urgent study and experimentation. Some of these will now be discussed.

Assessment

Interaction between pupils during cooperative group work can be highly complex. 'The talk seems to lack form and direction and it might even degenerate to squabbling' (Biott, 1984). It often seems to defy analysis, never mind assessment. Moreover the ethos of group cooperation often seems to contradict notions of individual assessment. For these reasons, assessment of pupils' progress has been a neglected element in group work approaches, especially in the context of everyday teaching, as opposed to research. Yet, this can be a mistake. Unless some form of assessment is undertaken, how can we be sure that individual levels of performance and awareness have improved? It might be that group work merely exploits those personal qualities that pupils initially bring to the group, but does little to develop such capabilities. It might be that performance actually deteriorates for some pupils. Biott (1984) has drawn attention to the importance of assessment and feedback in giving status and meaning to those cooperative activities, which pupils often denounce as 'not real work'.

We need to be clear about exactly which skills and qualities we are aiming to develop through group work. Criteria for judging individual progress have been summarised in Rudduck (1979) and Biott (1984). However, the issue of assessment raises two further concerns. First is the danger that cooperative group work could become too closely associated with just one particular cluster of normative social values, ie trust, cooperativeness and commitment. It is noticeable how frequently these qualities are mentioned in this publication and there is already evidence that assessment does sometimes focus upon these 'cooperative skills' (Biott, 1983). It needs to be remembered that these qualities are not necessarily valuable as a basis for behaviour in all social circumstances. There are times when it can be unsafe to be trusting, irresponsible to be cooperative and foolish to be committed. Thus, cooperative group work might sometimes seem to foster too much conformity to an idealistic world of warm, cosy, harmonious groups. As such, it could be in danger of misrepresenting the balance of skills needed to survive in a world where there are often painful divisions of gender, race, class, employment. Instead, should not schools be attempting to encourage values of independence, alertness, awareness, self-confidence, intelligent flexibility and the ability to confront as well as support?

It is interesting that two decades ago the emphasis of innovation was more explicitly upon education for independence and personal autonomy, in which the teacher was encouraged to protect individual and minority disagreements within the group.[4] Then it seemed more acceptable to be an 'outsider'. This is not to argue that the present advocates of cooperative group work actively subscribe to any of the above distortions, but rather that teachers need to be vigilant in considering the total social context of discussion, when assessing group work skills. This is especially important, since teachers themselves probably have the strongest personal vested interest in producing uncritically cooperative, committed and trustworthy groups in school (Pollard, 1980).

The second issue concerns the social context of assessment. How individuals behave and the level of participatory skill demonstrated, can depend fundamentally upon the chemistry and composition of the particular group in which they work. Pupils' group work skills can never be assessed in a hermetically-sealed and protected environment equivalent to the examination hall. This makes it important that assessment should always be offered in a sympathetic, fully negotiated and formative rather than summative context. Biott (1984) includes examples of how transcripts and tape-recordings can be analysed for feedback purposes and offers valuable suggestions for how teachers might best communicate their assessments.

[4] For example, The Humanities Curriculum Project (see Rudduck, J 1983).

The teacher's role

For most of the time, teachers are purposely not present as members of the pupils' self-directing, cooperative groups. However, they may often visit groups during the course of the work and will usually be in charge of introductory and concluding reporting-back sessions. This raises questions about when, how and in what role a teacher should intervene. It can be all too easy for the teacher, unwittingly, to undermine the autonomy and independence gained by pupil groups, through inappropriate interventions. The ORACLE research revealed that, in the traditional 'grouping' system of organisation, the nature of the teacher's interaction with groups was 'overwhelmingly didactic'. Harwood (1986), investigating interaction in lessons using ATW methods, found that the teacher invariably became the centre of attention, when present in a group. It is therefore surprising that, in most manuals, the role of the teacher has been regarded as relatively unproblematic. Most recent approaches advocate either commitment to or reliance upon the personal intuition of each individual teacher (Baldwin and Wells, 1979; Button, 1981; Brandes and Ginnes, 1986). In contrast, in the early 1970s, the Humanities Project (Rudduck, 1983) recommended the adoption of a consistently 'impartial' role for the teacher. Harwood (1983) has suggested a pattern of role flexibility, operated self-consciously within a preferred hierarchy of alternative roles. These different alternatives need to be debated openly. Action research involving the audio-taping and systematic analysis of classroom interactions could also be useful in identifying possible pitfalls in the conduct of the teacher's role (Ford Teaching Project, 1975).

The place of group theory

One feature remarkably absent from recent cooperative group work manuals is any reference to theories of group behaviour. Nor is there any evidence of its inclusion in in-service courses dealing with developmental group work, despite the fact that the new pedagogy is explicitly a process-centred innovation, in which the group's behaviour can constitute a potential element of subject matter during feedback sessions. Many of the problems undermining pupils' performance may have a group dynamic rather than

248

individual explanation. In addition, both Tann (1980) and Bennett (1985) have commented upon the 'paucity of group interaction process studies', although important findings concerning the importance of group composition, in particular supporting the superiority of heterogeneous groups, have been reported (Good and Brophy, 1987). There are a number of publications[5] dealing with group work in education, although these are usually directed towards adults and older students. Harwood (1981) has argued for the inclusion of experiential and theoretical group work within teacher-education. Such approaches could also contribute towards the objective of enhancing the awareness and sensitivity of teachers, mentioned by McGuinness in chapter 32. Finally, Rudduck (1979) includes a section on observing and responding to the problems of group behaviour, which might be useful to teachers new to the field.

The training of pupils

It has already been mentioned that the low levels of performance skills demonstrated by some of the groups studied, may be the result of pupil inexperience. The complex skills involved in participating effectively in a group setting means that the competence of pupils, especially at the younger age-levels, should not be taken for granted. It follows that children should not be left to find their own way through the labyrinths of self-directed discussion, but should be helped by some form of training. Such training ought to involve the recognition and practice of the major procedural skills, such as listening, initiating, questioning, using evidence, supporting, facilitating, confronting, expressing feelings, using personal experience, trying to include everybody, keeping to the task, etc. In order to avoid too much teacher direction in this area, pupils could be encouraged to brainstorm the skills they feel they need in order to be effective in groups. Teachers can also help by sometimes structuring work so that group members have to depend upon each other and

[5] Abercrombie, M L J (1979), *Aims and Techniques of Group Teaching (4th Edition)*, Society for Research into Higher Education, Guildford, Surrey; Bramley, W (1979), *Group Tutoring*, Kogan Page, London; Jacques, D (1984), *Learning in Groups*, Croom Helm; Richardson, E (1967), *Group Study for Teachers*, Routledge & Kegan Paul; Rudduck, J (1978), *Learning Through Small Group Discussion*, Society for Research into Higher Education, Guildford, Surrey.

are made accountable to other group members (Johnson and Johnson, 1984). In general, however, the approach should usually be away from too much individual role specialisation, especially with young children, so that pupils are encouraged to broaden their own personal range of skills as much as possible.

Conclusion

Cooperative and developmental group work strategies have become central to innovation in personal and social education and pastoral provision in schools. There is evidence that its use is being increasingly developed with primary teachers. This paper has attempted to identify some of the issues that may be pertinent to future work.

Group work is still a new and developing approach to learning, especially in the primary school. Clearly further research, practice and experimentation is needed to test and refine its theoretical claims and procedures. Much of the emphasis of the empirical research so far has been to find justification for its use as an alternative to other approaches. However, Barrow (1984) has warned that the case for group work will inevitably be difficult to prove in this way, because of the intrinsic empirical and analytical obstacles involved. Yet the justification for the use of collaborative group work does not depend entirely upon its superiority as a strategy over other pedagogies. Human beings have to spend most of their lives in small groups.

> To be human is to be in relationship with other people . . . in order to learn how to develop and maintain those relationships, a group of people must be available as an arena, in which they can be learnt and practised.
> (Button, 1981)

It is no preparation for adult life if schooling provides no opportunities for learning, through personal experience and reflection, about the processes and problems of work in groups.

Research should therefore focus on finding ways of improving and refining the pedagogical processes involved in cooperative group work and on examining the reasons for differences in response between pupils, especially at the younger age-levels. An approach through self-critical classroom action research would seem to be the most effective way of involving interested teachers fully in this process, provided that it is continually open to external scrutiny, so that a parallel critique can evolve at the same time.

References

Baldwin, J and Wells, H, 1979–84 *Active Tutorial Work* Oxford: Blackwell.

Barker Lunn, J, 1984 'Junior School Teachers: their Methods and Practice' in *Educational Research*, *26*(3), p 178–88.

Barrow, R, 1984, 'Problems of Research into Group Work' in *Durham and Newcastle Research Review*, *X*(52), p 122–5.

Bealing, D, 1972 'The Organisation of Junior School Classrooms' in *Educational Research*, *14*, p 231–5.

Bennett, S N, 1976 *Teaching Styles and Pupil Progress* London: Open Books.

Bennett, S N, 1978 'Recent Research on Teaching: A Dream, A Belief and a Model' in *British Journal of Educational Psychology*, *48*, p 127–47.

Bennett, S N, 1985 'Interaction and Achievement in Classroom Groups' in Bennett, S N and Desforges, C, *Recent Advances in Classroom Research*, Br. Journ. of Ed. Psych. Monograph Series No 2 Scottish Academic Press, p 105–19.

Biott, C and Clough, M, 1983 'Co-operative Groupwork in Primary Classrooms' in *Education 3–13*, *11*(2), p 33–6.

Biott, C, 1984 *Getting on Without the Teacher: Primary School Pupils in Co-operative Groups* Collaborative Research Paper 1, Centre for Educational Research and Development, Sunderland Polytechnic.

Biott, C, 1987 'Co-operative Group Work: Pupils' and Teachers' Membership and Participation' in *Curriculum*, *8*(2), p 5–14.

Boydell, D, 1975 'Pupil Behaviour in Junior Classrooms', in *Brit. Journ. of Ed. Psych.*, *45*(2), p 128–9.

Brandes, D and Ginnes, P, 1986 *A Guide to Student-Centred Learning* Oxford: Blackwell.

Button, L, 1981 *Group Tutoring for the Form Teacher* London: Hodder and Stoughton.

Central Advisory Council for Education (England), 1967 *Children and Their Primary Schools* (The Plowden Report) London: HMSO.

Ford Teaching Project, 1975 *The Castles Group* (K Forsyth), Cambridge Institute of Education, Shaftesbury Road, Cambridge CB2 2BX.

Galton, M, Simon, B and Croll, P, 1980 *Inside the Primary Classroom* London: Routledge and Kegan Paul.

Galton, M, 1981 'Teaching Groups in the Junior School: A Neglected Art' in *School Organisation*, *7*(2), p 175–81.

Good, T L and Brophy, J E, 1987 *Looking in Classrooms* Harper and Row.

Harwood, D L, 1981 'Group Dynamics and Teacher Education' in *West Midlands Journal of Pastoral Care* (2), p 25–38. (Available from the author at the University of Warwick.)

Harwood, D L, 1983 'Leader-Roles in Pastoral Groupwork' in *Pastoral Care in Education*, *7*(2), p 96–107.

Harwood, D L, 1986 *Evaluation of Personal and Social Education within Coventry TVEI*; Part One: Report on 'Active Learning', University of Warwick.

HMI, 1978 *Primary Education in England* London: HMSO.

HMI, 1982 *Education 5–9* London: HMSO.

Johnson, D and Johnson, R, 1984 *Structuring Co-operative Learning: Lesson Plans For Teachers* Minnesota: Interaction Book Co.

Mortimore, P *et al*, 1986 *The Junior School Project: A Summary of the Main Report* London: ILEA Research & Statistics Branch.

Pollard, A, 1980 'Teacher Interest and Changing Situations of Survival Threat in Primary School Classrooms' in Woods, P, *Teacher Strategies* Croom Helm.

Roth, E, 1983 *Group Processes in the Primary Classroom* Unpublished MA dissertation, Department of Educational Research, University of Lancaster.

Rudduck, J, 1979 *Learning to Teach Through Discussion* Occasional Paper No 8, Centre for Applied Research in Education, Norwich, University of East Anglia.

Rudduck, J, 1983 *The Humanities Curriculum Project: An Introduction* School of Education, University of East Anglia.

Simon, B, 1980 'Inside the Primary Classroom' in *Forum*, *22*(3), p 68–9.

Slavin, R E, 1983 'When Does Co-operative Learning Increase Student Achievement?' in *Psychological Bulletin*, *94*(3), p 429–45.

Stauffer, R G, 1969 *Teaching Reading as a Thinking Process* London: Harper and Row.

Tann, C S, 1980 *A Study of Groupwork in primary and Lower Secondary Schools* Unpublished PhD thesis, University of Leicester.

Tann, C S, 1981 'Grouping and Groupwork' in Simon, B and Willcocks, J, *Research and Practice in the Primary Classroom* Routledge and Kegan Paul, p 43–54.

Thacker, J, 1985 'Extending Developmental Group Work to Junior/ Middle Schools: An Exeter Project' in *Pastoral Care in Education*, Feb 1985, p 4–13.

Tough, J, 1977 *Talking and Learning: A Guide to Fostering Communication Skills in Nursery and Infant Schools* Schools Council Communication Skills in Early Childhood Project, London, Ward Lock Education in Association with Cardiff Drake Educational Association.

Webb, N M, 1982 'Student Interaction and Learning in Small Groups' in *Review of Educational Research*, *52*(3), p 421–45.

Yeomans, A, 1983 'Collaborative Groupwork in Primary and Secondary Schools: Britain and the USA' in *Durham and Newcastle Research Review*, *X*(51), p 99–105.

SECTION FIVE
Significant dimensions

One of the aspects of personal and social education that has worried many teachers is the apparently amorphous nature of the area; this is particularly the case when attempts are made to establish precise boundaries to the scope and content of PSE. There are a number of areas and questions that some would include within the framework of PSE and others would place elsewhere, or treat as separate areas in their own right. Whether or not the topics in this section are seen as essentially aspects of PSE, or as closely related areas of concern, might form the basis for a somewhat sterile debate. A debate of this kind is not our concern; wherever these topics are located, all can be seen to have a significant contribution to make to the personal and social development of pupils.

One feature of all the topics covered in this section is that in one way or another each has a controversial dimension and all may raise questions about what the role of the primary school and its teachers should be. Partly because of this the areas covered here tend to be the aspects of primary schools' work which are most often ignored or consciously avoided.

24 Personal and social education with particular reference to special educational needs

David Galloway

The Warnock Report (DES, 1978) and the 1981 Education Act have resulted in greater awareness that schools have a responsibility for a substantial minority of pupils with special educational needs. The widely publicised figure of 20% may be criticised as a statistical artifact resulting from the way tests and behaviour screening instruments are developed. It may also be criticised as a political compromise, reflecting the committee's view that teachers should be entitled to expect extra help in teaching the most difficult or disturbing 20% of pupils, rather than 10 or 30%. There is much less doubt that teaching these children is always challenging and potentially stressful. This is scarcely suprising given the range of special needs in most ordinary schools, from sensory and physical disabilities to the much more numerous cases of children presenting learning and/or behavioural problems.

It is implicit in the Warnock Report that the pupils benefiting least from their schooling are those who might be regarded as having special educational needs. Most teachers would probably agree on the importance of personal and social education for these pupils, even if they failed to agree on its definition, aims, scope and curriculum implications. It is argued in this paper that the functions of personal and social education are developmental, and require systematic planning as an integral aspect of the curriculum for all pupils. Currently, however, approaches to personal and social education may operate in the manner of a 'negative net'.

Primary school heads and deputies spend a lot of their time dealing with problems referred to them by colleagues. These problems may be of a 'welfare' nature, but are as likely to concern matters of discipline and classroom management. Certainly, though, they reflect perceived problems in the child's personal and social development. To anyone familiar with this negative net model, it may seem inevitable that pupils with special educational needs should, in some schools, monopolise the time and energy of senior staff. It is surprising, then, that there have been few attempts to establish conceptual links between the theory and practice of personal and social education and of provision for special educational needs.

This paper assumes a commitment to educate children with special educational needs in ordinary schools, and identifies the implications for their personal and social education. However, personal and social education for pupils with special needs cannot be divorced from discussion of a school's overall policy and practice. Hence, it is necessary first to identify some underlying issues. These will lead to discussion of specific issues concerning pupils with special needs, and some of the educational implications of special needs for the school's personal and social education programme.

Underlying assumptions

For theoretical and practical reasons, schools are unable to cater effectively for their pupils with special needs if they do not also cater well for the majority of pupils. A central aim of special education is to equip pupils to live as normal a life as possible. In this respect, integration is merely a step towards the more radical goal of 'normalisation' (Yesseldyke and Algozzine, 1982). Logically, this goal cannot be achieved if the mainstream of the school is not working well. The argument illustrates both the importance and the problems of a 'whole school' approach to special educational needs. This approach implies:

- a commitment to full functional integration for pupils with special needs, with a corresponding rejection of separate special classes and of withdrawal groups – except, possibly, for specific, short-term purposes;
- willingness to carry out a rigorous review of the school's organisation, curriculum and teaching methods;
- a mutual expectation that specialist staff (where they still exist) and class teachers will work together to ensure that pupils with special needs achieve recognition and success in the mainstream curriculum.

Just as effective teaching for pupils with special needs presupposes effective teaching for the majority, so effective personal and social education for pupils with special needs requires effective PSE throughout the school. It is not in the interests of children with special needs that they should monopolise the 'pastoral' time of their class teachers, let alone of headteachers, in the future. Nor is it in the interest of other pupils. Two questions arise from these considerations:

1 *What implications does the presence of children with special needs hold for the school's personal and social education programmes?*
2 *How can personal and social education contribute to a 'whole school' policy for special educational needs?*

The personal and social education programme

Personal and social education aims to help all pupils acquire a developing sense of their own personal identity, an awareness of their rights and responsibilities as fully contributing members of the class and of the wider community. Children cannot become fully contributing members of the class if their development is restricted by stereotypes of sex or ethnicity. Hence, personal and social development is concerned with self-image as a boy or girl, as a member of an ethnic group, as a member of the class. A major problem facing many children with special educational needs is their perception, sometimes accurate and sometimes not, that neither their teachers nor their peers expect them to achieve very much, or to contribute much to the life and work of the class.

Having defined personal and social education as broadly as this, we have said that everything that happens in the classroom contributes to it. Personal and social education, by definition, is something that occurs across the curriculum. The six year old girl who has 'learned' that she is no good at reading, and the five year old boy who has already discovered the benefits of being the clown of the class, have both received powerful messages about their personal and social identity. If, however, everything that happens in the classroom contributes, for better or for worse, to personal and social education, it is tempting to say that there is nothing to talk about and that the personal and social education curriculum has no content.

This is a dangerous *non sequitur*. The fact that personal and social education is all-pervasive increases, rather than diminishes, the need for clear thinking and conscious planning. How do we want children to behave to us and to each other? Why is it that the Wendy House is used mostly by girls in some classrooms while boys and girls play together in others, and does it matter? What do we want children to learn about themselves, for example regarding their health and care of their bodies, their cultural background, their physical development? How do we teach children to make choices? How do we teach them their rights as children, and thereby help them to protect themselves from abuse?

Questions such as these point to the richness of potential material for inclusion in the personal and social educational curriculum. It is worth noting that each one of these areas involves children in learning (and us in teaching) facts, skills and attitudes. This is a somewhat 'high-falutin' way of talking about the day-to-day activities of an infant or junior school classroom, but nevertheless it has very practical implications. Knowing who to tell if you have been threatened by another child or by an adult is essentially a fact. The five year old who never joins in other children's games may lack the skills needed to get along with other children. The girl who regards boys as boorish and the boy who regards girls as cissy are both showing sexist attitudes. All these children may be able to explain why it is important to brush their teeth, but lack the skill to do it properly, and think it is unimportant anyway.

It will be clear by now that resources for personal and social education cannot be bought as ready-made programmes, such as those provided by Button (1982) and Baldwin and Wells (1981). These were designed for secondary schools, but have also been used with older primary and middle school children. However unintentionally, these programmes may have fostered the view that personal and social education can safely be left in the backwater of a specialist activity, and hence that it has no implications across the curriculum. A further problem is that the materials are used very unevenly. Many schools have bought them, but many teachers feel uncomfortable with some of the activities proposed and resist using them. The difficulty seems to be the authors' implications that personal and social education requires a new set of skills, different from those required in classroom teaching. At least in primary schools, however, there is no alternative to starting with the class teacher's *existing* skills and resources, and considering how these may best be applied and extended in the area of personal and social education.

Welfare tasks with pupils with special educational needs

Following assessment under the 1981 Act, the LEA produces a statement indicating the nature of the child's special needs and how they should be met. While overall responsibility for the curriculum of children with statements is likely to rest with the headteacher, the needs identified will require the active involvement of *the class teacher*. More important, it should be recognised that children with statements account for a very small proportion of the school's children with special needs. The class teacher's responsibility for maintaining oversight of each pupil's progress across the curriculum places him or her in the front-line in identifying special needs. Uneven performance in different areas of the curriculum, or deterioration in progress, motivation or behaviour, are examples of obvious indications that further investigation is needed.

Dissemination of information

Ensuring a reliable and smooth interchange of information is a traditional task for headteachers, but still a necessary one. In the case of children with medical conditions such as epilepsy, haemophilia or catarrhal deafness the need is obvious enough, though even here failures of communication seem to occur with extraordinary frequency. As important, and more difficult, is the need to exchange information relevant to the teaching and management of children whose needs are less obvious, less acute, yet in many ways more complex. The danger here is that on hearing information, for example about home problems, some teachers may expect less from the pupil, and thus inadvertently reduce the potential benefits of success and achievement at school.

Help with particular problems

Some children require help of a more specialist nature than can be provided through the routine activities of the classroom. Obvious examples are family and medical problems. Class teachers and headteachers may not be able to offer such help themselves. They do, nevertheless, have a responsibility: for identifying the need; and for ensuring that it is met, if necessary by seeking support from agencies outside the school.

Counselling

Few headteachers and even fewer class teachers have had formal training in counselling. They do, however, need some basic counselling skills in order to promote pupils' personal and social education effectively. This is evident if we consider common problems such as lack of attention or pride in written activities. Possible reasons include dislike of the topics; lack of understanding; handwriting difficulties; dislike of the teacher; common or garden laziness; a more generalised feeling of disengagement from school, perhaps associated with tension at home, and so on. Often, the explanation is obvious enough. Sometimes more detailed inquiry is needed, requiring patience, tact, ability to see the pupil's point of view in a non-judgemental manner and the ability to pursue a line of inquiry without arousing defensive anxiety in the pupil. Perhaps the most important skill for class teachers, though, is to recognise the limits of their own competence, knowing when to seek assistance from a more experienced member of staff or from a member of an appropriate agency outside the school.

Liaison with LEA support services and other agencies

Referral to one of the LEA support services is sometimes seen as a last resort, indicating that responsibility must now be passed to someone else. The unstated reason for referral here may be to initiate a process resulting in the pupil's transfer to a designated special school or centre, thus equating the School Psychological Service with the Special School Removals Service. More constructively, teachers can seek a partnership with support services using their expertise to develop a clearer understanding of the pupil's needs, and of ways in which these may be met. This model assumes an equal partnership between teachers and members of the support services in which each shares experience and expertise with the other (Galloway, 1985).

Liaison with parents

The Warnock Committee's notion of parents as partners is a well-known piece of educational rhetoric that is not always reflected in practice. Developing active, mutually cooperative links with parents is a fundamental pastoral task. In the case of pupils with special needs it becomes a necessary ingredient in any effective programme. Links with the parents of these pupils will not, however, be possible in the absence of similarly constructive links with parents of other pupils. Schemes involving parents in listening to their children reading have had notable success (eg Tizard *et al*, 1982). Such schemes demonstrate to children the importance that teachers attach to their parents' help. By valuing the parents, the teacher is also valuing the child. The importance of these schemes may lie as much in their indirect contribution to children's personal and social development as in their direct contribution to their progress in reading.

Special needs and the personal and social education programme

The issues we need to consider here concern provision of personal and social education for pupils with special needs. First, though, we must note that the usefulness of anything provided through the curriculum depends on the social climate of the school. There is something more than faintly ridiculous in the spectacle of ten or eleven year olds practising Button's 'trusting' activities in a school at which smaller children are regularly bullied in the playground by older pupils. The point is that behaviour in one context, for example the classroom, does not necessarily transfer to other situations. A practical example of this is the enormously varied ways in which the same pupils may behave with different teachers in consecutive years. Nevertheless, acknowledging the importance of the school's social climate does not negate the desirability for personal and social education in the curriculum. Developing children's awareness as thinking, contributing members of their class, school, family and wider community is an essential aspect of personal and social education. To succeed in this task it is essential that the climate of respect between teachers and pupils throughout the school should be consistent with the climate in the classroom.

Awareness of disability

It follows from previous sections that effective personal and social education for pupils with special needs requires a climate throughout the school which accepts and respects individual differences and which values the achievements and efforts of the least able as highly as those of the most able. It also follows that the school should encourage all children to accept and respect exceptionality. As the Fish Report (ILEA, 1985) so clearly recognised, this has wide-ranging implications, requiring equality of opportunity irrespective of social class, sex or ethnic group, as well as a constructively sympathetic approach to special educational needs. The personal and social education programme has a central role to play here. It would include factual information about disability, and would seek to develop some understanding of related concepts. It would also aim to develop pupils' ability to recognise how they may help people with special needs, and to promote a willingness to do so. The key points here are that a personal and social education element can be incorporated in *all* project work; and that this requires conscious planning – it cannot be left to chance.

Conclusions

Headteachers and class teachers are jointly responsible for ensuring that their pupils' special needs are recognised and met. The way class teachers approach their pupils' personal and social education can create a climate which accepts and respects special needs, ensures that the achievements of children with special needs are valued, and creates opportunities for them to contribute, and be seen to be contributing, to the school community.

A school's provision for children with special needs can reveal starkly any shortcoming in the curriculum, teaching methods and personal and social education. The challenge for everyone with classroom responsibilities is to adapt and develop resources existing within the school to cater for the needs which are identified. This in itself would be a worthwhile exercise. Because provision of effective education for children with special needs is likely to improve the quality of education throughout the school, it becomes even more worthwhile.

References

Baldwin, J and Wells, H, 1981 *Active Tutorial Work. 1. The First Year – 5. The Fifth Year* Oxford: Blackwell.

Button, L, 1982 *Group Tutoring for the Form Tutor. 1. Lower Secondary School. 2. Upper Secondary School* London: Hodder and Stoughton.

Department of Education and Science, 1978 *Special Education Needs* (The Warnock Report) London: HMSO.

Galloway, D, 1985 *Schools and Persistent Absentees* Oxford: Pergamon.

Inner London Education Authority, 1985 *Equal Opportunities for All?* (The Fish Report) London: ILEA.

Tizard, J, Schofield, W N and Hewison, J, 1982 'Collaboration between teachers and parents in assisting children's reading' in *British Journal of Educational Psychology*, *52*, p 1–15.

Yesseldyke, J and Algozzine, B, 1982 *Critical Issues in Special and Remedial Education* Boston: Houghton Mufflin.

25 Integrating pupils with special needs into mainstream classes: opportunities for personal and social development

Margaret Heritage

In the wake of the Warnock Report (DES, 1978), there has been an emerging focus on the integration of children with special educational needs into mainstream schooling. The Warnock Report identified three forms or levels of integration: locational, social and functional – the last mentioned representing the fullest form of integration in which children from both groups jointly participate in educational programmes. This paper reports on aspects of a programme of integration undertaken between a mainstream primary school and a special school (severe learning difficulties). The paper will describe how the programme was initiated at the staff level, the course of its development and the opportunities which were created within the integration initiative for the personal and social development of the mainstream children. A separate paper will be required to identify the effects of the integration on the special school children and this will not be attempted here.

Background

The integration programme, which represented one strand of a continuing LEA policy, resulted from the wish of the headteachers of both the schools concerned to see initiatives in this direction. The schools involved were a 260 place primary school comprising children from nursery age to 11 years, and a 60 place special school (SLD) with children ranging from nursery to 16. The schools occupy adjacent sites, although access between them requires a half-mile road journey. The staffs of both schools were largely unfamiliar with each other's circumstances and teaching practices, but felt positive about exploring the possibilities of integration.

Initiating the project

It was accepted from the early stages that if any form of integration between the children was to be successful it would be essential for the staff involved to feel comfortable and positive about the initiative. To this end, the 'visitor strategy' was used to establish initial contact between the two staffs. In this process, the staffs of each school were divided into small groups of two to four people and were asked to 'plan a visit to their school for a staff member of the other school'. In accordance with this strategy, they were to consider how the visitor would be met, where the welcome should take place, where the hospitality would be offered and what the visitor would see and do during the course of the visit. The practical outcomes of each group's deliberations were different, but their planning activities converged in creating a constructive ethos in which the sense of threat to both host and visitor was minimised. Both the planning and the subsequent visits took place after school. Some groups decided to collect their opposite numbers from school, whilst others met their visitor at the school gate. What the visitors did and saw in school also differed substantially according to the plans of their host group. Subsequent to this, members of staff from both schools made further visits in pairs to their opposite number schools during the school day and had opportunities to meet the children and observe them working.

The strategy behind this sequence of meetings embodied a number of objectives. First, it was decided that relationships between the staffs of the two schools would be crucial throughout the initiative. A number of staff in both schools were hesitant about meeting the children in the opposite school and it was decided that meetings among staff without children present would be a valuable confidence-building exercise. This turned out to be the case and most of the teachers felt more comfortable about involving themselves with the children once they had had opportunities to meet and discuss the issues arising from the projected programme with their counterparts.

Second, the entire process was initiated on the premise that the staffs from the two schools would have joint 'ownership' of the project and would not see it as being externally imposed. It was essential therefore that, from the outset, the staff were responsible for making their own relationships, for establishing their own procedures and for determining the pace at which the initiative developed. The entire planning exercise and the subsequent meetings were geared to this objective.

Third, it was significant that the staff had, to some degree, undertaken a parallel experience to that in which the children would ultimately be involved. This first-hand experience fed into their thinking about how the children might feel in comparable circumstances and provided a framework for them to initiate the development of relationships between a number of the children. In effect, the adult experience served as a model for significant aspects of the kind of experiences the children would have. It raised the teachers' awareness of the range of issues which they might have to consider in relation to the needs of the children. Moreover, the experiences of the early stages gave the teachers from both schools a shared understanding of the problems to be faced, which was an important resource in planning the initial stages of the children's integration.

Developing relations between the children

The first stage in linking the activities of the children came shortly after several of the staff had made their reciprocal visits. One class from each of the schools was to participate in a LEA-wide music day and rehearsals for the ensemble singing that was to form part of the occasion were perceived by the teachers to be a useful opportunity to begin the process of collaboration.

Drawing on their own experiences, the teachers involved were very aware that the initial meeting of the children would be highly important. This first meeting took place in the mainstream school with mainstream children acting as hosts. The class teacher explained that there was an opportunity for the children to work together in their music sessions. The children were told about some of the difficulties which the special school children had and were able to ask questions about how the special school children might behave in their classroom. All the children were asked if they wanted to take part and all but one were very positive.

The model of the visitor, as outlined above, which the teachers had used was then implemented with the mainstream class. The children were divided into groups, each of which was to have one visitor. Each group decided what they would like to show their visitor in their classroom, if they would offer refreshments, and where they thought it would be best to meet their visitor. The subsequent visit involved some ten special school children who ended the afternoon joining in a singing session. Following this session, the children met on a weekly basis to prepare for the music day which they ultimately travelled to and took part in together.

This initial event was an effective ice-breaker and both sets of children decided that they wished to continue their interactions. The mainstream children wanted the special school children to continue to come to their classroom and planned a range of joint activity afternoons and a joint assembly. A number of them also undertook the role of visitor to the children in the special school and involved themselves in a range of activities there.

This involvement took place over the course of a whole school year and on a weekly basis. The initiating class continued its relationship with the special school children during the subsequent academic year and the procedures which were employed in its initiative became a model for other classes.

This approach to the integration of the children was adopted because it had the same positive elements as those which had characterised the earlier procedure involving the staff. As was the case with the staff, the children had 'ownership' of the project and took responsibility for its development. As a result, they were not passive in its processes and were able to make decisions which would shape its evolution and to choose the pace at which they would implement them in practice.

The impact of the integration experience manifested itself in a number of ways in the mainstream children.

1 Perhaps the most obvious primary effect of the integration project was that the children's level of awareness of handicap was dramatically raised. A survey of the children conducted by qualified teachers seconded for the BEd degree found that two-thirds of the children involved had had no personal contact or experience with a handicapped person prior to the project. Through the integration process, the mainstream children derived first-hand experience of children with handicaps. The survey showed that the mainstream

children had developed positive attitudes to the handicapped children. After the project was properly under way, 83% of the mainstream children were able to name one or more of the special school children involved. All the mainstream children perceived the special school children as friendly. The vast majority interacted frequently with the special school children and only one child said that he never spoke to them. Possibly more importantly, while most of the mainstream children said that it sometimes bothered them to see children who were handicapped, only one felt that he could not become 'good friends' with a handicapped person.

2 It has been stressed that the responsibility for planning and pacing the project remained with the children throughout. Although at times the mainstream children needed the help and support of adults to help them understand and respond to the special school children, there remained considerable scope within the integration for the mainstream children to take responsibility for planning activities and resolving the difficulties which arose. It soon became apparent to the mainstream children that the special school children did not necessarily respond to activities and events in the same way that they did. However, the mainstream children quickly began to make decisions without adult intervention about the best ways in which they and the special school children could work together. For example, the children readily resolved the problems of working with others who had limited mobility by changing the arrangement of equipment and sometimes furniture to be used in an activity. On other occasions they were able to adapt their expectations and the task to suit the circumstances without seeking adult intervention.

3 In their concrete interactions with the special school children, the mainstream children were compelled to look at familiar situations from the perspective of those who could experience considerable difficulties in dealing with routine activities and tasks. In this process of role-taking, the mainstream children found themselves looking at the constituent features of their joint activities in considerable detail and becoming aware of how these activities might be seen from the perspective of a handicapped partner. The mainstream children's developing tolerance faced by obstacles in the achievement of tasks is manifest in video recordings of the sessions and was the object of much comment by the children's teachers.

269

4 Finally, the mainstream children inevitably tended to serve as role models for the special school children. It was significant, however, that many of the mainstream children progressively became aware of their role in this modelling process and recognised that the special school children would learn by talking to them and copying what they did. The self-conscious awareness of the value of 'setting an example' is an important feature in any child's personal and social development and this interaction provided a sustained context for its emergence and growth.

Conclusion

This paper has described some aspects of an integration project from the perspective of its impact on the personal and social education of mainstream primary children. While the benefits of integration accruing to special school children have received considerable attention, it is not insignificant that the integration experience can also create an environment in which substantial personal growth can be achieved by mainstream children.

Reference

DES, 1978 *Special Educational Needs* London: HMSO.

26 Child abuse: how do we help?

Peter Maher

The abuse of children in our society is a widespread problem; whilst certain types of abuse might be associated with specific social, economic and environmental factors, there is increasing evidence to show that abuse, of one form or another, is no respecter of social class, creed or colour (Creighton, 1984).

Over the last five years, the developments in our understanding of what constitutes child abuse have been quite dramatic. The categories of problem which are now officially defined as child abuse are:

- physical abuse
- failure to thrive
- sexual abuse
- emotional abuse
- neglect.

The NSPCC records of children aged up to 17, show a recent dramatic increase in reported cases of abuse. This may not, however, reflect an actual increase but rather an increase in public awareness of the problem of abuse. The trends also show an increase in the average age of children suffering abuse (Creighton, 1987). There is no agreement about the proportion of children who suffer abuse; a conservative estimate would suggest that one in five of all children will have been abused by the time they leave the secondary school. Some estimates put the figure as high as 35–40%.

In one category of abuse at least – sexual abuse – children are at their most vulnerable between the ages of 9 and 14. This has serious implications for primary, middle and secondary schools. It is between these ages that most children transfer school and thus, without proper liaison between schools, are placed at greater risk.

Thirty-five per cent of abuse cases are first reported by schools. Yet there has been a tendency to underestimate the role played by teachers in detecting the abused child. Teachers are often the first adult that the child comes into contact with after abuse has taken place; further, teachers are trained in the normal development of children and therefore are ideally qualified to recognise abnormality in behaviour or development. However, the majority of teachers have had little or no training in child abuse issues; certainly the developments in thinking shared by other professional groups, have not been passed on to teachers.

Generally speaking, teachers are not aware of the range of abuse; of the physical or behavioural characteristics associated with the abused child; of procedures for reporting abuse; of the inter-disciplinary network of professional groups who work on abuse cases; or of the ways in which these groups operate. The need for in-service training is critical but given the lack of understanding of the importance of the teacher's role, the demand for such training is unlikely to be identified by either teachers or local authorities. As a consequence, training in child abuse issues needs to be a nationally determined priority.

The interdisciplinary setting in which abuse cases are dealt with is most important.[1] Yet teachers tend to have a very low opinion of some of the groups involved in such work. This cynicism is often mutual, other professional workers sometimes see teachers as of only peripheral value. They are reluctant to share sensitive information with teachers because they do not trust them to maintain the necessary confidentiality. These tensions between professional groups, of which this is just one example, inhibit and limit the effectiveness of interdisciplinary work and mitigate against the safety of children. We need to urgently explore the way in which these groups of professionals work together and consider in particular the prospect of *interdisciplinary training* in child abuse issues.

The reactive role of detecting and reporting cases of abuse and acting, as part of an interdisciplinary team, to support the child and family, is only one part of the contribution teachers can make. All groups involved are searching for ways of reducing levels of abuse in future generations. Teachers are uniquely placed to affect social

[1] 'Child Abuse – Working Together; A draft guide to arrangements for interagency cooperation for the protection of Children', DHSS, 1986. Available from DHSS, Room 1317A, Alexander Fleming House, Elephant and Castle, London, SE1 6BY.

attitudes through their work in schools and through the curricular experiences that they offer (Maher, 1987). The adults who will be abusing the next generation of children are sitting in our classrooms today; it is this group that we must influence if levels of abuse are to be reduced in the longer term. This proactive role has enormous potential; it is vital that we properly consider and research the ways in which this potential might most effectively be fulfilled.

A lot of work has been done in the USA, Canada and Australia to produce curricular material on child safety programmes. The potential financial gains of producing such materials are great and some of the commercially-produced materials have been developed largely for profit and are of dubious quality. We need to be alert to the danger of replicating this experience; one way of avoiding the dangers might be to establish national guidelines about the types of materials that are suitable and the context in which they should be used.

In the last two years some materials have been produced for the UK market, and more are due to come on to the market shortly. This material along, with some from the USA, Canada and Australia has been used in training sessions for teachers, parents and children, but at present there is national concern at the ways in which some of this work has been approached. Any such programme has to be set in context and with an understanding of the ways in which schools in the UK work; it needs to be implemented within an interprofessional supportive network and with a thoroughly researched understanding of the effects of the use of such materials upon both the abused and the non-abused child.

A range of attitudes have been identified as contributing to an environment where children are abused:

Attitudes to women: The perception of women as sex-objects and of men's domination of women through 'ownership' sanctioned within a relationship.
Attitudes towards violence: Violence is seen, individually, institutionally and nationally, as a legitimate activity. Recent generations of young people have been subjected to a diet of violence through a media which seems to condone violence towards property and persons (eg inner-city violence, picket-line violence, terrorist violence, international violence). Children are widely offered access to many examples of violence;

violence in video films and sex and violence in pop-videos. There is every indication that an acceptance of such violence increases the likelihood of violence within the family being seen as part of a socially accepted norm.

Attitudes towards parenthood: Our working definition seems to accept parenthood as the natural course for all children. Perhaps we need, instead, to offer the view of parenthood as an *option*. There is little systematic preparation for the role of parent; schools need to explore ways in which children of all ages can be helped to develop parenting skills. It is when these parenting skills break down that abuse often occurs.

Attitudes towards relationships: The vast majority of our students will form at least one long-term relationship, within or outside marriage. We give little help to young people in preparing them for the choice of partner or in preparing them for the stresses that develop at some time within the majority of relationships. Stress and instability within the relationship is usually present in an abusing environment.

Attitudes towards poverty and unemployment: Unemployment could be seen as the most violent experience suffered by a significant proportion of families. Whatever the financial background of the family prior to unemployment or redundancy, the financial hardship that follows is an increasingly common experience. The changes that take place due to financial constraint cause stress and we need to consider whether we adequately prepare our students to cope with such circumstances. Poverty may be experienced by a whole range of families who are in fact in full-time employment, and these issues equally pertain to them. Similarly, the stress caused by decreasing self-respect, personal confidence and motivation resulting from unemployment, can seriously affect the stability of the family. Stress caused by poor economic circumstances and unemployment is often present in an abusing environment.

Attitudes within the community: With the breakdown of the extended family, through social mobility and other factors, families are increasingly isolated within the community. We need to work towards a community that accepts responsibility for all its members, the old as well as the young. Schools can play an important part both in developing attitudes towards a supportive community environment and in acting as a focus for community activity and support. Isolation within the community is a factor often present in an abusing environment.

It may be possible for schools, through the curriculum, to affect these attitudes and thus to contribute to a long-term reduction in levels of abuse.

I do not suggest that schools or teachers have the sole responsibility for developing such strategies; they are just one part of a supportive infrastructure that needs to be further developed if abuse is to be reduced in the long term. None the less, schools and teachers can and should play an important part in developing such work. Artificial boundaries that exist between the different professional groups involved in child care will inhibit such developments. For the sake of the safety of many thousands of children in each coming generation we need to develop ways of creating a proper inter-professional relationship between these groups.

References

Creighton, S, 1984 *Trends in Child Abuse* NSPCC Publications, 67 Saffron Hill, London EC1N 8RS
Creighton, S, 1987 'Quantitative Assessment of Child Abuse' in Maher, P (ed) *Child Abuse: The Educational Perspective* Oxford: Blackwell.
Maher, P (ed) 1987 *Child Abuse: the Educational Perspective* Oxford: Blackwell.

27 Sex education in primary and middle schools

Dilys Went

The widespread debate about sex education in the media, and particularly the television coverage of issues such as child sexual abuse and AIDS (even portrayed in TV soap operas), has meant that children in primary classes are now raising the sort of questions about sex previously only anticipated at secondary level. No literary skills are required to absorb such visual and aural inputs, of course, so even young children are now 'aware' of certain sexual matters, in a way not encountered by previous generations. Many schools are therefore in the process of taking stock of the whole situation, not only in order to cater for the needs of the children but also to take account of the new statutory requirements and government suggestions on sex education.

The Education Act 1986 states:

> The local education authority by whom any county, voluntary or special school is maintained, and the governing body and head teacher of the school shall take such steps as are reasonably practicable to secure that where sex education is given to any registered pupils at the school it is given in such a manner as to encourage those pupils to have due regard to moral considerations and the value of family life.
>
> (Part IV, paragraph 46)

From this it can be seen that sex education has not in fact been made compulsory. Other sections of the Act make it clear that school governors have been given the sole responsibility for deciding the sex education curriculum, and the power to allow parents to withdraw their children from classes if they wish (though there is no statutory provision for this). The governors are also required to present an annual report to parents, where curriculum matters can be discussed. Under the Education (School Information) Regulations

(1981), governors have to publish information on 'the manner and context in which sex education as respects sexual matters is given', so this must be explained clearly in school brochures.

This would seem, then, an appropriate time to review the government guidelines and the overall rationale for sex education at primary level.

The HMI discussion document *Health Education from 5–16* (July 1986), strongly emphasises the value of sex education at both primary and secondary level.

The importance of sexual relationships in all our lives is such that sex education is a crucial part of preparing children for their lives now and in the future as adults and parents.

The draft circular *Sex Education at School* confirms and reinforces this commitment to sex education. Both documents stress that communication and consultation between schools and parents about the sex education policy and programme is fundamental, both at the planning stage and after. It is also suggested that teaching approaches and the materials used should be explained to parents and discussed with them. This then enables them to be aware of what the children will be covering, which may help with any questions that come up at teatime! Recent surveys have confirmed that the vast majority of parents do support the idea of sex education in schools.

Any questions parents may have can be raised and discussed, and hopefully an atmosphere of mutual trust and respect can be generated between them and staff, for the overall good of the children. It is important that schools should always make it clear that they are not trying to usurp the role of parents, but to supplement it.

The DES Circular, *Sex Education at School* elaborates on the role of governors, and suggests that teachers will need to continue to fulfil their responsibilities with skill and sensitivity, and use their professionalism and expertise when implementing the governors' policy at classroom level. Guidelines for sex education for early years are given in paragraph 15:

At the *primary level* particular care and sensitivity is needed in matching teaching to the maturity of the pupils involved, which may not always be adequately indicated by chronological age. At this level, teaching should aim to help pupils cope with the physical and emotional challenges of growing up and give them an elementary understanding of human reproduction. Pupils questions should be answered sensitively and with due consideration for any particular religious or cultural factors bearing on the discussion of sexual issues.

The general ethos of a school, and the attitudes of the staff to each other, are of course all part of a sex education programme. An open and relaxed approach can help neutralise any tendency to unduly focus on the 'sex' component in the curriculum. Sex education should be as much concerned with sexuality in relationships as with actual reproduction, but there can be some confusion about these two aspects. It is therefore important that all members of staff have a chance to discuss this issue together, whether or not they will be directly concerned with the programme (and no one should be forced to contribute if they are uncertain of their ability to cope). The teachers actually doing the work can then feel confident about an agreed approach and content, and sure of overall support. Discovering and considering the attitudes and wishes of minority group parents is extremely important, and the teaching should be flexible enough to accommodate them without compromising the validity of the programme. This is easy enough to say, of course, but in practice it may require considerable negotiation. One question raised by teachers and parents alike is, 'When should sex education start?'

Pre-school and infant children, 1-5 years

It may seem rather early to be thinking about sex education for this age group, but as many parents know, questions may crop up even before a child starts school. The Goldmans (1983) confirmed the fact that if children are not provided with correct information about human reproduction when they are ready, they invent their own explanations. These can be even more fantastic than the truth, and in the long term may promote anxiety and eventually require much un-learning.

The HMI report stresses the need to respond to children's questions naturally as they arise, and as all teachers know, this can be at any time and place! The aim of sex education for this group is

278

to provide information simply, and at the right level (for example in giving them names for *all* parts of their bodies), and to answer questions such as, 'Where do babies come from?', 'How do they get out?' and, 'How do they get in?'. Some questions may be 'asked' just by pointing, or staring, and these should be answered in the same way as verbal ones. Some books which may help are listed on page 282; but these should not necessarily be read all through at one go, as small children may have a short attention span and get bored with this subject as much as any other. Children will ask the same question several times, and a little more detail can be added each time as they become old enough to understand more. The curriculum should be a spiral one; children need to develop their concepts about human life cycles and sexuality in exactly the same way as for other complex issues. 'One off' inputs have been shown to be ineffective at all levels.

Infant and lower junior children, 6–8 years

These children ask similar questions to those above in the younger age-range and many more besides, including ones about values and attitudes. As pre-pubertal children tend to identify with babies rather than adults when human reproduction is considered, work on animal young of all kinds, parental care, family life of all varieties, growth and development, personal relationships and caring for others, are all particularly appropriate at this level. Sex education should be integrated into the curriculum fully, and not isolated, taken out of context or over-emphasised in any way.

Junior and middle school children 9–13 years

Many of these children will begin their pubertal changes during this time (a few girls begin their periods as early as nine) and it is reassuring if all girls and boys learn about the stages their bodies will soon go through, and how these may affect their emotions, their relationships and their potential as adults. The HMI report emphasises the need to prepare girls adequately for the onset of menstruation, 'which might otherwise cause them unnecessary stress'. There is evidence that in the past schools have not always fulfilled this role (see Went, 1986).

279

The aims of sex education in the primary school should include

- to generate an atmosphere where questions about reproduction can be asked and answered without embarrassment on either side; these questions may now well include overt or covert ones on the nature of AIDS, and/or condoms, and it is important that they be answered simply, but truthfully, and without creating extra anxiety or fear;
- to provide acceptable vocabulary for *all* parts of the body (including those in the undercarriage);
- to counteract myths and folklore, some of which is gained directly from adult lies (storks and gooseberry bushes?) and some in the playground, or from TV (The Colbys, Eastenders?)
- to elucidate the nature of human reproduction in gradually increasing detail;
- to stress the value of 'family' life (taken in its widest definition) and the need for proper care for all young things. In this context it is salutary to remember that we are living in a society where 1 in 3 marriages break down, over 14% of children (1 child in 8) in England and Wales are in one-parent families, the family size mean is 1.6 children, and only 3% of the population have families of six or more. These are the daily realities faced by teachers, who know the children in their class may have very complex family histories. '. . . moral considerations and the value of family life' have therefore to be treated diplomatically;
- to help children understand they have rights, and should have control over who touches their bodies, and to increase communication skills about these (sadly needed sometimes in cases of child abuse. All adults should take children's stories about interference seriously.)
- to raise awareness of the danger of going with 'strangers';
- to aid communication about forthcoming pubertal changes and all their implications, including communication between parents and children;
- to enable children to accept *variation* both in size (overall and parts!), in growth rates, and in the age when puberty starts;
- to provide constant reassurance that body changes, physical, emotional and social, are normal and acceptable, and give help in adjusting to these changes, particularly for early developers;

- to help children accept their sexuality as a part of their whole personality;
- to develop communication skills in personal relationships, including those necessary for getting help if things go wrong;
- to raise awareness of potential sexism, and the value of equal opportunities for males and females;
- to help parents understand the nature of sex education at primary level, and develop their own skills as sex educators.

In all this work teachers must of course keep within the given school policy and the guidelines in the DES Circular, which include:

19. The Secretary of State considers that the aims of a programme of sex education should be to present facts in an objective and balanced manner so as to enable pupils to comprehend the range of sexual attitudes and behaviour in present day society; to know what is and is not legal; to consider their own attitudes, and to make informed, reasoned and responsible decisions about the attitudes they will adopt both while they are at school and in adulthood. Teaching about the physical aspects of sexual behaviour should be set within a clear moral framework in which pupils are encouraged to consider the importance of self-restraint, dignity and respect for themselves and others, and helped to recognise the physical, emotional and moral risks of casual and promiscuous sexual behaviour. Schools should foster a recognition that both sexes should behave responsibly in sexual matters. Pupils should be helped to appreciate the benefits of stable married and family life, and the responsibility of parenthood.

(*Sex Education at School*, DES, 1987)

Resources

The following resources may be available from the local Health Education Department (contact your District Health Authority, Health Education/Promotion Unit).

Curriculum material
1 Schools Council Health Education Project: *All about Me* (5–8) (Nelson), *Think Well* (9–13). Unit 1 'Myself' (9–13), Unit 2 'One of many' (11–13). Teachers' books and work cards for children are

included in these two units, which can form a sound basis for sex education in the junior school.

2 McNaughton, J 'Health Education for slow learners' *Fit for Life* (Macmillan), Level 1, 5–8, Level 2, 9–13. This includes teachers guidelines and excellent visual material specifically designed for less able children, but most useful in a wider context too.

3 The Clarity Collective, *Taught not Caught* (Learning Development Aids). Some of the strategies for sex education suggested here are for children from 9–13 years.

4 Future publication: Health Education Council, *Primary Schools Project* for 4–12 year olds. This will have three main corner stones:
- Relationships (sex education is included here)
- Looking after self
- Community and environment

Enquiries to Health Education Unit, University of Southampton.

Television programmes

1 *BBC Sex Education*, 1983 series, three 20 minute programmes:
- Growing
- Someone new
- Life begins

Very comprehensive teachers notes are available, with background information and suggestions for preparation and follow up work for each programme.

2 *ITV*

'Good Health' series, programme 10, What next? (9–11).

'Living and Growing' Series of eight programmes for 10–13 year olds on the human life cycle, growth and reproduction. Very full teachers notes available. These programmes are now being revised and updated, and a new series of six, plus two which form a special unit on Relationships and Decisions, will be broadcast in the Summer 1988.

Books

For Teachers and Parents (T = particularly relevant for teachers); (P = particularly relevant for parents).

DES *Health Education from 5–16*. (T)

Dallas, D, 1972 *Sex Education in School and Society*. NFER (T)

Allen, I, 1987 *Education in Sex and Personal Relationships* Policy Studies Institute. (T)

Farrel, C, 1978 *My Mother Said* Routledge and Kegan Paul. (T)

Goldman, R and J, 1983 *Children's Sexual Thinking* Routledge and Kegan Paul. (T)

NCW Report, 1984 *Sex Education – whose responsibility?* Report by the National Council of Women of a survey of 81 schools. (NCW, 34 Lower Sloane Street, London, SW1W 8BP.) (T)

Went, D J, 1985 *Sex Education – Some Guidelines for Teachers* Modern Teaching Series, Bell and Hyman. (T/P)

Pickering, L, 1981 *Parents Listen* Cassell (Companion volume to *Boys Talk* and *Girls Talk* books). (P)

Chovil, C *How did I grow?* BBC Publications. Parents book, companion to children's book of same title, for children 8–10. (P)

For children from 4–12

Changing Baby Hollie Phototalk, ILEA Learning Resources and from Nottingham Education Supplies.

Concertina books: 1 *Waiting for baby.* 2 *What about me?* 3 *The Nuisance*, Nottingham Educational Supplies. (All pre-reading books.)

Spiers, H, 1971 *How you began* Dent & Sons Limited.

Hegeler, S, 1967 *Peter and Caroline* Tavistock Publications.

Berger, Terry, 1974 *A New Baby* Macdonald Raintree.

Althea, 1975 *A Baby in the Family* Dinosaur Publications.

Althea, 1976 *David and his sister Carol* Dinosaur Publications (about an adopted baby).

Jarner, Bo, 1977 *My New Sister* Adam & Charles Black.

Nilsson, L, 1975 *How you began* Kestrel.

Jessel, Camilla, 1982 *The Joy of Birth* Methuen.

Fagerstrom, G and Hansson, G, 1979 *Our New Baby* Macdonald Educational Limited.

Althea, 1973 *The New Baby* Dinosaur Publications.

Chovil, Claire, 1977 *How did I grow?* BBC Publications Children's Questions Answered.

Berger, Terry, 1979 *Big sister, Little brother. Being alone, being together, A friend can help* Macdonald Raintree.

Rankin, C, 1984 *How Life begins* (Animals) Collins for Oxford Scientific Films (biology book).

Bailey, J, 1979 *Nature in Action Series* 1 *How creatures multiply* 2 *Growing up* Purnell (biology books).

References

Allen, I, 1987 'Education in Sex and Personal Relationships', Policy Studies Institute.

Brand, J, French, J and McLaren, S, 1985 'Health Education in West Sussex Schools' in *Education and Health*, *3*(4) September.

DES, 1980 The Education Act HMSO.

DES, 1981 Education (School Information) Regulations 31 1981/636.

DES, 1986 The Education Act HMSO.

DES Draft circular 'Sex Education at School' (August 1986).

DES 'Sex Education at School' Circular 11/87, Welsh Office Circular 45/87.

Elliott, M, 1985 *Preventing Child Sexual Assault*, Bedford Square Press.

Goldman, R and J, 1983 *Children's Sexual Thinking* Routledge and Kegan Paul.

HMI discussion document 'Health Education from 5–16' *Curriculum Matters 6* DES, July, 1986.

Went, D, 'Questionable Assumptions' in *Times Educational Supplement*, 30.5.86.

28 'Are you sitting comfortably?': Under five in a multiracial society

Tricia David and Jenny Clements

Are you sitting comfortably? Then I'll begin.[1]

Once upon a time there was a town where all the inhabitants had brown eyes. The town was a busy, thriving place with growing industries – so much so that they became short of workers.

'Let's invite some blue-eyed people to come and live here', suggested the mayor, 'A good idea', came the reply, 'They need work and they'll be glad to have jobs'. So the blue-eyed people moved in and took on the tasks which the brown-eyed people didn't really want to do.

When the blue-eyed children went to school, they were disappointed to find that all the books and pictures told of the clever exploits of the brown-eyed people. Sometimes the brown-eyed children wouldn't play with them and even called them names to make them feel unwanted and unimportant. Even some of the teachers reinforced this view, treating them as though they were a 'problem'. When blue-eyed people appeared on television they were rarely shown in serious debates. In fact, they found themselves the subject of unkind and incomprehensible jokes.

Then, hard times came to the town. Many of the brown-eyed population and even more of the blue-eyed, if the truth were told, became unemployed. But because some of the blue-eyed people still had jobs, the brown-eyed people began to protest,

'Why has she/he got a job while I'm unemployed?

Why don't they go back home?'

---

[1] 'Are you sitting comfortably? Then I'll begin.' was the phrase which always preceded the story on *Listen with Mother*, a BBC radio programme for preschool children.

285

Of course, our 'story' isn't really about blue/brown-eyed people. Like the above quotation from Sarup's *The politics of multiracial education* (1986), it is about the consequences of the way human beings have been classified by other human beings. We have labelled these groupings as 'races'. Sometimes the groupings have been made according to state or country of origin, but most often the categories are white and black (ie non-white) skin colour. When you begin to think about it, our story about eye-colour prejudices doesn't seem quite so ridiculous. The repercussions of such divisions in society can be the negative and harmful attitudes bred when, as Sarup continues,

> Such racist beliefs are an attempt to understand and explain daily experience but . . . these socio-economic processes cannot be grasped in terms of daily experience.

In our posts as headteachers at two nursery schools, we became aware that perhaps we were guilty of 'sitting too comfortably'. The black children we taught were growing up not only disadvantaged but as victims of prejudice and the white pupils were actually learning to show uncaring attitudes towards non-whites, so that they too were being subjected to a system which did not foster their emotional, moral and cognitive development as fully as we should expect in a democracy.

Kozol warned us 20 years ago, in 1968, that we cannot turn back the clock and restore to a child a year in which their life has been destroyed, yet we continue to do little towards the development of curricula which will alter this situation. Schools are notoriously conservative in their rates of change. This can be a strength, but Little and Willey's (1983) report on the development of multicultural perspectives in primary schools indicates that, despite changes in attitude, the action has occurred in the majority of schools has been negligible. For those children attending our schools now, both black and white, this does not bode well.

There may be those who believe that to develop antiracist practices in nursery schools amounts to indoctrination – we would counter such an argument by saying that *not* doing so amounts to indoctrination, since the transmission, by a whole range of processes and practices, of the belief that another person can be treated as inferior because of skin colour is the reality, when an antiracist perspective is absent. Further, those who believe that three and four year olds are unaware of differences have long been proved incorrect. Goodman (1952) and Milner (1983) describe the way in which three year olds are aware of those differences and further-more, of the power relationships which have been vested in such differences. It is not enough to think we can 'correct' prejudice when children are older and capable of abstract thought. Racist attitudes comprise deeply embedded emotional responses as well as beliefs rooted in our history of imperialism and colonialism.

When we are young we learn that in order to belong to a group, we too must develop the group's attitudes, particularly if those attitudes relate to a retention of status or power within 'our' group. We often transmit such attitudes to our young through non-verbal communication, even though we may deny them by what we say. The ambiguity of these experiences is likely to have a lasting impression on the young child. In their search for reasons to explain such incidents, children are likely to jump to conclusions which fit, according to their experiences of life so far. They find it difficult to understand how their loving parent or teacher can be uncaring or even hateful towards other people, identified simply by a different skin colour. They probably conclude that non-whites must have done something wrong. At this stage children will accept the judgement of a revered adult as absolute, so unless we consciously foster the cognitive processes that govern moral development, as Kohlberg urged (Munsey, 1980), the terrible cycle will go on.

Preschool provision is patchy and inadequate. There have long been calls for fairer allocations of nursery education and for the coordination of services, from the campaign of the McMillan sisters in the early part of the century through Blackstone's (1971) detailed study and later work, to the Rampton Report (1981), Tomlinson (1984) and Austen et al (1984). The school hours of opening when a nursery is available make attendance difficult for working mothers, and ethnic minority group mothers are more likely to work outside the home than are white UK mothers. One survey reported 75% of Afro-Caribbean mothers in paid employment at some time during their child's first five years, compared with 45.2% of white mothers (Austen et al, 1985). The CRE reports detail the widespread employment of childminders, ethnic minority children often being found in overcrowded homes, with minders who neither shared the child's language nor had any respect for cultural differences. We need more nurseries, some with extended day facilities and all with positive anti-racist policies and genuine parent participation.

The importance of establishing parent-teacher partnerships in the early years relates to far more than setting up links which will prove beneficial in later home-school cooperation. By enabling the parent-child dyad to develop autonomy in matters of the child's educational progress, rather than feeling that the parent must hand over the job of education to the 'experts', we may be fostering a system with greater long-term gains, as well as 'here and now' satisfaction. Some of the parent-involved *Headstart* programmes in the United States, reported by Lazar *et al* (1982) and Berruetta-Clement *et al* (1984), have apparently resulted in long-term benefits in the areas of personal and social maturity. Earlier studies of the long-term effects of preschool provision had focused on cognitive aspects of school performance. Mortimore and Blackstone (1982) describe the way in which the hopes of improved performance in later school tests were unfulfilled. Both in Britain and the US, preschool provision seemed to offer nothing of lasting value to the children who were deemed disadvantaged. Interest in what would be costly nursery expansion waned. We must ask, however, as the American researchers did – are test results the only way of measuring success? They claim that earlier studies had myopically examined narrow outcomes. The now 19 year old 'graduates' of certain *Headstart* programmes, when compared to non-preschool counterparts, were more likely to have a job, to have studied for or gained qualifications, to have avoided involvement in crime and to have succeeded at school without remedial teaching. Evidence now available from British research by Osborn *et al* (1987) supports the view that preschool provision offers positive long-term benefits.

It was with data of this kind in mind that we attempted to articulate an effective approach to multiculturalism. Of the nursery schools where we (the writers) were teaching, one had all white pupils, the other 70% black, mainly Asian, pupils; both would in earlier times have acquired the designation EPA schools. We hoped to provide the children and their parents with an education service which would not only be appropriate and exciting now, while the children were three and four years old, but which would also enable them to move on to each new educational stage, or experience, with joy and confidence. Within this curriculum, multicultural antiracist perspectives would be inevitable if our pupils were not to be destined to bear the scars of the racist attitudes they could otherwise develop (if they were white) or suffer (if they were black).

Developing multicultural perspectives in the nursery curriculum

The problem for us was that most of the DES and HMI documents urged teachers to espouse multiculturalism but we had to look elsewhere for help on where to begin and how to encourage others to join such a reappraisal. Like Perry (1986), we found widespread reticence, resulting in the relegation of multicultural perspectives to one of the lowest priorities for curriculum development initiatives. We perceived that a certain amount of the reluctance was due to lack of knowledge – teachers seeing multicultural education as yet another subject area to tackle – and a certain amount to a fear of being 'wrong-footed', blundering on in good faith but finding oneself frequently doused with cold water, from all sides. We believed it to be essential and exciting work, which would run like a golden thread through every aspect of the children's experience in school. This meant we had to begin with our own education, primarily its personal and social aspects, most of which had been effected through the hidden curriculum during our earlier years. We began to see connections between the limited knowledge we had of our own families' histories and the movements of people subjugated by various forces. The famine in Ireland is a pertinent example. We became aware of the links between racial disadvantage and working class disadvantage and realised that multiculturalism alone is not enough. Thus we deliberately chose to call our article 'Under five in a multiracial society', because we wished to emphasise the very real and damaging effects of racism.

Like Sarup (1986) and Cole (1986), we believe that by dwelling on ethnicity and culture we are concentrating on lifestyles and ignoring aspects of society, and particularly of education, which may increase life-chances. Curriculum development in the schools may begin with the celebration of cultural diversity but there has to be an awareness that without antiracism we will probably fall into the same trap as that of the 1960s when 'cultural deprivation' was blamed for the school failure of working-class children. The need to extend the above developments became obvious as we continued our own personal education. Literature for staff to read and discuss (eg VOLCUF (1986), ALTARF (1984), Interracial Books (1983), Development Education Centre (1984)) and in-service training for new and existing staff teams were essential. We found we needed to join a network of contacts who would help and support us, both locally and nationally.

Each of the two nurseries entered an independent programme of curriculum development, some of the elements described below occurred in both, others in one of the schools.

Weekly staff meetings were set up to discuss children's progress. At these meetings we were able to review both the ways in which we were making judgements about children's abilities and the actual assessment instruments and record sheets which we were using. During these discussions we were able to ensure support for each other in our growing awareness of the ways in which a system can militate against certain children, labelled at the age of three or four! Parents were already part of the everyday life of both schools but we realised that we needed to engage their cooperation in more meaningful ways and that the feedback we gave them about their child's progress must be more than the blithe 'she/he's doing very well'. Most parents are happy to be involved in varied tasks, for example, school investment in a couple of cameras can result in lovely books about home and family, which will interest all children because of their intimacy and relevance. Asking parents to tell stories in mother-tongue encourages all the children to admire bilingualism and to be more conscious of language and its power. We felt that staff needed more information about the difficulties faced by bilingual children, and that we must have positive policies to encourage ethnic minority representation on training courses. The need of staff at all levels who have experience of minority communities, culture, needs and child-care, has grown as we have become more aware of our own inadequacies. We also found that to achieve antiracist multicultural permeation of the whole curriculum we needed staff with a commitment to develop antiracist practices and challenge racism, as well as reviewing resources so that books and equipment reflected multi-ethnic Britain.

290

Personal and social education in the early years

The nursery sector has, for over 50 years, claimed that paramount in its aims are the social and emotional development of young children. The study by Taylor *et al* (1972) indicates that nursery teachers believe it is part of their role to influence growth in these areas. More recent work by Roberts (1986) sadly refutes this, since she observed that in practice children are being made to repress their feelings, rather than being helped to come to terms with them. Lang (1986) has reported that teachers will frequently claim that personal and social education and pastoral care are implicit in their practices. Some would no doubt agree with Johnson's (1985) comment that by developing conscious, structured approaches to these aspects of a child's education, there may be a danger that these areas will be regarded as separate from the fostering of cognitive and physical abilities.

Ken David (1981) described pastoral care as 'concerned with helping families to socialise children and to develop attitudes which will support and improve society'. There is, as Pring (1985) points out, an enormous responsibility involved in any intervention in the personal growth of individuals, for who is to decide what will 'improve society' and how is such a choice of values manifested in classroom practice?

The nursery sector was given little attention by the Swann Report (1985), and indeed trivialised by suggestions such as those in paragraph 6.8, suggesting that bilingual teaching could be undertaken by 5th and 6th formers. Despite this we need to examine the aims and practice of early childhood education in relation to personal and social education for all.

Although we accept that there is a need for changes outside the school in order to achieve greater equality of opportunity, for children under five the home and the nursery constitute the majority of their world. The young child coming to school for the first time is in a unique situation. However gentle the admissions procedure, however good the preparations by parents and staff, the child is undeniably alone, encountering an environment in which there will be new experiences, new relationships, all of them having the potential to induce powerful feelings. The ways in which the child adapts to and learns from these will depend on the help, sensitivity and support of the adults within and without the school situation.

The children in preschool groups at the present time are the future Citizens 2000. They are already living in a technological, multicultural and multiracial society. If they are to benefit from these attributes of the society they share, should not all of us serving their current needs be talking together to improve our work? We find no challenge in the idea of explicit policies relating to personal and social education in the early years but if we examine our practices, preferably by systematic mutual observation with trusted colleagues, using tape-recorders and even video cameras, we may discover that our stated intentions and aims are being subverted.

Conclusion

Our own and others' observations and experiences confirm our belief that we must begin antiracist multicultural education in the nursery and that this involves the personal and social education of us all, staff as well as children. Young children know about love, affection and caring, fear and anxiety. In the nursery they are encouraged to share feelings of joy, to sympathise with sadness, to empathise with the children and adults in school, and with the imaginary characters they meet in stories. Personal and social education must not be permitted to become the equivalent of valium or the analyst's couch, where people are changed because they are a 'problem', due to the pathologising of views that are different from those of the dominant ideology. By developing a conscious approach to PSE in the nursery we will be more aware of stereotyping and of the unintentional transmission of racism. Part of the action to promote antiracist policies must be the involvement of parents and ethnic minority group leaders, so that areas of possible disagreement can be debated. PSE is a field which could be open to misuse when race, class and/or gender influence decisions.

We urge the need for sensitivity, for the assistance of trained advisers to join in work in situations which are potentially volatile. We acknowledge the pointlessness of policies issued from 'above' – although these are often a vital element in the legitimation of the efforts of those on the 'chalk-face' who may have little power or support in their own workplace.

The current pressures for education for industry, CDT and technology are signs of the re-emergence of an education system which is geared to the needs of the State. We may be optimistic in thinking that the needs of the State and those of the individual do not necessarily lie at the opposite ends of a continuum, but we are certainly pessimistic about a society which ignores unequal treatment and lack of consensus among its members concerning respect for other human beings. We neglect the personal and social education of all our pupils at our peril.

References

ALTARF, 1984 *Race in the classroom*. ALTARF.

Berruetta-Clement, J R, Schweinhart, L, Barnett, W, Epstein A and Weikart, D, 1984 *Changed lives: the effects of the Perry Preschool Program on youths through age 19* London: The High/Scope Press, or the NCB.

Blackstone, T, 1971 *A Fair Start: the provision of preschool education* Penguin.

Cole, M, 1986 'Teaching and learning about racism: a critique of multicultural education' in Modgil, S, *et al* (eds) *Multicultural Education. The interminable debate* Palmer Press.

David, K, 1981 'Pastoral Care in Local Education Authority' in Hamblin, D H (ed) *Problems and Practice of Pastoral Care* Basil Blackwell.

Committee of Inquiry into the education of children from ethnic minority groups, 1985 *Education for All (The Swann Report)* HMSO.

Commission for Racial Equality, 1978 (revised edn) *Caring for Under-fives in a multi-racial society* CRE.

Community Relations Commission, 1975 *Who minds? A Study of Working Mothers and Childminding in Ethnic Minority Communities* CRC.

Development Education Centre, 1984 *Starting Together* DEC, Selly Oak Colleges, Birmingham.

Goodman, M E (1952, 1964) *Race Awareness in Young Children* Anti-defamation League of B'hai B'rith.

Interracial Books for Children, 1983 *Childcare shapes the future: anti-racist strategies* Council for Interracial Books Inc., N.Y.

Johnson, D, 1985 'Pastoral Care and Welfare Networks' in Lang, P and Marland, M (eds) *New Directions in Pastoral Care* Basil Blackwell.

Kozol, J, 1968 *Death at an Early Age* Penguin.

Lang, P, 1986 *Primary and Middle School teachers' attitudes to the provision of personal and social education*. Conference Paper, University of Warwick, Oct 1986.

Lazar, I and Darlington, R, 1982 *Lasting effects of early education: a report of the Consortium for Longitudinal Studies*. Monogram of the Soc. for Res. in Child Dev. 47 (2–3, No 195).

Little, A and Willey, R, 1983 *Studies in the Multi-Ethnic Curriculum* Schools' Council.

Milner, D, 1983 *Children and Race – ten years on* Ward Lock Educational.

Mortimore, J and Blackstone, T, 1982 *Disadvantage and Education* Heinemann.

Munsey, B, 1980 *Moral development, moral education and Kohlberg* Religious Education Press, USA.

Osborn, A F and Millbank, J E (1987) *The Effects of Early Education* Clarendon Press.

Perry, A, 1986 'Amalgamation – the facts' Letter reporting research findings, in *Child Education*, *63*(8).

Pring, R, 1985 'Personal development' in Lang, P and Marland, M (eds) *New Directions in Pastoral Care* Basil Blackwell.

Rampton, A, 1981 *West Indian Children in our schools* HMSO.

Roberts, M, 1986 WEF Conference London, May 1986.

Sarup, M, 1986 *The Politics of Multiracial Education* Routledge and Kegan Paul.

Taylor, P H, Exon, G and Holly, B, 1972 *A Study of Nursery Education* Schools Council Working Paper 41, Evans/Methuen.

Tomlinson, S, 1984 *Home and School in Multicultural Britain* Batsford.

Voluntary Liaison Council for Under Fives (VOLCUF), 1984 *Unequal and Under Five*. Prepared by the Centre for Research in Ethnic Relations, University of Warwick, for VOLCUF.

VOLCUF, 1986 *A Guide to Anti-racist childcare Practice* by Celestine, N for VOLCUF.

29 Personal and social education – a black perspective

Cas Walker and others

This paper has been developed from the discussions and meetings of a Black Women's group in Birmingham. The term 'Black Women' includes Asian, Afro-Caribbean and Middle Eastern Women. The group came together as a form of mutual support as many of the members found themselves working in isolated situations, especially those women who are involved in education.

What is written attempts to give a flavour of the discussions which took place over a period of six months. The thoughts and concerns presented reflect both the collective and individual experiences of the group. Some women also drew on the wider experiences of family, friends and parents with whom they had contact at schools. The arguments and issues presented are mainly subjective. The interesting thing was that there were many common experiences, both past and present. Some reference was made to the material available on multicultural education issues. However it was difficult to find personal and social education material which focused on the experiences of black children and their parents.

The group felt very strongly that education is an important issue but this whole area of personal and social education is something which many black parents are unaware of, as it is perceived by white teachers and other educationists. As black women we have a cultural tradition of being involved in the educational debate as it affects our young people. The educational experience of many Afro-Caribbean parents and their children are highlighted graphically by Bryan, Dadzie and Scafe (Bryan, B, *et al*, 1985, p 59). Black people in general have viewed education as important for self advancement. We believe it is every child's right to have a good education and to develop whatever talents and skills they have. As many black children in this country seem to end up in some educational difficulty, many black women have been in the front line giving their children the necessary encouragement and support. They have often resorted to alternative education, such as supplementary schools, in an effort to help their children achieve.

Personal and social education – a black perspective

Apart from personal and social education generally the group also engaged in discussions about the hidden curriculum in primary schools as they have experienced it. One important fact which was gained from our discussions is the importance of the hidden curriculum as it affects black children. There was a general consensus that black children in primary schools are being disadvantaged in their personal development.

Personal and social education in primary schools was seen to offer good possibilities for many black children. The features about which the group felt positive were:

- good relationships between school and the local community;
- good teacher/parent relationships;
- good teacher/pupil relationships;
- positive peer group interaction, in and out of the classroom;
- positive ideas of self;
- feeling valued as an individual.

Having discussed our personal and collective experience of what it means to be black in the primary school we felt that it was important for schools to consciously promote those features.

Many black children 'suffer' from the fact that many teachers are unaware of the 'oppressive' conditions which can exist in a primary school, especially if the child happens to be black. Quite a lot has been written about the 'problems' of teaching in a multicultural classroom. The BBC publication, *Multicultural Education*, illustrates this point (Twitchin and Demuth, 1985). The focus of attention has usually been on the teacher and their needs not extensively on the need of the pupils. The overall emphasis in many publications has been on 'content' rather than on 'process' and 'structures'.

The group felt that any thoughtfully designed personal and social education course or general curricula approach for the primary school could take on 'content' and 'process' and in so doing engage in exploring the feelings and experiences of black children 'seeing' themselves on equal terms. The group felt that an effective and conscious approach to personal and social education offered a way of primary schools valuing black children without seeming to patronise them or viewing them as a 'problem'. Black parents have been expressing their concerns about their children's educational attainment for some while (Rampton, 1981). On the whole many secondary schools were seen as causing black pupils problems. Primary schools, on the other hand, have usually been seen as providing a good educational foundation in areas such as reading. The research conducted by Cecile Wright illustrates the point that even if Afro-Caribbean pupils are successful in the primary phase they are very likely to fail at secondary level. The whole point of this failure is 'racism' (Eggleston, 1985).

The group felt strongly that some primary schools isolate themselves from the reality of life for many black children. Many of our children in primary schools have direct experience of racism. Some black children encounter racial abuse in the classroom or in the playground. The group accepted the argument that many young children do not fully understand some of the things which happen to them. They were able to draw on many personal recollections of experiences in the early years of schooling. Even in nursery and reception classes there are incidents which arise because children bring their home attitudes about other people to school. Many black children realise very early on that their skin colour can prompt negative reactions in other people.

Teachers are often unaware of these incidents or even dismiss them as 'meaningless name calling'. This can lead to conflict at home between black children and their parents. There is often a disagreement between parents and school about how these situations should be handled. This has implications for attitudes towards black children in school. Children often find it difficult to explain their hurt to adults, even their parents. The group feel that personal and social education could provide the structure where such 'sensitive' issues as name calling could be handled and black children could have the support they need to cope with the negative experiences relating to their colour and culture which they encounter.

Many primary school teachers argue that they do not see 'colour' differences, they only see children. They suggest that if they focus on 'colour' this will cause divisions. They prefer to ignore that particular 'difference' with the aim of creating a 'happy classroom atmosphere'. The group are worried by this often used argument. This is a denial of black children's identity. Implicit in this denial is the refusal of some teachers to admit the importance that this society places on skin 'colour'. Many black children suffer from a lack of positive self-identity and become confused. They lack confidence in themselves as individuals. Research evidence seems to conflict about the importance of the whole issue of self-image (Milner, 1983; Stone, 1981). However, the group were agreed that many black children were muddled about their identity. Black children even felt at times that they had to make choices about being a black person. There were many personal and painful recollections by the group about incidents which had taken place in some schools. The group discussed their experiences with bewilderment. Some of the women are now very concerned about the attitudes of their own children to their skin colour.

The group feel that it is important for those teachers in schools which adopt a 'colour blind' approach to understand that schools are a part of the wider community and that society is a multiracial one. The world is multiracial. The group identified some typical examples of the difficulties black children face and their questions (mainly posed to their mothers) which result from these dilemmas.

Why do I have to be this colour?
If I scrub hard will I go white?
I want to be white when I grow up.
What does blackie mean?

Many black women were at a loss to know how to deal with these situations. They felt unable to discuss these matters with their children's teachers. They were often very embarrassed and upset.

Black children are forced to live in two cultures. Many primary schools view this situation somewhat negatively and this attitude becomes transmitted to black children, who may have to cope with emotional tension as a result. The minority home culture also makes demands. The black child has to attempt to meet these demands without much support from school and teachers who sometimes have little awareness of the problems at home.

There is a sad lack of black teachers in most primary schools. This reflects the lack of black professional involvement in education at all levels. It is also rare to see black non-teaching help in the classroom.

Many of our group felt that this further mitigated against their children, especially the very young ones. They suggest that there are two important consequences of this imbalance. First, black children do not have any positive reinforcement of themselves. Second, white children do not have any exposure to a black adult in a caring and supportive role. The hidden curriculum implications are that many black children do not realise that black people can be teachers. They do not have any role models. They do not have someone who is able to understand their home language and culture. The group felt that many teachers and workers in primary schools are unable to empathise with these very real situations which black children face.

This seems to be an area that primary schools endeavouring to develop a planned approach to personal and social education could explore. They could engage the help of black parents and community leaders to advise them. Parents and the black community can be encouraged to be actively involved in schools. We would hope eventually that the gap is filled by black educationists, especially in those schools where there is a substantial proportion of black children.

There still seems to be a lack of accurate information about family life and the homes from which black children come. Until this situation changes black children will continue to be viewed as a 'problem'. Because much of what is written depicts the deficit model of black families, black children in the classroom are handled in an inappropriate way. Schools still have certain assumptions about what being black means, eg 'having a working mother', 'one parent family', 'no language', 'withdrawn', 'noisy', 'good rhythm', 'likes physical activity', 'poor home', 'working class' . . .

The culmination of this is that black children are seen as having *no* academic potential and having *little* to offer in personal or social terms. A consciously developed approach to personal and social education in a multicultural anti-racist context could provide the framework for combating some of the group's concerns. For example, problem-solving activities could encourage black children to develop the confidence to articulate their ideas. They could explore with white children moral questions affecting themselves as children. The group were concerned that many schools fail to realise the value that black people place on the education of their children. But there are certain differences in the ways they thought schools must act. Black parents want to be involved; they want to be supportive, but no-one bothers to tell them how to do this. Teachers sometimes react defensively when their values are questioned. This makes it difficult for black parents to feel free to speak honestly or to develop a rapport with teachers.

Of course many primary schools argue strongly that they 'treat them all the same'. We feel that while this sounds well in theory it acts to the disadvantage of many black children. They are not the 'same' as white children they are different in many ways. We feel that personal and social education could make all children aware of the positive aspects of cultural diversity. Attitudes and values are transmitted by schools and it seems very odd to the group that white attitudes and values are acceptable in primary schools while those associated with black people are often rejected as being 'political'. All children can be encouraged to adopt attitudes which include making judgements about other people based on facts and information *not* on prejudice.

Many black children bring knowledge and skills to the primary classroom. Teachers are often unaware of this. Consequently black children never have the opportunity to demonstrate what they know and what they *can* do. The primary classroom possibly has the best flexibility to foster and encourage positive personal growth.

One member of the group gave an example of her nephew who seemed very unhappy in the reception class. The teacher was concerned about his lack of progress and diagnosed him as 'withdrawn'. The class started a topic on food and the teacher brought in some spices, including ginger. The teacher was amazed as this child explained how his mother made ginger beer. He gave a detailed description about buying and preparing the ingredients and the processes involved. He had hardly spoken to anyone in the class before that. This led to greater communication between the child and his teacher and his work improved.

The group felt very strongly about the importance of the relationships which teachers (mainly white) develop in the classroom. Teachers' attitudes towards black children can have long-term repercussions on black children's educational attainment and black children's attitude towards schooling.

Conclusion

Teachers should make every effort to develop their knowledge and understanding of the black presence in Britain. They can start with their own school situation. But they should not only limit themselves to this. It is possible in schools which have large numbers of black children that they will develop a one-dimensional view of black people in general.

This obviously means greater in-service provision by LEAs. It is important that any such provision should be task-orientated and goal directed. For some time now, awareness has been raised, but this has not been followed through by changes in practice. Black children still face difficulties in the primary school.

There should be a clearly and consciously articulated approach to personal and social education at primary level. Teachers' Associations have expressed concern about the problems faced by teachers at primary schools. Personal and social development cannot just be left to individual teachers who have an inclination in this direction.

Value systems do conflict and primary school teachers should be aware of and accept this. Racism affects both black and white children but in different ways. Ignoring this life situation in a formal structure does not drive it away. Personal and social education should acknowledge diversity and cultural pluralism but this is not an end in itself. The wider issues have to be tackled.

References

Bryan, B, Dadzie, S and Scafe, S, 1985 *The Heart of the Race: Black Women's Lives in Britain* Virago.

Eggleston S J *et al*, 1985 *The Educational and Vocational Experiences of 15–18 year old Young People of Ethnic Minority Groups* University of Warwick, Trentam Books.

Milner, D, 1983 *Children and Race – Ten years on* Ward Lock Educational.

Rampton, A (June 1981) *West Indian Children in our School* (Interim Report) Cmnd 8273 HMSO.

Stone, M, 1981 *The Education of the Black Child in Britain: The Myth of Multiracial Education* Fontana.

Twitchen, J and Demuth, C (eds), 1985 *Multicultural Education: View from the classroom* BBC Publications.

30 Learning about gender in primary schools

Mary Jane Drummond

Who plays with the Lego? a true story

> The local authority was organising a week's in-service pro-
> gramme on the theme: 'Equal Opportunities'. The head-
> teacher of a progressive first school, with a reputation for good
> practice on gender issues was invited to lead a session on *Play in
> the nursery/first school*. She involved the staff in preparation for
> this event and Miss W volunteered to make some classroom
> observations to illustrate the mixed-sex play established in her
> reception class. To her astonishment, during the first three
> afternoons of observations, she saw no girls playing with the
> Lego, small construction toys or big building blocks; and,
> correspondingly, no boys involved in domestic play or
> dressing-up.

The week's in-service course duly took place, and I was thunder-
struck when Miss W opened the session on *Play* by telling this story,
openly admitting her role in it as unwilling heroine. There are very
few road-to-Damascus moments in week-long in-service courses,
and this one was all the more surprising to me, for, like our heroine I
had been blissfully certain that all was well. Miss W's story dis-
lodged that certainty, and I suspect it may never be reinstated.

At the time I was, professionally, the headteacher of a Group 4
infant school, and personally, a long-standing card-carrying member
of the women's movement. As a teacher, I considered myself well-
informed about the disabling outcomes of sex-stereotyping and discrimination in the early years at school. Judith Whyte's account of
the process in *Beyond the Wendy House* (1983) had given me new
material to quote to my colleagues and to parents, but little in the
way of new insights into my professional responsibilities.

I had been entertained by Ronald King's satirical observations in

All Things Bright and Beautiful? and was sensitive to echoes, in my
own workplace, of what he had heard:

> Teachers publicly differentiated between two groups of
> children – girls and boys. In every classroom boys hung their
> coats separately from the girls. They were lined up in separate
> rows at the door.
> 'Oh, Philip is a little girl. He's in the wrong queue.'
> They were divided for activities.
> The class is acting Humpty Dumpty. Mrs. Pink makes the girls
> horses and the boys king's men. Later on during music and
> movement, boys are houses and girls are rats.
> Histograms of height or foot length were usually colour coded
> for sex. The bureaucracy was sex differential: the official record
> cards were colour coded, the registers listed boys and girls
> separately. These practices were completely taken for granted
> by the teachers, who, when I talked with them, generally said
> they had 'never thought about it', and that to divide the class by
> sex was 'convenient' and 'natural'. They were sometimes
> puzzled by what to them were my silly questions like, 'Why do
> you line the boys and girls up separately at the door?'.
> Sex differentiation was also used to promote competition
> among the children.
> 'Boys don't sing. Listen to the girls, make certain they sing
> nicely. Now it's the boys' turn. Get your best singing voices
> ready. See if you can beat the girls.'
>
> (King, 1978, p 67/68)

Outside the school, the women's group I had joined in 1971 had
undertaken various local projects, that had ranged from the small-
scale and practical – a campaign for allowing push-chairs into the
public library – to the more ambitious and educational – producing
a local schools radio series for fifth year pupils, *Not Just a Pretty Face*.
Some of us had worked with other nearby women's groups with a
particular interest in education, and together we had written what
was probably the first attack to be published on the stifling sex-
stereotyping to be seen in the infant reading schemes of the day
(Wandor, 1973). So my credentials were impeccable. I was not only
certain that all was well, I was certain that I was certain.

The road back from Damascus

Miss W's story invited me to think again. Back at school I tried to imitate her calm observer's behaviour, and began to see patterns in incidents and activities that I would rather not have seen. We did not (any more) line the boys and girls up separately to move around the school; but at the end of windy play times, there was often a little group of boys standing by the playground steps, waiting to be dealt with. We did not select girls for cleaning jobs, or boys for furniture-moving ('I need three strong people, please'); but the children who stayed behind after school to help their teachers clean up were all girls. Boys and girls shared all their activities – so why were we so especially proud of Alistair who was exceptionally good at sewing? When I looked in my folder of notes on 'crime control' to check on my responses to bullying at dinnertime, floods in the toilets, gangs in the cloakrooms, why didn't I find any notes on girls? Why had the teacher in Class 2 organised her reading groups as single-sex groups? Why hadn't we talked about it? Groups of fifth form and sixth form pupils from the next-door comprehensive came regularly to work in the school: why had we done nothing when we noticed the fifth form group (the much-despised CSE 'homemakers') were all girls? Why did we get so excited about the two boys in the Sixth Form Community Service group? Why had I never noticed that *One Two Three and Away*, the reading scheme that we'd used to replace *Through the Rainbow*, was every bit as unbalanced as the notorious *Ladybird Readers* or *Janet and John*?

I began to worry out loud about these questions, and was not reassured by the assurances I was given by my colleagues. They told me, kindly, gently, supportively, not to worry. 'We've been through all this already', they said (though what they probably meant was, 'You've dragged us through all this before'). In any case, Everything is All Right.

I decided that we would have to have a full, frank staff-meeting on the subject: so we did. We began by reporting to each other about the workshop sessions that some of us had attended during the Equal Opportunities in-service week. As discussion continued, lively, agreeable, reasonable, I began to sense that something was going wrong with my plan: instead of reflecting on our need to learn and to improve our practice, we were using the self-satisfied tones of those who know they are in the know. *We* are the converted; it was *other* teachers, 'them', out there, who needed in-service training to convince them of the error of their ways. In desperation, I produced a sheet of questions that had been passed around as a hand-out during one in-service meeting, and invited my colleagues to answer the questions,[1] to comment and discuss. The questionnaire was treated with outright contempt. The staff meeting broke up in unusual disarray.

Over the next few days, several members of staff approached me to explain the sense of insult and affront they'd experienced at having it suggested to them that anything more needed to be done. The questionnaire in particular was singled out for abuse: 'these questions are out of the Ark!' concluded the Deputy Head. The staff made it clear that they were prepared to overlook my ineptitude in handling the issue, but that the incident must be regarded as closed.

Learning about gender

Since that time I have been involved in a good many in-service sessions on gender issues, led by myself, and by colleagues from the in-service institution where I now work. I have learned that what I saw and heard and felt so painfully in that particular staffroom, in the company of my trusted and respected colleagues, was not the unique experience I took it to be at the time.

I have come to see how likely it is that teachers will respond negatively to the topic of gender if it is broached in certain ways – of which mine was certainly one of the clumsiest. Within a generally hostile staffroom or in-service group response there will always be local and personal variations, but the main themes remain constant. The argument goes something like this:

> We know all about gender issues, thank you. Besides, it doesn't happen here. Besides, lining boys and girls up separately is

[1] The questionnaire consisted of some 40 questions, which teachers were invited to answer by ticking columns marked Always – Sometimes – Never. The list included: *Do you line boys and girls up separately? Do you expect girls to be more verbal and artistic than boys? Do you think boys and girls expect to be treated differently? Do you excuse behaviour in boys you would not tolerate in girls?*

completely irrelevant – *that* doesn't affect A level results. Besides, boys and girls *are* different. Besides, they learn sex-roles at home. And from the media. And what about our Muslim families? I think you've got to be very careful. Besides, we can't change society. Besides, women have got the vote. Besides, women teachers are the worst. Besides, our girls don't want to play football. Besides, we've got a woman prime-minister . . .
And so on.

I have here summarised, very crudely, attitudes I have heard expressed many times in staffrooms and teacher centres. But I do not want to ridicule the teachers who express them, nor to emphasise their difference from me, or any of my colleagues, past and present. I would argue that these attitudes must be taken very seriously, and their meanings honestly explored, if we are to make progress on gender issues in primary schools. Attitudes are learned, not dropped intact from the skies, and if teachers' attitudes are to be unlearned or modified, then we need to take into account what it is we know about how teachers learn.

My present understanding of teachers' professional development has come partly from my own experience as a practising teacher, but also from other teachers' accounts: there is a surprisingly large area of common ground. Effective learning seems to take place when motivation is high, when there is a perceived need to learn – a *sense of purpose*. Teachers who select the content of their learning, focusing on the themes most relevant to their teaching, feel an enabling *sense of control*. In small groups, teachers quickly discover that learning is a social activity: they appreciate the *sense of support* that other learners can give. If workshop sessions are used in which teachers can report on their experiences in classrooms, rather than listening to the accounts of the 'visiting expert', teachers come to feel a *sense of self*, of personal involvement and growing self-confidence. And the opportunity to move directly from reflection outside the classroom to action and experiment within the classroom brings an awareness of the practical outcomes of analysis and evaluation – even, sometimes, a *sense of success*.

It is these factors that will help us or hinder us when we embark on any staff development work. We may not yet have a fully developed model of how teachers learn, but we have at least begun to recognise affective elements in our learning, to realise that professional development is also personal – and so, inevitably, emotional, untidy, difficult, risky, and sometimes downright unpleasant.

Power, process and persons

I am arguing that for teachers, if not for everyone else as well, learning about gender issues is always personal as well as professional. The growing literature of the subject offers a range of description and analysis: some authors (for example, Delamont, 1980; Paley, 1986) are concerned with the process; others (for example Spender, 1982) investigate the distribution of power in schools and classrooms. Important as these issues are, I believe it is only through a personal approach that effective learning can be achieved. This is not to say that a personal approach makes it easy to establish the sense of purpose and control I have referred to above: in fact it seems to make it all the more difficult.

The Reverend Nash – another true story

You are the headteacher of a group 4 infant school, and you and your staff are known to be committed to the principles of equal opportunities. Mr Nash, a parent governor, comes to see you, bringing with him his 6-year old daughter Lucy-Anne's topic book, in which she has written: 'My mummy is kind. My mummy wears an apron. My mummy cooks the dinner. My Mummy sweeps the house.' He reminds you of what you know already – that Mrs Nash is not this kind of person at all. Mrs Nash is a professed non-conformist Minister; she works in a busy church and parish, writes weekly articles for a local paper, and has a regular Sunday morning radio programme. He asks you, in the nicest possible way, what is happening to his daughter in the process of studying the class topic *My Family*. What are you going to do?

I wish I could report that the minute Mr Nash had gone home I took this story to the whole staff group, that we debated it long and seriously, that Lucy-Anne's teacher's eyes were opened, that Lucy-

Anne made a public recantation, and that we expressed our gratitude to the whole Nash family for having helped us learn . . . but it would not be true. What I can report is that after some more or less effective attempts at crisis management I stored the incident away in a part of my memory reserved for difficult, it not impossible, problems and abandoned it there for quite some time. But when I became involved in in-service work on gender issues away from that particular school, I took it out, dusted it down, and offered it to groups of teachers for discussion and resolution. I added to the 'Nash' incident a number of other factional stories, all first-hand, recent, and relevant.

At first the teachers in these groups saw the purpose of the discussion as being to establish an agreed action-plan for each incident. Teachers are, typically, task-oriented people, and after apparently business-like discussion, alternative courses of action were reviewed, rejected, and one specific set of strategies approved. Then, prompted by questions from me, the focus of the teachers' talk shifted: had the discussion been a difficult one? In what ways? Why? Which had been the most difficult issue to resolve?

At this point, I felt, we began to move a little nearer to learning something about gender issues in primary schools. For each of the stories, the teacher groups were able to see different reasons for experiencing difficulty in discussing what action to take, and even in handling the discussion.

Mr Nash and the Reverend Mrs Nash had come in for some hostile comments during the session; and when we reviewed these responses we found that the Nashes had raised the question of how we, as professionals, and as individuals, can cope with criticism, even when sensitively offered. As we talked around the implications of Mr Nash's questions (complaints?), we glimpsed our common professional defensiveness, always ready to be wheeled into place against parents (or others) who seem to be on the attack. If we are to take control of our learning, as I've argued we need to, we may find it very difficult to learn when we feel attacked or threatened by others, however well-intentioned they may be.

When we discussed the *Who plays with the lego?* story, with which this chapter began, we considered the implications for our self-esteem if classroom observations were to throw up such unwelcome results. Gradually, as the groups of teachers became able to open up to each other a little, individuals began to offer personal anecdotes, giving instances of occasions when they had learned something valuable, if painful, about themselves, by looking again at taken-for-granted events. We discussed the climate of trust and sympathy that would be necessary to support such re-examination; and we warned each other of the dangers of assuming that one observation, or moment of insight, can radically alter a routine or set of practices established over months or years. Alongside the dangers and difficulties of learning to look again at our own practices, we cautiously noted the sense of achievement that self-evaluation can sometimes bring. The guilty excitement of proving oneself in the wrong, and establishing the extent of one's misdeeds, may help one to recover from the initial discomfort of self-discovery.

During one such discussion, a nursery teacher talked about how, researching her own practice for an M Ed dissertation, she had uncovered evidence of her differential treatment of boys and girls. She reflected on the feelings of anxiety and inadequacy this had caused her, and some teachers present were clearly uneasy about the emotional impact of her research on her as a person. But it seemed to me that the emotions she was describing, and, to some extent re-living, were an inseparable part of her learning: it was her decision not to allow her feelings of anxiety and inadequacy to cripple her as a teacher that had made it possible for her to tackle the problem in hand. She continued her investigations into the way she treated boys and girls, making more detailed observations of the time she spent with them, and classifying the type and style of her interactions: the positive sense of purpose that held her to this programme derived, I believe, from the very negative emotions she had experienced at the outset.

In the staffroom – yet another story

Julie has been clearing out her bookshelves and has brought into the staffroom a girls' annual, *Mandy*, dated 1974. She is reading out extracts from 'The ABC of jobs for girls' (Air hostess, Ballerina, District Nurse). There is general conversation about how times have changed for the better. Suddenly Margaret interrupts:
"Mind you, I think it's all gone too far. Personally, I like being a woman; and being treated as a woman is very important to me. I don't *want* to wear dungarees and share the cooking."

There are cries of protest from Julie, but Maureen joins in, supporting Margaret. The discussion becomes very acrimonious, with small groups muttering in corners. Some comments are very close to personal abuse. Maureen and Margaret are clearly very upset.

The story of Margaret and Maureen raises other questions, particularly it seems to me, the part that sense of self can play in learning. Margaret and Maureen were speaking not just as experienced teachers, but as middle-aged women, with family commitments to husbands, children, and, for Maureen, a new grandchild. I believe that the staff group of which Maureen and Margaret (and I) were members had a joint responsibility to respect this personal dimension and to honour the lives our colleagues had chosen to lead. When gender issues come into the staffroom, this respect must be maintained, even if tensions and contradictions seem to be inevitable. The division of labour in society, or in the home, is not a neutral topic for any of the people who take part in a staffroom discussion. They are all deeply involved in it, and to question their views may be to question the whole structure and foundation of their family life. I am not suggesting that we should, therefore, avoid such discussions; but I do believe the connections between the personal and the professional, the personal and the political, are far too complex and far too important to ignore. Indeed I would suggest that only by examining these connections in *ourselves*, rather than in our colleagues, can we begin to learn about gender in our schools and classrooms. A sense of personal involvement can certainly be used as an excuse for not looking into the dusty cupboards and dark corners of one's private life, but it can also be the stimulus for facing up to difficult questions about oneself.

Conclusion

In this chapter I have tried to describe, in as personal a way as the conventions of the printed page will allow, something of the process of my own learning about gender. I have attempted to avoid the impersonal jargon of many accounts of institutional development, which are littered with concepts like 'paradigm shift' and 'change agents'.

310

I have emphasised instead the notion of *learning*, because it is by using this concept, it seems to me, that we can understand most about the enterprise of creating schools and classrooms where children can work and play without suffering from sexual stereotyping, discrimination and harassment. If we agree that there is learning to be done (in our own schools and classrooms), and not just reforms to be instituted, or practices stamped out (in other peoples'), then we may find it easier to accept responsibility for our own learning, and to concentrate on that, rather than embarking on the conversion of the rest of the world.

I have tried to argue that all teachers are learners in this development, since all of us have been reared and educated in a society divided and constrained by sex-roles and stereotypes. All of us have attitudes and prejudices to un-learn, and all of us have preferred styles of learning. Each of us will come to the project with different definitions of what needs to be done and why. Some people will want to begin by clearing out the curriculum cupboard, abolishing books, pictures, and resources that depict the world in an unacceptably sexist way. Others will have the self-confidence to begin at a less practical level, exploring their value systems and the tacit beliefs that underly their own behaviour. Others again will explore the gender issue with the active involvement of the children they teach, opening up to their pupils, for example, questions of school rules, entitlement to space, time and resources, and sex-differences in achievement and ability. (Detailed accounts of teachers' explorations, using these and other approaches, can be found in *Primary Matters*, ILEA, 1986).

None of these approaches is right, or wrong, or better than any of the others. They are all parts of a process of learning which, for any individual teacher or group of teachers, will very likely be circular, confused, repetitive, and at times discouraging. And, of course, always incomplete. We will have learned nothing about gender issues if we believe that one day there will be nothing left to learn.

References

Adams, S, 1986 *Primary Matters* ILEA.
Delamont, S, 1980 *Sex-roles and the School* Methuen.
King, R, 1978, *All Things Bright & Beautiful? A Sociological Study of Infants' Classrooms* Wiley.

Paley, V G, 1986 *Molly is Three* Chicago: University of Chicago Press.
Spender, D, 1982 *Invisible Women: the schooling scandal* Writers and Readers.
Wandor, M (ed), 1973 *The Body Politic: Writings from the Women's Liberation Movement in Britain 1969–72* London, Stage 1.
Whyte, J, 1983 *Beyond the Wendy House: Sex Role Stereotyping in primary Schools* Longman.

Further reading

Aspinwall, K, 1984 *What Are Little Girls Made Of?* NNEB.
Browne, N and France, P, 1986 *Untying the Apron Strings* Open University Press.
De Lyon, H and Widdowson, F, 1987 (in preparation) *Women Teachers* Open University Press.
Deem, R, 1978 *Women and Schooling* Routledge and Kegan Paul.
Kelly, A, Whyte, J and Smail, B, 1984 *GIST: Final Report* GIST, Dept. of Sociology, University of Manchester.
NATE, 1985 *Alice in Genderland* NATE.
May, N and Rudduck, J, 1983 *Sex-stereotyping & the Early Years of Schooling* CARE, University of East Anglia.
Oakley, A, 1981 *Subject Women* Fontana.
Sharpe, S, 1976 *'Just like a Girl': How Girls Learn to be Women* Penguin.
Spender, D, 1980 *Man-made Language* Routledge and Kegan Paul.
Spender, D and Sarah, E (eds), 1980 *Learning to Lose: Sexism & Education* The Women's Press.
Steedman, C, 1982 *The Tidy House* Virago.
Whyte, J and others (eds), 1985 *Girl Friendly Schooling* Methuen.
Woolf, V, 1933 *Three Guineas* The Hogarth Press (reprinted 1977).

SECTION SIX
The preparation of teachers

It sometimes seems that whatever innovation is suggested in school, teachers' automatic response is that it will be impossible to implement unless adequate training is provided. In the case of personal and social education they would probably be right.

This final section includes papers that are concerned in one way or another with the implications of the development of personal and social education for the training of teachers at both initial and in-service stages. Clearly, if unsupported by appropriate training and resources, much of what is being proposed in this book may be impractical. A consideration of training raises many questions about resourcing, priorities, and the appropriate stage and location for training to take place. Many of these questions will need to be addressed by training institutions, LEAs and primary schools, individually or working together.

The contributions to this section provide some valuable examples and raise a number of issues that might be taken into account when training initiatives are being planned. Snow and Nelson's brief description of the work being undertaken in Coventry provides a valuable example of an operating model of training at the in-service level. Both Bond and McGuiness highlight the issues and problems raised by the fact that, if it is to be fully effective, training for PSE cannot just be concerned with how to do things with and to pupils. Training also involves a consideration of the sort of person *you*, the teacher, are, your own attitudes, beliefs and feelings, and how these relate to what you are doing. As a result of such consideration, the teacher may need to work toward some degree of personal change.

The most important message that emerges from this section, and perhaps from the book as a whole, is that personal and social education is for teachers as well as for pupils; if you teach it, you cannot avoid being affected by it. When this takes place as an unconscious process, and you are also unaware of the effect that the sort of person you are is having on the way you teach the PSE in which you are involved, what you do may well be counterproductive. The point that has to be stressed is that developing personal and social education should entail increased awareness, including self-awareness, and a degree of personal change among all those involved, both pupils and teachers.

31 Personal and social education – approaches to in-service training for primary teachers in Coventry

Anne Nelson and Ruth Snow

There are many features of primary education which have special relevance to the personal and social development of children. Some of these features are:

1 The organisation of the school day and year. Primary children spend a long period of time with one adult or a small number of adults.
2 The general acceptance by the primary class teachers of their role in the all-round development of children in their care.
3 An emphasis on children's learning rather than the teaching of separate subjects.
4 Recognition of the importance of offering children first-hand experience as a means of furthering learning.
5 The basic form of class organisation. In many primary classrooms children work in small groups.
6 The children spend most of their time working with other children whom they know well.
7 The children spend the majority of their day in the same area and attention is given to the creation of an attractive personal environment by, for example, displays of children's work.
8 Parental involvement and contact in the early years of schooling is much greater than in later years.
9 The relatively small number of children and adults who form the school community.

In the light of such accepted practice it was clear that any in-service initiative for primary teachers should be developed from a deep understanding of primary education. This was achieved by primary teachers themselves being involved in planning and providing the in-service provision. We brought together a group of experienced primary headteachers who were interested in exploring issues within personal and social education for themselves and in considering how other primary teachers could be helped to further develop their insights and understanding of this area. This group of seven headteachers had met regularly for a year with other head-teacher colleagues to consider the nature of personal development, they had been involved in an exploratory course which used developmental group work approaches. The group of headteachers, together with a Primary Adviser and the Adviser for Personal and Social Education, met to evolve an in-service support structure. After discussion it was decided to offer a short introductory course (two and a half days duration spread over a three to four week period) to interested schools. A requirement was that the headteacher attended the first course together with another member of staff. Schools who were involved would be offered a number of opportunities to participate so that the majority of staff from a school could attend, two members of staff from the same school attending together. There would also be opportunities for follow-up support and, when the school was ready, for consideration of whole policy and strategy.

Some of the main principles around which the course has been designed are:

- to offer first-hand experience to teachers which is then used as the means to promote a process of review of their own classroom practice in relation to personal and social education;
- to offer a course in which the style of the course is in sympathy with the ideas being considered;
- to build understanding from existing practices and therefore not to give the feeling of 'bolting on' another aspect of education.

Emerging issues

Through the stimulus of the introductory course, teachers have raised many issues about personal and social education of which the following are some examples:

1 The nature of group work and how it can be managed so that each child has a significant part to play in group tasks.

2 The climate of classrooms and how this can be made more supportive to children – perhaps by giving consideration to the beginnings and endings of the school day.
3 The transition of children from class to class or school to school.
4 The organisation of the school day and how this can create or limit children's opportunities for choice. Are the opportunities for choice about what activities they do, who they work with, where they sit, how they approach a task and the order in which they engage in activities, fully exploited?
5 The formation of different groups for different purposes and how this can be used to enable learning.
6 The acknowledgement and recording of learning and giving feedback.
7 The importance of reflection in learning.
8 The positive use of situations involving conflict.
9 The creation of opportunities for the expression of feelings.
10 The creation of opportunities for children to take real responsibility within the everyday life of the school.

Development in school

The issues raised by the course are closely linked to classroom practice. Teachers are asked to:

- think about an aspect which is important to children's personal growth and development, such as decision making or taking responsibility, and consider the opportunities which are already provided in their classroom for children to develop their learning in this area;
- share their practice with other teachers so that more ideas are generated;
- consider some aspect of work they are planning to develop in the next few months and explore how further opportunities for pupils could be provided;
- plan how this could be implemented, thinking about the opportunities that could be provided for individual children and groups.

After an appropriate period of time the teachers come back to share and discuss what they have learnt about their pupils and the opportunities that have been provided for them to develop personally and socially. This process is being used both to help individuals review and develop their practice and also to help the whole staff of a school review aspects of their work.

With support, teachers were encouraged to record their planning and work. These case studies have been published in a booklet entitled *Decision Making: Approaches to Personal and Social Education in the Primary School*. Within the case studies there are examples of:

- all children in a class being given the opportunity to decide individually how to structure part of their week;
- the youngest and oldest children in primary school working as a pair to decide what they will do for part of a session;
- all children in a school choosing from a range of practical activities on offer during the afternoon session;
- groups of children being given the responsibility for organising an important school event on behalf of their class or the whole school;
- children being involved in making decisions about how their school should be regulated.

Summary

Developments to date in Coventry have gone through the following stages:

1 The identification of aspects of primary practice which are important within personal and social education.
2 The raising of teacher awareness of their role in personal and social education and of particular issues within it.
3 The facilitation of a review of existing practice in the light of increased awareness.
4 The support of on-going development and review in schools.
5 The sharing of ideas and practice with colleagues.

32 Let's start at the very beginning: primary school teachers and PSE

John McGuinness

I am not a primary school teacher, and therefore feel something of an intruder in a book addressed chiefly to them. I am, however, a psychologist who is interested in the way human beings can help each other to grow. My interest in that area has recently taken me into practice-focused contacts with business and industrial managers who want to be able to communicate more effectively with colleagues, employees and customers; with psychiatric nurses who hope to respond more competently to the interpersonal challenge their patients pose; with general practitioners who want to make space in their busy consulting schedules for a more human contact with their patients; with careers officers who find that beneath the specific skills of counselling the unemployed 40 year old and the jobless school-leaver lie a number of generic interpersonal issues about the nature of authority, respect for others and so on. Each of these professional groups, in defining the issues they wanted to explore, helped me to re-learn something that is central to all of us who work as helpers, developers, facilitators of change in other people – that if we want to be able to stand close to another person, to *be* next to that person as s/he struggles with a range of complex challenges, then we must have learned to stand close to ourselves, to know and be comfortable with ourselves – warts and all. Egan (1986) calls it 'coming to terms with the problematic in ourselves'. I would like to argue that Egan's task is as much one for teachers as it is for managers, nurses, doctors and careers officers.

This book's focus on the social and emotional development of children in primary schools reminds me of the burgeoning interest in and analysis of secondary school pastoral issues in the 1960s and 1970s. It was not at all that Circular 10/65 suddenly revealed to secondary colleagues that their pupils had social and emotional potential as well as academic talents. It was rather that well-established practice in secondary school was subjected to close professional scrutiny to analyse the extent to which socio-emotional development was being helped by the school experience. This is now happening in primary schools – the well-establshed concern in primary schools that pupils grow emotionally and socially is being flagged as an area for professional scrutiny.

An attractive aspect of a sense of *déjà vu* is the way it confers a sense of security and stability. It can thus encourage and underpin adventurous exploration (Piaget, 1958; Heisler, 1961). In some ways, the current interest in personal and social education in the primary school has that feel of 'been-here-before' about it, in that it parallels the early days of research into pastoral issues in the secondary school (Best, Jarvis, Ribbins, 1980). A similar, important consciousness-raising is underway, the teasing out of key issues and research problems is beginning. This, I suggest, takes us to a less reassuring aspect of *déjà vu* – there is a danger that unless great care is taken, the very stability of the known (our work so far on pastoral care in secondary schools) will fetter our perceptions in a way that leads us to reapply the categories, filters, structures and analyses which have helped us at the secondary level, to the new issue of primary schools and pastoral care. While this use of previously garnered insights is, of course, desirable and useful, it must not allow us to forget that pastoral care at secondary school level is still a contentious issue – even among ourselves – and that there are still important areas as yet unresearched, unanalysed. We are still too young to establish an orthodoxy. I hope we will always be too young for that.

My hope is that just as previous work in secondary schools will illuminate nooks and crannies in the primary school, so work done on primary school pastoral care will shine illuminatingly into some of the still dark corners of the secondary school. One of my major anxieties about our work at secondary school level is our tendency to concentrate on structures, delivery systems, procedures and so on. It fits the tenor of the times. There is (strangely, given the context) an implicit hint that methods of organisation and structures have some kind of priority over the human dimensions of children's social and emotional development. We might even begin to suspect that we have fallen into the 'lamp-post' syndrome of research. (The kind passer-by who sees a man searching on hands and knees for a lost 50p piece and gets down to help. After a fruitless ten minutes he asks, 'Are you sure you dropped it here?' 'Oh no' replies the man. 'I dropped it over there in the dark – it's just that it's lighter over here.')

The real research questions tend to be in the dark, especially when human subjects are involved.

The delightfully infinite number of uncontrolled variables in any group of humans must make us pause before we over-generalise about them on the basis of traditional research methodologies. In a review of Best, Jarvis, Ribbins and Oddy's excellent (1983) *Education and Care*, I commented that while they were asking the right questions, their way of structuring the data collected seemed insufficiently to take account of the enormous idiosyncrasy of human relations. I would like to suggest that while the search for structural descriptions goes on we open a new front in our research into children's growth as persons.

Leslie Button, writing on pastoral issues (1983) makes the very challenging comment that 'a value position is inescapable, and it is no less a value position if it remains unacknowledged'. He plops us uncompromisingly into the human, the individual and cuts off possible escape routes with that final comment. We must not, cannot, says Button, avert our gaze from the value implications of personal and social education. He challenges us to ask ourselves how far we have looked inward before acting outward. He realigns our research priorities. Not so much *What is being done? What roles/functions/posts need to be distributed? What models/structures/programmes facilitate personal development of pupils?* Rather, the much less clear, more challenging (darker?) issue: *Who am I in this encounter? What kind of people do teachers need to be to work at pastoral care? What personal growth by me is needed to respond to pupils' personal growth?*

It is possible to detect a process in the development of pastoral care in our secondary schools. Initially there was a critique of the 'watered-down grammar school curriculum' (Dent, 1949), a growing awareness that our offer to pupils missed many important targets, and omitted much significant data from its planning (McGuiness, 1983). Psychological, sociological and philosophical critiques created the kind of climate in which Hemming (1980) could call his book on the secondary curriculum, *The Betrayal of Youth*. These theoretical perspectives fell on fertile ground – relatively new comprehensive schools with their new pedagogical challenge, rising youth unemployment and the challenge of preparing young people for a post-industrial society. Thus a demand grew for new materials, new approaches – a demand richly fed by the Schools Council, Baldwin, Wells, Hopson, Scally, Button himself and many others.

Despite warnings from these authors that *radically different pedagogy* was needed to use these materials effectively, it is unfortunately the case that some teachers reached out for them as if they were a Whitmarsh French textbook. Of course the result was frustration, feelings of being de-skilled and the occasional disaster. So, we arrived at the next stage in the process – an acceptance that these new materials, so pressingly sought, could not be used in the old teacher-centred way – important new skills were required. The INSET providers responded with courses on Tutorial Work, Group Leadership Skills, Experiential Learning, Negotiated Curricula and so on.

Despite excellent critical analysis from writers like Jonathan (1982), a series of historical accidents led the Manpower Services Commission to provide, via its TVEI scheme, a powerful legitimation of a skills view of learning. We were falling into the trap of thinking that new skills would be a sufficient base for new pedagogy – a tendency to value people on the basis of what they can do (profile checklists, teacher appraisal checklists?) rather than on the basis of who they are. Perhaps we can consider turning that on its head. Not – *We are what we can do*, rather – *We can do what we are*. I would like to argue that where practitioner complaints have emerged that group work does not work, that sharing responsibility leads to chaos, that experiential learning diminishes the quality of learning, the cause is that (necessary) skill performance, even when enhanced by INSET work, is not sufficient. Carefully developed skills can be undermined where they are built on inappropriate, unexamined values, beliefs, attitudes and feelings. The problem may be illuminated by considering the contrast between having sex and making love. Thanks to skill-focused INSET work, we are all getting good at having sex, but still struggling about making love. Button insists (1983), as do many others (Healey, 1984; Munby, 1985; Hibberd, 1984; Lloyd, 1984) on the centrality of the 'self' in pastoral issues. Yet INSET still gives it scant consideration. Thus my proposal is that a fundamental aspect of preparation for work in personal education is to help the teacher explore the issue 'Who am I?'. In addition, we need to devise a research process designed to help us evaluate the appropriateness of such a focus.

Secondary schools are working very hard to focus on the personal development of the child. An instrumental view of education holds a philosophical ascendancy at the moment – people, not to put too fine a point on them, are tools. Yet there is research evidence that must make us pause, both at primary and secondary level. Three recent attempts to identify aspects of a child's school performance that might serve as an accurate predictor of later success as an adult came independently to the same conclusions. Kohlberg (1977), Nicholson (1970) and Heath (1977) found respectively that 'school academic achievement made no *independent* contribution to successful life adjustment', that 'scholastic aptitude was not related to life success', and that 'academic achievement was not significantly related to a broad and multiple definition of life success'. The argument is not that academic work is not important; it is that if academic development takes place without social and emotional development, it will not help, and may harm, the child. Put more prosaically – the greatest gift we can give to our pupils at school is not academic success, but a mighty sense of personal dignity and worth, coupled with an ability to operate in a variety of social situations. Yet the most cursory examination of initial training courses (CATE led), and even INSET, finds scant practical recognition of these findings. How much time is given on B Ed and PGCE courses to sensitivity training, value clarification, personal development work? To what extent are students helped to stand close to their own attitudes to race, gender, class, authority, sexuality? How far are they encouraged to analyse how such values underpin our interpersonal behaviour? Are we, their lecturers, any more in touch with such fundamental aspects of our humanity than the students are?

We have tried at Durham, in both initial and in-service training, to give such questions centrality. We do some work on sensitivity training and values clarification with B Ed and PGCE students and with teachers on a range of courses from part-time certificate work to full-time MA courses. This inevitably brief paper signals the area of personal growth as having important implications, and lets colleagues in other institutions following a similar line know that we would like to share our insights with them. Looking specifically at primary school teachers, I find most illuminating a comment from one of our fourth year junior specialists. 'I have been here for over three years,' she said. 'I've studied curriculum theory, texts for children, psychology, the family and all that – this (the sensitivity work we had just completed) is the first time I've been invited to look at myself. But surely, I must be a crucial factor in the classroom equation.' My hope is we do not allow that crucial factor to slip through our training net.

It would be dishonest of me to pretend that at Durham we have been able to do anything more than nibble at the edges of this issue. This brief paper allows me to do no more than share one of our nibbles.

Imagine a group of 30 young men and women about to embark on a professional training course to become teachers. They bring with them memories of their own schooling, recent experience of the authoritarian atmosphere of university undergraduate life, clear (but differing) expectations of the status of the post-graduate teacher trainee at the feet of the experts, both in school and in the department. They know about teaching and learning – they've been at it since they were five. It is locked in with perception of authority, control, knowledge, convergence, caution, orthodoxy and a host of other potential inhibitors. They are waiting for a lecture – the title on the programme says 'Learning and Teaching Styles'. Heads are ready; hearts are about to get a shock.

> Please decide with your neighbour who will be A and who B.
> OK. If it helps close your eyes. Try to draw to mind any teacher from your past about whom you would say 'you damaged me, diminished me, hurt me'. Run that person through the fingers of your mind. Re-live some of your encounters.
> Now. A, invest B with the personality of that destructive teacher you remember. Tell him (her) 'you hurt me, harmed me when/because . . .'. You have two minutes to vent your anger.
> OK. Now B do the same.
> The noise is enormous. An explosion of pent-up, half-humorous, often deadly serious articulation of buried resentments.
> Right. Close your eyes again and draw to mind any teacher who you feel helped you grow, who was special to you, who helped you to see things in yourself you didn't know were there. Run that person through your mind. Re-live some of your encounters.
> Can you re-do the same structure. Tell your partner – 'you really were special for me because/when . . .'.

Sadly, this is often quieter, and occasionally a participant will say 'I can't think of anyone like that'.

The final part of the exercise is to collect the characteristics drawn from the whole group of both types of teacher. My most recent group came up with these lists:

Destructive teachers . . .	. . . while good teachers
Bully	Are sympathetic
Are sarcastic	Inspire
Humiliate	Care
Are insensitive	Are full of enthusiasm
Make you feel guilty	Listen
Frighten	Are humorous
Demean you	Have time for you
Hit	Respect your ideas
Have favourites	Are really interested in you
Are impatient	Encourage
Flaunt their authority	Make you feel good about yourself

The exercise, or a variation of it (good/bad manager, good/bad ward sister, good/bad doctor), produces a remarkably consistent response. When pushed within a brief fantasy to identify key elements in effective teaching, nursing, doctoring and so on, groups identify interpersonal qualities as central. Subsequent conversation makes it clear that they *do* value task skills (passing exams, producing goods, nursing well, treating illness) but that the central, generic hope in these relationships is for a respecting/respectful interpersonal encounter – and that the quality of the encounter radically affects the task aspects. Rogers (1962, 1969, 1983) has made this point far more eloquently than I could.

The consequence seems to me to be an acceptance that a central part of teacher education ought to focus on personal development, at both initial and in-service levels. Concretising the issue, we can pose the question: what learnings, experiences and opportunities should be offered to us as professionals-in-practice or in training to help us eliminate our destructive qualities and enhance our facilitative qualities? Can we help people learn how to care? To listen? To communicate respect? To be esteem-developers? Now there, it seems to me, we *do* have a problem worth tackling.

References

Best, R, Jarvis, C, Ribbins, P and Oddy, D, 1983 *Education and Care* Heinemann.

Best, R, Jarvis, C and Ribbins, P, 1980 *Perspectives on Pastoral Care* Heinemann.

Button, L, 1983 'The Pastoral Curriculum' in *Pastoral Care in Education*, *1*(2), p 74–82.

Dent, H C, 1949 *Secondary Education for All* Routledge and Kegan Paul.

Egan, G, 1986 *The Skilled Helper* (3rd ed.) California: Brooks Cole.

Healy, M, 1984 'Developing a Social Education Programme', in *Pastoral Care in Education*, 2(2), p 93–7.

Heath, D H, 1977 *Maturity and Competence* New York: Gardner.

Heisler, V, 1961 'Towards a Process Model of Psychological Health' in *Journal of Counselling Psychology*.

Hemmings, J, 1980 *The Betrayal of Youth: Secondary Education Must Change* Marian Boyers.

Hibberd, F N, 1984 'Does Pastoral Care Need a Theory of Self?' in *Pastoral Care in Education*, 2(3), p 174–7.

Jonathan, R, 1982 'The Manpower Service Model of Education' in *Cambridge Journal of Education*, *13*(2).

Kohlberg, 1977 'Moral Development, Ego Development and Psycho-educational practices' in Miller, D (ed) *Developmental Theory* St Paul, Minnesota Department of Education.

Lloyd, T, 1984 'Does Pastoral Care Need a Theory of Self? A Reply' in *Pastoral Care in Education*, 2(3), p 178–81.

McGuiness, J, 1983 'Secondary Education for All?' in Coffield, F, Goodings, R (eds) *Sacred Cows in Education* Edinburgh University Press.

McGuiness, J, 1984 'Education and Care: A Review Article' in *Pastoral Care in Education*, 2(2), p 151–4.

Munby, S, 1985, 'Value Judgments in Pastoral Care' in *Pastoral Care in Education*, *3*(1).

NAPCE, 1986 *In-service training for the pastoral aspect of the teacher's role* Blackwell.

NAPCE, 1985 'A policy statement on the initial training of teachers' in *Pastoral Care in Education*, *3*(1), p 73–7.

Nicholson, E, 1970 *Success and Administer Criteria for Potentially Successful Risks, Project Report* Brown University, Providence RI, and the Ford Foundation.

Piaget, J and Inhelder, B, 1969 *The Psychology of the Child* New York: Basic Books.

Rogers, C R, 1962 *On Becoming a Person: A Therapists View of Psychotherapy* Constable.

Rogers, C R, 1969 *Freedom to Learn* Ohio: Merrill Publishing Co.

Rogers, C R, 1983 *Freedom to Learn for the Eighties* Ohio: Merrill Publishing Co.

33 'Hunting the woozle': an exploration of personal and social education and the questions it raises for teacher education

Jean Bond

If you seek to understand the whole universe
you will understand nothing at all.
If you seek to understand your Self
you will understand the whole universe.

(From Lazloff, 1987)

The above statement represents an ancient belief which lies at the root of many current philosophies and emerging programmes of personal transformation (see Ferguson, 1980). In essence it seems to be saying that without an understanding of the Self, then the universe, or perhaps life itself, has no meaning. In the western world the importance of understanding the 'Self' has only recently begun to gain some appreciation and acceptance. Within the education system in this country it is barely recognised at all. Educationalists are beginning to recognise the importance of the self-concept with respect to academic performance (see Burns, 1982; Purkey, 1970) but the Self is a different matter. Yet if the above statement has any truth in it then it is the understanding of the Self (rather than the raising of self-esteem) which is central to all learning, gives meaning to life, and is, therefore, a crucial component in the educational process.

In a recent research project Niemi (1987) reports that '*the significance of most school subjects were evaluated* (by the pupils) *to be very slight in the search for the purpose and meaning of the pupils' own lives*' (my brackets). Perhaps this goes some way to explain the apathy and 'lack of motivation' which overtakes many pupils once they have transferred to secondary school. It is suggested here that the implementation of effective programmes of personal and social education could and should lead to the development of self understanding and thereby give direction and purpose to the lives of pupils, attacking at the roots the problems facing adolescent (and increasingly younger) children in our schools today, namely drug abuse, truancy, vandalism, underachievement etc. Yet it seems that the growth of PSE in schools is extremely slow. Some possible explanations for this emerged during a recent conversation with a middle school head and four of his staff, and are summarised below.

One of the major obstacles to implementing a PSE programme in that school was that the staff did not have a clear idea of what it was they were being asked to teach. First, they thought that it was already an integral part of their daily interaction with the pupils, and to some small degree this was true. There was also some confusion between PSE and pastoral care. Obviously a clear distinction needs to be drawn between these two areas, for, although planned programmes of pastoral care can (and do) cover the essential features of PSE, the type of pastoral care usually carried out in primary and middle school education is seen as part of the teacher's role and is not, as a rule, formally structured and 'taught'.

Another objection raised was that there were obviously some people who 'needed' courses in PSE and only teachers who 'needed' them should have to take them. The teachers who needed training were those who had 'problems'. Related to this was the notion that it was better to leave well alone and not discover 'who you are' because you might find out that you were the horrible person you secretly suspected you might be – that is, you might discover you did have problems after all. This attitude is not peculiar to teachers. From personal experience of running courses in self-awareness it is clear that many adults of all ages and from all walks of life have similar feelings about taking part in such activities.

Perhaps the most revealing comment made about PSE during this discussion was that there was no need to be trained to teach 'something' like that. When it was pointed out that teachers might not feel so confident to teach a subject, such as physics, if they knew nothing at all about it, the response was that subjects like physics, unlike PSE, had a whole body of knowledge associated with them.

The implication, then, is that PSE is not grounded in any theoretical context. It is not surprising that this attitude prevails, since the most popular programmes currently available are remarkably thin on theory, concentrating on exercises and activities that teachers can carry out. The *Tacade* scheme, *Active Tutorial Work*, and books designed to raise self-concept of pupils (eg Canfield and Wells, 1981) present only a scanty theoretical context for their programmes. Consequently teachers may have been encouraged to believe that carrying out these exercises with children is all that is needed to produce a personal transformation. This would be tantamount to the notion that children should carry out physics experiments without having any idea about the concepts, principles or theoretical issues involved. It would become a series of meaningless exercises which did not develop any understanding of the Universe. Similarly PSE, if taught in this way, cannot help pupils develop an understanding of the human psyche. It is small wonder that many teachers view it as a waste of time and simply go through the motions. Presented in this superficial and uninformed way it *is* a waste of time. PSE is not simply a matter of raising self-concept and 'getting on' with others. There is more to it than that.

After a while, the conversation with these teachers (not dissimilar to others I have had) began to feel like 'hunting the woozle'.[1] Each person had a totally different picture of what this thing called PSE was and each one was pretty sure that they were 'right' and could recognise it when they saw it. So far, however, it had eluded them. Nearly all were in agreement on one aspect of this strange 'animal', however – it was, beyond doubt, very dangerous indeed. Maybe that was a good reason for making no serious attempt to pin it down; could they handle it if they caught up with it? This, then, is another major obstacle to the implementation of PSE in schools. If teachers are to be persuaded to take in-service courses in this subject, and if these are to be effective, we must explore this key issue. *What makes it so dangerous and who will suffer the damage?*

The clue perhaps lies in the objection that teachers (those mentioned above included) frequently raise to teaching PSE in secondary and primary education, ie, that it will require them to 'bare their souls' and they are not going to do so in front of their colleagues and *certainly not* in front of their pupils. What does this

[1] This refers to an incident in A A Milne's *Winnie the Pooh*, where Pooh and Piglet discover some strange footsteps (the woozles) which they follow round in circles, only to discover that they are joined by others (their own) as they go round and round.

phrase 'baring your soul' imply to teachers? It is strange that it has such sinister connotations for people (and in my experience this is fairly common, and by no means exclusive to the teaching profession). It seems to be taken to imply that we must dig all the skeletons from our cupboards and reveal our worst and darkest secrets to the world – tantamount to a confessional.

Does 'baring the soul' really require you to 'reveal all'? Erich Fromm (1985) and Alan Watts (1978) would describe the 'soul' as the pure and innocent 'essence' of human beings, the powerful energy source at the centre of our being. To 'bare' this surely implies stripping away from it all the clutter with which it is surrounded so that this essence can shine forth. Stripping away the doubts, fears, beliefs, images, expectations and other 'baggage' implanted by our social conditioning can be an uncomfortable process as it requires a readjustment of our construct of reality. Certainly the experiences and thoughts that we harbour in the mind constitute the barriers to an experience of our true 'Self' and one has to bring those self-destructive thoughts to the level of consciousness or into the 'light' in order to begin the process of self-awareness. As Overstreet (1962) points out *'Fear is not a private affair because it stands like a road-block between us and reality'*. However the realisation of our human errors need not be revealed to others, as long as we are willing to reveal them to ourselves; this is the nature of enlightenment. Revealing them to others might simply help to speed the process up (see Cirese, 1977, p 137, 138) and it does not need to be a distasteful experience. It can be comforting as we discover that we are definitely not alone in the way we think and feel. When you begin to realise that other people have similar weaknesses and 'faults', somehow your own become much less significant and almost inconsequential.

At various times I have worked with groups of immigration officials, in-service teachers and undergraduates using an exercise known as the *Johari Window* (taken from Cirese, *op cit*). Participants are asked to write down on a piece of paper a 'thought, feeling or motivation that they know about themselves which others do not know'. Inevitably several of them reveal that they are afraid of failing at their job or being seen by others as being weak and inadequate. Once these are read out, anonymously, a good 75% of the group usually own up to having the same thoughts and experience great relief that they are not alone in that. This openness subsequently gives them far more opportunity to discuss their fears of failure with their colleagues without the sense that they will be judged adversely if they do so. They no longer need to struggle to keep up appearances.

PSE could perhaps best be described as a journey to one's centre, in the process of which subliminal thoughts about ourselves and others, which are irrational and unproductive, rise to the surface and can be disarmed, enabling us to get closer to reality and become healthy and vital human beings who can relate to others without hostility, suspicion and violence. It is the process of 'self-actualisation', which, according to Fritz Perls (1972), means developing our potential as human beings, accepting what we are, rather than trying to be what we are not, to experience '*The wholeness of a real person*', rather than '*the fragmentation, the conflicts, the despair . . .*' that usually accompany our human condition (p 8).

For teachers to acquire the expertise to enable pupils to become 'self-actualised' would require the exploration of a number of areas of study related to human development and the functioning of mind and spirit. There is insufficient space to discuss these in detail here, but broadly speaking they cover various schools of psychology and philosophy, including constructive alternativism (which addresses the idea of what constitutes 'reality'); humanistic psychology (eg Maslow and Rogers); behaviourism; post-Freudian psychologists (eg Fromm and Horney); existential psychology; philosophy of East and West (eg Krishnamurti; Alan Watts; Heidegger). Understanding human behaviour demands an eclectic approach.[2]

Could one possibly expect pupils aged from eight upwards, to grasp these complex abstractions? It is my contention that they can and *must* if programmes of PSE are to be effective. In order to examine the feasibility of this proposition a research project was set up in the middle school previously mentioned, in the spring term of 1987.

A PSE programme was designed which was based on the theoretical areas outlined above. Eighty-five pupils aged from 11–12, four fourth year teachers, one teacher/adviser and the head of the school took part in the programme, which took place on Friday afternoons for a $2\frac{1}{2}$ hour period each week.

The staff participated in the same way as the pupils (with the

---

[2] A selection of references with respect to the areas mentioned can be found in the bibliography.

exception of one exercise where they supervised a group) although they sat together at the back of the room and if partner work was entailed they worked with each other.

In the space available here it is not possible to comment on the children's responses to all of the areas we explored, but one of the conversations which related to the unconscious mind (and subliminal thoughts) is detailed below:

> *Course tutor : For example you are in bed and you wake up and hear noises downstairs and you suddenly decide (**conscious thought**) you need a drink. So you shout to your mum/dad, Do you really want a drink?*
>
> *Pupils : (Chorus) No.*
>
> *C/T : What do you want?*
>
> *Girl pupil : Well you really feel lonely don't you – you feel left out. You want love.*
>
> *C/T : Yes you want love. (**Subliminal thought**)* So why don't you ask for it?
>
> *Girl pupil* : Well if you ask for a drink and you don't get it that's OK, but if you ask for love and your mum says don't be silly that's awful.

As a result of this and subsequent sessions pupils began to realise that demeaning others was a way of attempting to overcome feelings of inadequacy in yourself and so was a symptom of feelings of inferiority. They began to see how their self-image had developed and how much of it was based on their interpretation of other people's view of them rather than on fact. Exploring Maslow's theory of motivation (Maslow, 1970) enabled one child to realise that she was afraid of incurring her teacher's disapproval and that this made her keep quiet rather than say how she really felt about a situation that arose in the classroom. She went home and thought about it, realised what she had been doing and spoke to the teacher the next day, telling him how she had felt and why she did not tell him at the time.

At the end of four weeks the head and one of the county advisers questioned the pupils to see how much they had learned from the course at this stage. Children reported improvements in confidence, improvements in school work, better communication with parents and teachers and that they were finding it easier to speak in front of strangers. Those who had not spoken to the whole group said that they had benefitted greatly from what others had said and that they were more able to understand themselves and others, which improved their relationships. This was an impromptu interview with a randomly-selected group, so the pupils had no chance to rehearse their answers.

In contrast to their pupils, the teachers were cautious and non-committal in their response to the course. Eventually the head decided to stop the project when it was less than half way through. It became clear that insufficient groundwork had been carried out with parents and staff before the project was started. The main reason for the head's decision was that the staff found it very difficult to cope with the course. The teachers were being doubly challenged, first by being asked to reconstruct their view of reality alongside their pupils and second by being required to change their role with the pupils.

Work with groups of in-service teachers at the University of Warwick has produced varied reactions. Some teachers find it incredibly useful and report changes in their relationships with others and a marked change in their understanding and feelings about themselves and their teaching role. Others find it too uncomfortable and cannot bring themselves to explore the workings of their own minds and the identification of their defence strategies when surrounded by their contemporaries.

More positive results have been produced with undergraduates and one year post-graduate certificate students, mainly because these students take this subject as an option and have a clearer idea of what is entailed before they embark upon it. The following extract from a fourth year student's assignment was written after 20 weeks of a course which was designed to raise the self-awareness of students. They were also placed in a school to work with a couple of disaffected pupils. This excerpt indicates the impact that self-discovery can have on teacher attitudes and the teacher's role. This particular student found Kelly's 'Personal Construct' theory (see Fransella, 1972) to be extremely useful to her understanding of teacher/pupil interaction.

Again and again I noted my anger and realised that I was taking their behaviour personally. . . . But I began to realise that I was hostile in a much more insidious way that was affecting the way the children behaved. It wasn't as simple as certain behaviour provoking me to lose my temper, therefore if the children could stop behaving in those ways I would stop being angry with them. What I began to realise was that it was my perception of these children that was the main cause for the hostility. . . . A construct can take the form of a word, a label. If the word 'disaffected' was a construct I was using, then the bi-polar opposite of this word would be 'interested'. . . . In this case I was inferring that all disaffected pupils were uninterested, unmotivated and bored. When I applied this to how I was feeling, the fear and the anger that these children were producing, I realised that to be 'boring' was one of the greatest fears of my life, I was taking their behaviour far more personally than I have previously thought. I was converting the fear that I was boring into 'I'm going to reject you before you can hurt me'. . . . When viewed like this it is easy to see how teachers, who after all are only human, can allow their own fears to affect their pupils' lives.

(Cole, 1987)

The middle school pilot project was a useful learning process, since it exposed the fundamental problems which are inherent in implementing PSE programmes with practising teachers. Mistakes were made, but that is an inevitable feature of learning. One of the mistakes was to attempt to run an in-service course for the staff alongside the course for the children. It seemed a very nice idea, which evaded the problem about finding sufficient time and saved on money too, but it was too ambitious to achieve without much more thorough preparation and follow-up with teachers. Fear of failing, fear of looking inadequate, a need for approval of colleagues (and pupils) and a protection of their own self-image are usually the dominating motives behind the actions of those who teach, at all levels (including university lecturers). There is nothing 'wrong' with this; it is simply human. The road to psychological freedom and self-actualisation is not easy. It demands the confronting of fear, the abandonment of pride and self-preservation and the development of trust in the people (staff and pupils) around us – not easy when all the evidence points to the fact that they are not to be trusted and will take advantage of any weak spot that presents itself. Obviously a lot of groundwork has to be done before teachers can begin to cope with the adjustment that has to be made for this change in role to occur.

One of the comments made to me by a disappointed pupil after the project had been terminated was:

It was the first time we could say what we were really thinking and you just listened. Now we have to go back to being told what to do.

These pupils were beginning to experience the joy of self-expression in an atmosphere free of fear. In order to produce this type of environment teachers have to learn to understand themselves and the reasons which lie behind the way they relate to pupils in the classroom.

Although this project was prematurely terminated, I was not discouraged. I believe that, in spite of their worries, the staff did begin to realise what PSE was and that there was more to it than their idea of 'baring your soul'. It also raised some important questions and implications for in-service training, perhaps the most important being, 'Who is to do this training?'. Does it not require that those who educate teachers go through the same process of self-awareness? How may of them have done so, or are willing to do so? Since PSE is so central to success in learning, should not every teacher teach it? If so, that will demand a large number of personnel who are educated in this area for teaching both initial and in-service courses. How many advisers/lecturers are so qualified? I suspect the answer is very few, for they will find it as alarming to contemplate as teachers do. The lessons learned also point to the importance of making this area a priority in programmes of initial teacher education.

Perhaps PSE can be likened to walking on the moon – a small step for (wo)man – a huge step for (wo)mankind. And perhaps, like the journey to the moon, it demands total commitment, courage and creativity. If PSE is, as many believe, the key to creating lives which are satisfying, exciting and fulfilling and eradicating the need for violence, drug taking and self-destructive impulses, that arise from fear and ignorance of our own functioning, then perhaps it will be worth teachers taking that 'small step' into the unknown in order to contribute to the quality and development of human existence.

References

Burns, R, 1982 *Self-concept, development and education* Holt, Rhinehart and Winston.

Canfield, J and Wells, H C, 1976 *100 Ways to enhance self-concept in the classroom* Prentice Hall.

Cirese, S, 1977 *Quest: A search for self* Holt, Rhinehart and Winston.

Cole, Sally-Anne, 1987 unpublished essay, B.A. (QTS) Warwick University.

Ferguson, M, 1982 *The aquarian conspiracy* Paladin, Granada.

Fransella, F, 1972 *Personal change and reconstruction* Academic Press.

Fromm, E, 1985 *To have or to be* Abacus.

Krishnamurti, J, 1974 *Krishnarmurti on education* Longman.

Lazloff, B, 1987 *We're all doing time* Prison Ashram Project.

Maslow, A H, 1970 *Motivation and Personality* Harper and Row.

Niemi, 1987 'The meaning of life among secondary school pupils' in *Research Bulletin*, 65 University of Helsinki.

Overstreet, B W, 1962 *Understanding fear in ourselves and others* Collier Books.

Perls, F, 1972 *In and out the garbage pail* Bantam Books.

Purkey, W W, 1970 *Self-concept and school achievement* Prentice Hall.

Rogers, C, 1980 *A way of being* Houghton/Mifflin.

Watts, A, 1978 *The meaning of happiness* Rider.

Endpiece

The nature and purpose of this book is such that a traditional conclusion would both be inappropriate and somewhat contrived. The purpose of a conclusion is normally to draw together and review what has gone before. A conclusion often seeks both to reiterate briefly the key messages that have been contained within a book and, in the light of this, point the reader in the right direction for future thoughts and actions.

The idea behind *Thinking about . . . personal and social education in the primary school* does not lend itself to a conclusion of this kind, for the intention is not that the book should first be read and then acted upon. The aim is rather that it should serve as a companion to both thought and action. This endpiece, then, points the reader in two directions: forward towards their own thoughts, analysis and actions; and back to a further consideration of relevant sections of the text. The writers whose work is to be found in this volume would hope to provide others concerned with primary education with a starting point for their work in personal and social education, but they would hope for more than that. It is also important that what they have written should serve as a 'sounding board', a 'measure' for work already underway, whether this had been started independently or as a result of this book.

Finally, one further important development should result from the increasing concern for and interest in personal and social education in the primary school. Many of the contributions to this book have highlighted the need for a national network of those either already taking initiatives or intending to do so. Through this network, ideas, insights and information should be shared as should examples of effective practice. Perhaps ultimately the members of such a network might be encouraged to write about their work, thus adding to a literature of which this book is offered as a forerunner.

Notes on the contributors

John Berridge has been a Head of Personal and Social Education Department and a Deputy Headteacher in a comprehensive school. For the past five years he has been a member of the Advisory and Inspection Service of Nottinghamshire LEA where he has become increasingly interested in the application of person-centred principles to curriculum and professional development within the Education Service. Currently he is seconded to the post of Education Officer Training and Personal Development where he is responsible for developing training programmes for support staff.

During her years as a lecturer in education at Warwick University **Jean Bond** has set up and run a part-time truancy unit and a full-time unit for disaffected pupils in local schools. This demonstrated to her the necessity for teachers to become self-aware and self-actualised if the development of disaffection in schools was to be avoided. Most of her work is devoted to this goal.

Sylvia Braddy has been teaching infants over a period of 30 years in schools in the North East and North West of England and now teaches in Inner London. She was able to study PSME in depth when her Authority was awarded an Education Support Grant. Along with others she was seconded for six months to develop this area of curriculum.

Joan Brier is Headteacher of a large first and middle school in Sheffield, in an inner city area of extreme deprivation. During her work in education with children from aged two years upwards, she has developed an interest in social development, being particularly interested in developing social skills, early identification of potential behaviour problems, and preventive intervention in classroom situations.

Jim Campbell is Senior Lecturer in Education at the University of Warwick, and co-ordinator of the MA in Primary Education programme. He is editor of the journal *Education 3–13*. His publications include *Developing the Primary School Curriculum*, Holt Rinehart and Winston 1985, *The Routledge Compendium of Primary Education*, Routledge 1988, *The National Curriculum; Primary Questions*, Scholastic 1987, and (with J Tomlinson and V Little) *Public Education Policy 2, 4*, 1987. He is currently writing a book on primary schools and political socialisation, and editing a book on the humanities in primary education.

Tony Charlton has taught in primary, secondary and special schools, and is currently a principal lecturer in the Faculty of Education at St Paul and St Mary's College of Higher Education, in Cheltenham. He is the co-author together with Kenneth David – of *The Caring Role of the Primary School* which deals with aspects of pastoral care and personal and social education in primary schools.

Jenny Clement, MEd, has taught throughout the primary age range but her real love is the early years. After several years as head teacher of a multiethnic school, Jenny now leads the staff of a large 'mono-cultural' nursery. She enjoys the challenge of developing multicultural perspectives and the chance to be involved in Staffordshire's multicultural and in-service training programme.

Tricia David is a Lecturer in Primary Education at Warwick University. Like Jenny, her co-author, she is passionate about education in the early years and equal opportunities. She has spent the last twenty years involved in this field.

Mary Jane Drummond is Tutor in Primary Education at the Cambridge Institute of Education. She started teaching in an over-crowded infant school in Hackney in 1966 and since then has worked in infant schools in Sheffield as teacher, deputy and headteacher. She spent four years with the *Communication Skills* project, directed by Joan Tough. Her present interests include gender issues in schools, and the education of four year olds.

David Galloway is a Lecturer in the Department of Educational Research at the University of Lancaster. He worked as a residential social worker, teacher and educational psychologist before undertaking contract research on disruptive behaviour, truancy, and stress and satisfaction in teaching. He is author of seven books, the most recent being *Schools, Pupils and Special Education Needs* and *The Education of Disturbing Pupils*.

Professor **Philip Gammage** trained at Goldsmiths' College, London and taught in London schools for almost ten years before studying psychology and teaching at Bristol University. He has taught in the USA, Spain, Australia, Canada and Malta and has published various books on curriculum, psychology and primary education.

Doug Harwood is Lecturer in Science Education at Warwick University. For many years he has worked on conferences studying Authority and Role in Groups and Organisations. He has published in the fields of pastoral care, personal and social education, political education and geographical education.

Margaret Heritage is County Adviser for Early Childhood Education in Warwickshire. Previously she was Headteacher of a primary school in Coventry and a part-time Lecturer in Education at the University of Warwick. She has been concerned for a number of years with the new ways of developing opportunities for personal and social education in the primary school.

David Ingram is Research Fellow in the Centre for Social and Moral Education at Leicester University. He joined the Schools Council's ME Project, Director 1976–78, at Cambridge, after school teaching. With the SMC he produced a plan for ME commissioned by Shirley Williams when Secretary of State. He co-edited *Stimulation of Social Development in Schools* for the Council of Europe.

Peter Lang is Lecturer in Education at Warwick University; previously he taught in both primary and secondary schools. He has a long term interest in Pastoral Care and Personal and Social Education, running courses in the area and co-editing with Michael Marland the book *New Directions in Pastoral Care*. He is also features editor of the journal 'Pastoral Care in Education'.

Peter Maher is Principal of Harold Hill Community School, London Borough of Havering. He is editor of *Child Abuse; the Educational Perspective* and co-author of *Leading a Pastoral Team* and 'Preparation and support for pastoral care' in *New Directions in Pastoral Care* all published by Basil Blackwell. He has been National Executive member of NAPCE since its foundation in 1982 and National Secretary since 1983.

John McGuinness has taught the full range of children (5–18) in several countries. Now a Senior Lecturer in Education at Durham University, his particular interests are counselling, pastoral care, responses to disruptive behaviour and the personal development of trainee teachers. He wrote *Planned Pastoral Care* in 1982 and has contributed to several books since then.

Alysoun Moon is a senior team member and trainer with TACADE. A trained nurse and teacher, she was formerly a member of the Health Education Authority's Primary Schools Project at Southampton University. Her long term interests include health education and PSE in the primary school and the need to start with the children and with what they bring to their learning.

Jane Needham has been a primary school teacher in Nottinghamshire for 14 years and during this time has developed a growing committment to person centred education. Recently she has been on a two year secondment to the classroom support service in Nottingham, working on a PSE development project with children and staff in a group of local primary schools.

Anne Nelson is a primary adviser in Coventry with particular responsibility for the early years. She has been involved in a series of initiatives concerned with personal and social education in the primary school. Anne was a primary head in Oxford for seven years and has been involved in in-service with teachers nationally and internationally, mainly in the USA.

Andrew Pollard is Reader in Primary Education at Bristol Polytechnic. He has taught across the Primary age range and among his books are *The Social World of the Primary School*, *Reflective Teaching in the Primary School* (with Sarah Tann) and *Children and their Primary Schools*.

Richard Pring is Professor of Education at the University of Exeter School of Education and currently Dean of the Faculty. He was author of *Personal and Social Education in the Curriculum*, published in 1984. He edits the British Journal of Educational Studies.

Tony Richardson is Headteacher of Green Lanes Junior and Infant School in Chelmsley Wood, Birmingham. He has taught in a variety of primary schools in the Midlands. He has an active interest in promoting pupils' personal development through the use of new technology, flexible teaching strategies and pupil based record and profiling systems. The school is currently involved in an SCDC sponsored project concerned with the continuity implications of developing Pupil Autonomy in Learning (PAL).

Heather Rushton has been a primary school teacher in Nottinghamshire since 1981. Her interest in personal and social education evolved from a personal wish to provide an atmosphere in the classroom/school whereby children and staff felt valued and valuable. She acted as a support teacher in her own school, on behalf of the Curriculum Development Support Service.

Ruth Snow is an Educational Adviser in Coventry with responsibility for a group of schools in the north of the city. Her area of specialist responsibility is for Personal and Social Education and she is currently co-ordinating the Authority's development work in Records of Achievement. She previously taught in Northern Ireland, Kenya and Coventry and she has worked as Senior Project Officer for the research and development phase of the Schools Council Project *Home and Family Education 8–13* and directed the dissemination phase.

Pam Stoate used to be an advisory teacher in personal, social and moral education in Devon. The training aspect of the role raised issues which she explored in her doctorate. She now combines work with young people, students and teachers with research and writing.

Delwyn Tattum is Reader in Education at South Glamorgan Institute of Higher Education. He runs an initial teacher training course on Social Education and Personal Development, and has written about Pastoral Care. His main interest is in aggressive behaviour and his publications include *Disruptive Pupils in Schools and Units* (1982). He has edited *The Management of Disruptive Pupil Behavior* (1986) and *Bullying in Schools* (1988).

John Thacker is a Lecturer in Education at Exeter University and is a Course Director of the professional MEd Course for Educational Psychologists. He has published curriculum materials on interpersonal problem solving entitled 'Steps to Success' and edited a book with Richard Pring and David Evans entitled *Personal, Social and Moral Education in a Changing World*. He is currently researching the use of group work techniques in personal and social education in the primary school.

Patsy Wagner works as an Educational Psychologist for the London Borough of Waltham Forest where she works with the teachers of nursery, primary and secondary schools. She was originally a teacher of modern languages and a Head of a Compensatory Education Department. She is a trained family therapist and co-author of *School Discipline: A Whole School Approach* with Chris Watkins.

Cas Walker is a Curriculum Adviser with Birmingham LEA. Her teaching experience has covered primary and secondary phases and includes some recent nursery involvement. Her interest in pastoral care and personal and social education has developed out of close observation of the educational experience of many black youngsters. Cas has recently been involved in planning courses for class teachers.

Dilys Went is a Lecturer in the Science Education Department of the University of Warwick and is involved in biology, science and health education teacher training, and in-service training for teachers. She has specialised in sex education and has wide experience over many years of working in this field with pupils, parents, teachers, health professionals and youth groups. She has written numerous papers on health and sex education, and is the author of *Sex Education, Some Guidelines for Teachers*, Bell and Hyman (1985).

Noreen Wetton is a Senior Research Fellow in the Education Department at Southampton University and currently co-directing the Health Education Authority's Primary Schools Project. She has taught across the whole age and ability range and was a Headteacher before moving into teacher education to develop an early years BEd. Her particular interest is in how young children perceive and explain their worlds.

She is the co-author of a new language scheme for the primary school (Open Door, Nelson 1987) and has published stories for young children.

Patrick Whitaker has been a general adviser in Derbyshire since 1979. He has written several books on the management of schools and articles on counselling in education, personal and social education and experiential learning. In recent years his in-service work with teachers has increasingly focused on human relations training and person centred learning.

Arthur Wooster is a clinical psychologist who teaches Human Relations at the School of Education, Nottingham University. His areas of interest include social skills training, counselling, cooperation, group work and friendship and he has published books and research articles in these areas. He has taught at universities in England and abroad.